Food and Drink
in History

Food and Drink in History

Selections from the

Annales

Economies, Sociétés, Civilisations

Volume 5

Edited by

Robert Forster

and

Orest Ranum

Translated by

Elborg Forster

and

Patricia M. Ranum

The Johns Hopkins University Press
Baltimore and London

This book has been brought to publication with the generous assistance
of the Andrew W. Mellon Foundation.

Manufactured in the United States of America

The Johns Hopkins University Press, Baltimore, Maryland 21218
The Johns Hopkins Press Ltd., London

Library of Congress Catalog Card Number 78-21920
ISBN 0-8018-2156-8 (hardcover)
ISBN 0-8018-2157-6 (paperback)

Library of Congress Cataloging in Publication data will be found on the
last printed page of this book.

Contents

Introduction

Why study the history of food? A number of reasons come to mind. Food is the most basic of human needs, and obtaining enough of it has been the most pervasive human activity since "Dawn Man." No history that claims to recapture the lives of the mass of the inarticulate can ignore it. Moreover, the need for adequate nutrition in our own time and in the century ahead has made the study of food much more than an object of historical curiosity. Does a knowledge of the past provide us with any "tools" or "warnings" for the future? At the very least it demonstrates how our ancestors have grappled with the production, distribution, and consumption of a commodity that has almost always been in short supply. Finally, for the historian, anthropologist, sociologist, and social psychologist, a study of food habits in the broader sense serves as a useful point of entry into an investigation of a wider culture.

The Annales School has a special reason to emphasize the last of these justifications for the study of food in history. The Annalistes—if one may grant some cohesion to a very diverse group of historians—have stressed the need to establish relationships (*rapports*) and ties (*liens*) among many long-run trends in history—climatic, demographic, productive, technological, cultural. Food can serve as an indicator of broader social and cultural phenomena (not that food habits simply reflect other situations or patterns of behavior in a given society). As an integral part of a wider popular culture, dietary customs and the attitudes and values they embody are active agents in their own right, helping to fashion the peculiar tone and direction of society. In short, food is one of the "ties" in the intricate tissue of history.

Maurice Aymard outlines three approaches to the subject of food and history: economic, nutritional, and "psychosociological." All of these, and perhaps a fourth we might simply call cultural history, are represented in this collection of articles from the Annales. The economic approach emphasizes not only the production, processing, and marketing of food, but also consumption, including consumer choices and tastes. This approach has obvious links with the long French tradition in agrarian history ranging from the price studies of the Labrousse School to the local and regional monographs launched so successfully by the original editors of the Annales, Marc Bloch and Lucien Febvre.* This legacy is reflected in the use of many of the same kinds of sources employed in local and rural history—price series, tax rolls, population data, administrative reports, institutional and private account books, and, perhaps most important, the notarial archives, including inventories of property made after someone's death.

Nor are older debates forgotten. Michel Morineau's article on the potato is a contribution to the issue of productivity and the characteristics of a "progressive" or "pioneering" agriculture. Morineau is among those who doubt that French yields per acre increased at all from the fourteenth to the nineteenth century. Whatever the other successes of the Netherlands' agriculture, he also doubts that the potato was the wonder crop Belgian and other historians would have us believe. His article is a careful comparison between Belgian and French Flanders designed to determine the relationship among the "agrarian regime," population growth, and standard of living. Agricultural growth is complex and rarely characterized by unqualified "breakthroughs" in which single crops "revolutionize" production. There are always trade-offs.

The Annales stamp is also apparent in a concern for social classification in order to determine which social groups ate what and to chart long-run—century-long if possible—changes in food consumption among occupational and income groups, and between the inhabitants of town and country. Jacques Revel traces a double process of reallocation of food supplies from *campagnia* to capital and from the poor to the well-to-do by investigating the food consumption of Rome from 1600 to 1820. By modern nutritional standards, Rome was a well-fed city throughout most of this period, better fed than Paris, consuming a diet of meat (especially veal, mutton, and pork), olive oil, bread (white for the rich, dark for the poor), and close to 200 litres of wine per capita per year. In addition to his substantive findings, Revel indicates how misleading it is to draw conclusions about the "average diet" of a city dweller on the basis of aggregate price and demographic data alone. Food consumption and the components of diet do not follow price trends in any automatic or symmetrical way; the reallocation of consumption priorities and the substitution of other foods is a very "sticky" process, to borrow an economist's word.

Like Revel, Jean-Jacques Hémardinquer, a pioneer in food history,† traces changes in food consumption over the *longue durée*, focusing on the history of pork in France over the three centuries after 1500. An initial glance at death inventories and sharecrop contracts of peasant families may evoke the picture that still decorates folkloric postcards, the succulent roast pig cooking on the spit surrounded by smiling peasants. Statistically speaking, this rosy image became more and more imaginary as generations succeeded each other. The sixteenth century may have witnessed such culinary spectacles at royal feasts in Loire châteaux; for the rest of rural France, the century brought accelerated population

---

*See volume 3 in this series, *Rural Society in France* (Baltimore: The Johns Hopkins University Press, 1977).

†See *Cahiers des Annales* 28 (1970).

pressures on food supplies, deforestation to make way for maximum cereal production, and rising salt taxes (the *gabelle*), all of which discouraged pig production. By 1750, pork had disappeared from the tables of the peasantry —even before coffee—and, like white bread, had become a sign of affluence. Like Henry IV's famous "chicken in every pot," the "family pig" had become another myth from an idealized rural past.

Behind much of the first research in food history is a desire to determine the subsistence level from direct evidence of food consumed and not from inferences, no matter how sophisticated, drawn from national and regional price series for staples such as grains and from calculations of the "net" harvest of the "average" family farm. A knowledge of the full range of foods eaten—or at least purchased —makes it possible to assess the quality as well as quantity of food consumed. This in turn leads to the application of modern nutritional science. Aymard, in his methodological article, urges historians to take full advantage of the findings of the World Food and Agricultural Organization (FAO) and the World Health Organization. Some Annalistes add the adjective "nutritional" to their older "Malthusian" and "agrarian" Old Regimes, analyzing the nutritional components, food values, and dietary balance of actual food consumed. A new set of tables now garnishes the pages of the Annales, with such column headings as "proteins," "lipids," "glucids," "trace elements," and "calories," not to omit the crucially important "ratios" of calcium to phosphorus or of animal to vegetable protein, both related to the weight of the individual food consumer.

But nutritional analysis does not end with an elaborate classification of food intake among the great mass of people. More central is the desire to determine what proportion of the population was undernourished and vulnerable to disease, who they were, where they lived, and what their total environment was like. Pushing a step further, what acute and endemic illnesses was a given population most likely to contract? Nutritional science has met the history of medicine and public health, two of the most promising new areas of history today—"new" at least by their integration into a much wider social and cultural context. This "social history of medicine" has also drawn upon many of the conclusions of international health organizations. It seems agreed, for example, that famine itself is not the direct cause of high mortality rates, but rather that chronic malnutrition weakens the body's capacity to resist certain diseases. Thus, by using the present to understand the past, the historian is much closer to identifying the link between diet and disease, and more broadly, between agriculture and demography, than ever before.

Willem Frijhoff and Dominique Julia, by analyzing the food value of the diets of four French *collèges* in the eighteenth century, not only expose the inaccuracy of the timeless student complaints about institutional food, but also demonstrate that the sons of elites received an adequate supply of calories (all above 3,800 per day), protein, fat, and most vitamins. Meat consumption of 300 grams daily was ample and well above the national average. The only conspicuous shortage was of dairy products, especially milk, to improve the calcium/phosphorus balance.

Of course, there was some regional variation, reflecting in part local agricultural production. Auch in Gascony, for example, was short of animal protein and vitamins A and C. Molsheim in Alsace had the best-fed student body from a nutritional point of view, with a variety of food that would appear fabulous to any rural villager: meat (30%), wine (20%), bread (only 20%), and vegetables, fruits, butter, eggs, sugar, spices, and cooking oils (the remaining 30%). There was no hunger here, despite rising food prices after 1750. The authors even show that the diet was improving each decade at Molsheim, and they consider the increasing consumption of apples and potatoes the mark of a "modernizing" diet. A knowledge of modern nutritional science could not have solved the problem of chronic shortages of food in the eighteenth century, but it might have rectified certain imbalances in the diets of the lucky few.*

There is more to food history than the issues of agricultural growth and distribution of food, of nutritional deficiencies and public health, fundamental as these are. Consumer "taste" may seem like an elitist luxury when we recall that at least three-fourths of Europe's population was close to the subsistence level from the sixteenth to the late nineteenth century and that dietary imbalance had been worsening since the population explosion of the sixteenth century and the diminishing proportion of animal protein and fats in the diet of most Europeans. But the significance of "taste" and consumer preference is not restricted to the lives of a few rich and well-born, even in those grim times. Until quite recently, food has been ranked not by its nutritional value or even by its availability, but by a hierarchy of status peculiar to locale and culture. In seventeenth-century Rome, for example, bread eating was a source of municipal pride to be contrasted with the *pasta* consumption of Neapolitans and other inferior "foreigners." White bread, like white rice, was a privileged food, preferred because it was associated with social status, the hallmark of the *bourgeois* table, only slightly behind the silver service itself. White bread still holds a privileged position in most French households, though its food value is no greater than that of rye or whole wheat; to eat *pain de seigle* or *pain noir* is to lose social status or perhaps even national identity.† The obsession with bread as the staff of life has also had something to do with retarding the adaptation of forage crops to French rotations, though its precise effect is difficult to assess. Potatoes, in France especially, were long viewed as a pauper's fare, fit for the pigs but not for the table, despite the efforts of Parmentier, a persistent propagandist, to make the bland tubers palatable. The French fry is a very recent culinary success in history. The reader may even wonder whether Morineau's invidious comparison between Belgian and French Flanders in 1800 is overly influenced by the conviction that eating potatoes was a sure sign of rural deprivation and might even perpetuate low living standards in

*For a nutritional analysis of a French peasant diet, see R. J. Bernard, "Peasant Diet in Eighteenth-Century Gevaudan," in Elborg Forster and Robert Forster, eds., *European Diet from Pre-Industrial to Modern Times* (N.Y.: Harper and Row, 1976), pp. 19-46.

†The contrast with the German *Bürger* family who eat *Schwarzbrot* and other varieties of "dark bread" with their evening meal comes to mind immediately. No stigma is attached to rye bread in Germany.

general. Similarly, it may come as a surprise to some North Americans that pork products have not always been below beef on the status scale. In Europe after 1500 pork gained in status as it left the peasant's spit for the notable's cuisine. The social standing of various foods has obvious connections with a wider culture, often helping to define a national culture as well. National cuisine is a deeply emotional issue. Who would dare maintain, for example, that wine is only wine?

Food history is, therefore, not restricted to ties with economic and medical history. Jean Leclant's article on the introduction of coffee into Paris in the seventeenth century has more to do with flamboyant Turkish emissaries like Mustafa Raca and imaginative Italian entrepreneurs like Procoppio Coltelli than with market analysis in a systematic economic sense. Leclant presents a Parisian "world" in order to explain the ultimate success of the "arabesque liquor" in the café and coffeehouse. His description of this milieu is much more a contribution to the history of urban *sociabilité* and cultural interchange than that of economic growth or public health.

Ostensibly, Jean-Paul Aron is concerned with "networks of distribution" and the unhappy effects of a trade in "hazardous" and spoiled leftovers on Parisians in the nineteenth century. But Aron's obvious love for *haute cuisine* and his zest for the eccentric and picturesque make his essay a fascinating insight into a clandestine and often fraudulent trade in secondhand foods, the "venerable *débris*" of a three-star restaurant or a famous Parisian caterer. Indeed, the trade included even thirdhand leftovers, for the hucksters off the Place Maubert put the half-decayed dishes from the second-class restaurants back into circulation. "Fish-heads, fragments of pastry, bones with a bit of meat left, mixed pell-mell and disguised in twenty gravies," were peddled to pretentious but impoverished "sidewalk gourmets" who would have been well-advised to remain content with the simple staples, bread and potatoes. Alas, the scourge of adulterated luxury food did not end with La Belle Epoque.

If Maurice Aymard in his introductory essay invokes a "nutritional Old Regime," Guy Thuillier coins an "Ancien Régime of water." Nevers, an average town in central France in the nineteenth century, seems closer to a city on the Ganges than to one on the Loire. The primitiveness of its water supply, the total absence of public hygiene, and the lethargic indifference of its citizens to public (or private) health measures makes Thuillier's story somber reading indeed. But like Leclant's coffee and Aron's leftovers, Thuillier's water supply (or lack of it) serves as a vehicle for a broad-gauged inquiry into the problems of urban history. Thuillier describes 140 years of effort by public health officials and physicians to reduce pollution of the city's wells and fountains, to drain stagnant pools and fens, remove manure piles from doorways, and seal leaking septic tanks—all in the hope of providing pure water and curbing the chronic outbreaks of cholera and typhoid fever. Yet as late as 1910 only 3,000 of 27,000 inhabitants of Nevers had running water in their homes, and only a few hundred had indoor toilets. Nevers presents a dismal record of the frustration of a few dedicated and persistent administrators and physicians in the face of massive popular indifference to public health. For the availability of pure water is not only related to sanitation and personal hygiene but to food preparation and drinking habits as well. In the absence of good water, a diet of cooked meat and fermented wines may be "superior" to fresh fruits, vegetables, and drinking water in more ways than one. "Natural foods" are not the most healthy foods when the water supply is inadequate or polluted.

The last three articles might be classified as "psychosociology," to use a phrase of Roland Barthes. But while all three are more concerned with the "language of food" than with its economic or social role, each author approaches the subject quite differently. It would be misleading, therefore, to force these three articles into any rigid category.

Jean Soler attempts to explain the dietary laws of the Hebrews. His is an essay in intellectual history, a textual exigesis of the Bible using the newest techniques of semiotics. Through a careful analysis of the logic of the Old Testament, Soler demonstrates how dietary distinctions follow and "fit" a coherent system of thought. The reader is led step by step from the basic proposition that the Garden of Eden was vegetarian through the Biblical treatment of meat eating, the distinction between flesh and blood, the substitutive function of animal sacrifice, and finally, by logical deduction and analogy, to a basic taxonomy distinguishing "clean" from "unclean" food. The "unclean" and prohibited foods are "blemished," "altered," or perverted from their pristine place in the ordered, rigorous system of the Mosaic law. They are "unclean," not because they are dangerous to public health but because they do not conform to a very tight logical system. Soler ends his article by suggesting that this "logic of choice of food" is a key to understanding a wider society, that is, Jewish culture to this day.

Like Soler, Jean-Claude Bonnet invokes Lévi-Strauss and the "structuralist approach" to food. But unlike Soler, Bonnet does not have a single authoritative text to elucidate and interpret. Instead, he attempts to collect a widely scattered number of references to food preparation in the articles of Diderot's *Encyclopédie* and to identify an ordered structure, tying these references to other intellectual tendencies or thought patterns in French society in the mid-eighteenth century. At the end of this substantial article, Bonnet himself concludes that he has not uncovered a coherent structure in the same sense as Soler's dietary code. Yet he has demonstrated that the treatment of the culinary arts by Jaucourt, Diderot, and other authors of the *Encyclopédie* illustrates various preoccupations of the wider culture, its intellectual concerns in particular, in a curious amalgam. Moral and religious objections to a self-indulgent, luxury-loving *haute cuisine* are mixed with utilitarian caution about the physically damaging consequences of a "treacherous art," summarized in the word *"ragoût."* The rules of fasting were relaxed, but temperance was emphasized. In fact, there was a great deal of ambivalence toward elaborate food preparation. *"Gourmandise"* was defined as a "sophisticated and immoderate" love of good food, surely not an unqualified condemnation in contemporary Paris.

Although these Encyclopédistes would reject the voluptuous sensuality characteristic of the nineteenth-century gourmet literature in the generation after Brillat-Savarin, the oracle of *haute cuisine,* they approved of the refined cooking that evoked exotic produce (mangos of South America or cane sugar from "les Iles") and required manipulation of ingredients that, after all, reflected an open, experimental, scientific frame of mind. References to a nutritional science based on a balance of the humors went side by side with a new set of poetic and sensual metaphors that left the older prosaic taxonomy of natural science behind. In short, the culinary "discourse" of the *Encyclopédie* reflects the wide range of concerns of Diderot and his associates, exposing many different levels of contemporary knowledge ranging from religion, morals, and literature to utility, technology, and the biological sciences. In the end, Bonnet characterizes the "Encyclopedic view of eating" as neither obsessive nor guilt ridden, but rather a "learned game combining knowledge and sensual enjoyment." Although those raised in what remains of a puritan tradition might find less cohesion in this "culinary system" than those reared on Descartes and coq au vin, all would agree that Bonnet has deftly probed the *Encyclopédie*'s attitudes toward food and opened another window on eighteenth-century culture.

Roland Barthes's essay is less a historical investigation than a suggestive essay, a pronunciamento that food is not simply a collection of products that can be used for statistical and nutritional analysis, but "a system of communication, a body of images, a protocol of usages, situations, and behavior." More speculative than either Soler and Bonnet, Barthes signals the qualities or "labels" people give to their food—"sweet," "crisp," "succulent," "moist"—and attempts to relate these labels to a larger set of "themes" and "situations" in the society. Arguing that modern advertising is a reflection of a collective psychology, Barthes identifies a series of themes "signaled" by food ads such as commemoration of the national past, sexual awareness, and health. He suggests that different social classes look for different qualities in their food; it is these qualities he wishes to distill and relate to other social and cultural values and attitudes. He extends this differentiation to entire national cultures. The language of food, he insists, is an expression of a civilization, and the words we use to describe it are keys to other attitudes as basic as those we have toward activity, work, leisure, and celebration.

One of the hallmarks of the Annales School has been the melding of historical problem, source, and an ancillary social science in new and imaginative ways. In this selection of articles the meld seems especially successful. Old and new sources—"serial," qualitative, linguistic—about food and drink have been joined by economics, nutrition, medicine, urban and rural sociology, and social psychology. Yet all the authors have retained their identities, formulating the problem in a unique way, often building on previous research. None has followed a rigid methodology or a set plan imposed from the outside. Happily, "food in history" has many recipes.

Robert Forster
Orest Ranum

Food and Drink
in History

1
Toward the History of Nutrition: Some Methodological Remarks

Maurice Aymard

Taking Stock of the Problem

The appeal launched by the *Annales* in 1961 has been widely heard. But the history of nutrition is in danger of suffering from its very success. The proliferation of studies has given rise to a number of problems that can only gain from being stated clearly and faced honestly.[1]

The local data available now, often amounting to no more than spot checks and based on such sources as happen to have survived, still leave large blank areas on the map of western Europe, despite the cumulative efforts of many patient scholars. Moreover, these data are imprisoned, as it were, by their very precision, so that it is difficult to compare them to each other in time and space; and it is clear that no comparative evaluation will be possible without a considerable effort at unification and abstraction.

Owing to the need for reliable statistical sources, the main body of observations concerns a "long nineteenth century" (1780-1920), a situation that is bound to produce a certain slant. Approached in this manner, the high point of a hypothetical "nutritional Ancien Régime"—a notion that is as convenient as but even more debatable than the so-called "demographic Ancien Régime"—is seen to precede and prepare the mutation of the contemporary era. The "boom" in source materials has not yet, some groping attempts notwithstanding, been able to lead us beyond the descriptive stage toward interpretative hypotheses or an attempt to classify the data. Yet this is a necessary methodological step that was taken by both price history and historical demography at this stage in their development.

In a deeper sense, the history of nutrition appears to be undecided in the face of a number of approaches that offer themselves. Here are the three major avenues that are open to it. First, there is the psychosociology of diet: human

Annales, E.S.C. 30 (March-June 1975): 431-44. Translated by Elborg Forster.

beings do not live on nutrients but on food items, and these are arranged in a relatively rigid code of values, rules, and symbols, a code that is very slow to change. Then there is the macroeconomic approach, which seeks to ascertain, or at least to establish the statistical parameters of the "outer limits of productivity" by the roundabout way of data concerning consumption, population, international trade, and prices. Finally, there is the study of the nutritional value of the foodstuffs of the past and of their deficiencies in quantity and quality. This is the most obvious but not the easiest approach, for here the simplest, most banal questions can bring an investigation to a halt. This can be the fault of the sources: there are cases where a few vegetables or a little fruit, which may not have been mentioned, would be enough to make for a balanced diet.[2] But it can also be a matter of the system of reference used.

The fact is that all historical tallies concerning the intake of calories, proteins, vitamins, and minerals are normally measured by the standards of the nutritional *optima* established by experts in public health and nutrition for the contemporary world. This tends to distort our perspective, as I shall show by three examples.

1. *Meat.* Meat, or more generally the proportion of animal proteins in the diet, has rightly been used as a measuring device, for it is a sure sign of nutritional improvement in developed countries, and it is closely correlated with improved sanitation and an increase in average physical stature. Applied to the past, however, this criterion would above all have the effect of assigning a privileged status to periods of demographic decline (fourteenth-fifteenth century) and to nomadic or seminomadic societies of stock breeders. Moreover, the range of oscillation in meat consumption is probably frequently exaggerated, for we know from J. C. Toutain's calculations for France[3] that the proportion of animal proteins did not rise from its traditional level of 25 percent of the total protein intake until after 1880-90. But most historians relegate everything that happened before that date to a kind of nutritional prehistory.

2. *Wheat.* Every one of us has wrestled with the matter of converting wheat into bread: In principle, each quintal [100 kilograms] of wheat should correspond to 120 kilograms of black bread, but one usually finds only 100 kilograms, often less, and in rare cases 105 to 110 kilograms. In terms of equal weight, 600 grams of wheat always corresponds to 1,980 calories in the form of grain, and 1,440 calories in the form of bread; in other words, 20-25 percent of the calories are unaccounted for when we convert the available supplies into actual consumption. If this is the case here, one wonders whether all our other calculations will not also be condemned to spurious precision. This is particularly likely with respect to vitamins and trace elements, which are infinitely more difficult to measure.

3. *Calcium.* Thus, it is questionable that a listing of calcium intake based on a minimum daily requirement of 900-1,500 milligrams[4] and a calcium/phosphorus ratio of 0.6 to 0.8 is a valid approach. Like the historian L. Stouff, contemporary statisticians have doubts about the value of their sources, which are often incomplete. Fruits and vegetables in particular are always underreported;[5] moreover, their mineral content is extremely variable. In fact, the listing of fruit and vegetable consumption is no better than that of dairy products, which can be estimated with some precision only when they are commercialized. Contemporary

data place only developed countries of Caucasian race above the threshold of 900 milligrams (compared to 350 milligrams in 1960 Japan). Yet "no specific disease attributable to calcium deficiency has ever been described in male humans" (F.A.O./W.H.O., *Besoins en calcium,* p. 20), even when their intake is close to the threshold of 300 milligrams. Only the requirements of women during pregnancy and lactation can be calculated with some precision, and it appears very difficult to isolate a possible calcium deficiency from all the other factors contributing to the slow growth of children in developing countries. As for the calcium/phosphorus ratio, its variations are felt to "have no discernible effect on human nutrition" (ibid., p. 16). Moreover, "in every part of the world, most apparently healthy individuals, children as well as adults, develop and live satisfactorily on a calcium intake ranging between 300 milligrams and more than 1,000 milligrams (ibid., p. 10).

With the exception of the very small privileged groups that existed in every country, the world's population before 1800 lived to an overwhelming extent below our contemporary optimum standard of nutrition, which was beyond the reach—and indeed, until quite late, beyond the aspirations—of even the wealthiest. Most people lived close to the same minimum standard that is the lot of half or three-fourths of the present-day inhabitants of our planet. These minimum standards have now become well (or better) known through the studies of the United Nations Food and Agriculture Organization (F.A.O.) and the World Health Organization (W.H.O.). These studies establish thresholds of outright undernutrition and of the whole complex and differentiated gamut of malnutrition. For our purposes, these thresholds constitute much better points of reference than our anachronistic optimum standards.

The Classification of Data

We will be well advised to arrange our sources and our tables of quantitative data according to principles taken from contemporary statistics, which do not necessarily have access to better data than the historian. Thus, various categories can be distinguished under the headings of available supplies and consumption.

1. *Available supplies*
   - At the level of production: records of harvests, tithes [which represented a certain percentage of the harvest], etc.
   - At the aggregate level: import statistics, levies paid at city gates, stockpiling or purchases by government agencies.
   - At the individual level: rations in armies or navies, prisons and schools; free distribution or sale of food by municipalities; food pensions for aged members of families (which should list the quantities stipulated, regardless of whether they were actually provided).

2. *Consumption*
   - Either by a population as a whole (not including the privileged of every kind, and with due allowance for inevitable cases of fraud): taxes on salt (*gabelles*) and various other items of consumption

—or by social or demographic groups, provided that their value as a sample is first discussed: aristocratic or royal tables (including the redistribution of leftovers illustrated by J. P. Aron);* religious houses such as convents, seminaries, or hospitals; bourgeois families (household and account books); working class (cf. Fréderic Le Play, ed., *Les Ouvriers des Deux-Mondes* [Paris, 1857-85]) and peasant families; workers employed by specific agricultural, industrial, or mining enterprises that either provided all their food or paid part of their wages in food. In agricultural enterprises, a distinction should be made between the daily fare and the more exceptional meals provided at the peak of the harvest.

Actually, this classification should be used with some caution, for as the sample is enlarged, the accounts become increasingly likely to tell us about "available supplies" under the label of consumption, given the losses and discrepancies due to fraud, the dishonesty of shopkeepers, and hoarding. And in any case, however close they may come to the actual facts, these measurements fail to account for three potential causes of overestimation:

—The discrepancy between the product "as bought" and the edible part, which may be null, as in the case of flour, but can vary from 10 to 15 percent (meat) and amount to as much as 40 percent (poultry and game), indeed 50 percent (certain vegetables and fruits). The tables of composition of foodstuffs for international use published by the F.A.O. in 1949 have attempted to establish at least the approximate percentages for the various foodstuffs.

—Losses occurring between the retail and the "physiological" level due to spoilage, loss in cooking, discarding of food, and so forth. Such losses can amount to as much as 10 to 12 percent.[6]

—Uneven distribution, regardless of whether one extrapolates the findings of a limited sample or establishes an average for the consumption or the available supplies of a population as a whole. The impact of this factor will vary according to the social structure and the percentage of well-to-do families, but it does necessitate raising, by 10 to 15 percent at the very least, the quantities needed to fulfill the average requirements.

Under these circumstances, a twofold approach is indicated. On the one hand, we must study "cooking" in the widest sense, that is, the entire area of food preparation. The case of bread is an example: As bread becomes increasingly whiter, the discrepancy between available *supply* and *consumption* becomes more pronounced; yet at the same time the share of bread in the diet also tends to diminish. We also know how much long cooking affects the nutritional value of vegetables. Inversely, the admixture of chalk to corn [maize] meal in the preparation of Mexican tortillas is known to compensate for its low calcium content.

On the other hand, however, any comparison in time and space that goes beyond limited social groups (Tuscan oarsmen and Dutch sailors) and seeks to encompass entire populations implies that we must turn from actual consumption

*See chapter 8 of the present volume.

to available supplies, from real people to the "statistical unit" (the healthy, moderately active, adult male between 20 and 30 years of age) before we can deal with the wide variety of concrete situations.

Nutrition and Diet

While it is necessary to isolate the various components of human nutrition for the purpose of analysis, they assume their meaning only within the framework of a dietary regime, just as a culture assumes its meaning within a system of cultures. Only the diet as a whole can bring about a more or less satisfactory nutritional balance. A dietary regime has all the characteristics of a "structure" as Fernand Braudel uses this word, for it evolves very slowly over time and has very limited flexibility. Moreover, the dividing lines between the different dietary regimes must have been even more rigid and clear-cut a century ago than they are today, when diets are usually classified according to their main sources of protein. Under the current scheme of classification, the diets of the various countries are listed in a decreasing order according to the main source of protein. They are:
—products of animal origin (54-70 percent of the total protein intake)
—wheat and associated cereals, barley, rye, etc. (42-66 percent)
—sorghum and the various kinds of millet
—maize
—the wheat-maize-rice combination
—rice
Finally, at the very bottom of the list, there are the countries where roots, tubers, and plantains are the mainstay of the diet, since they need complementary products to supply most of their proteins.[7] In all these cases, except the first (products of animal origin) and the last (tubers), the main source of proteins is also the main source of calories, in other words, the basic staple of the diet.

This hierarchy matches the hierarchy of diets based on the percentage of calories from proteins (the ratio of calories from proteins to total calories), and the main cleavage is between the wheat-millet group on the one hand—which can supply quite as much protein as animal products, provided the rations are sufficiently large—and the maize-rice group on the other. The only foodstuff capable of closing this gap is rice, which provides a smaller quantity but a superior quality of protein than the other cereals. What is important for our purposes is the fact that from the Middle Ages to the early-modern period virtually all of western Europe was part of the second group, that of the wheat-based diet. And while it is true that occasional spurts of increased meat consumption occurred in periods of great demographic decline, Europe has only very recently moved up into the first group, where animal products furnish more than half of the proteins. This change took place in France after 1900, according to J. C. Toutain's calculations, and is occurring in Italy only today. The various kinds of millet, which had never played a very important role, were eliminated relatively early. Potatoes appeared or gained acceptance too late, fortunately, to bring about a catastrophic slide into the last category, a diet based on tubers. Historically, potatoes were successful in Europe only as a complement, and not as a substitute for bread; and even at the peak of their importance in France, between 1935 and 1960, they still furnished four times fewer calories than bread. The few enclaves that specialized in maize (Aquitain basin, Venetia, etc.) date from the seventeenth and eighteenth centuries, and, as we shall see, maize was prevalent enough there to cause the widespread incidence of pellagra.

Historians find that these dietary regimes remained unchanged over centuries and millenia, and their findings are strikingly similar to the conclusions reached by observers of the twentieth-century situation: At the top of the scale, in rich countries, "income ceases to be the decisive explanatory variable for food consumption,"[8] and the new dietary model—the daily meat—tends to be followed by virtually the entire population. At the other extreme of the scale, the dietary archetypes are also adhered to by everyone; and in nonmonetary societies the prevalence of self-sufficient farmers even tends to reduce, if not to obliterate, the difference [in dietary habits] between rich and poor.

Between these two extremes, however, a wide area of instability is created whenever money becomes the basis of the economy. The disruption of the traditional balance leads to increasing inequality in food consumption, with improvement for some accomplished at the price of the pauperization of a part of the population, especially in the cities. For we know that this disruption often coincides with migration to the cities, which breaks down dietary and culinary habits and changes the traditional channels of supply. And if our sources often show us cities that were in every respect privileged in relation to the surrounding countryside, this advantage of city living was effective above all in the largest cities, those that were closest to the seats of political power and hence the most threatening. (See figure 1.1).

It was in such a zone of instability that western Europe lived between the fourteenth and the twentieth centuries, and such quantitative data as we have suggest that two phases should be distinguished. The outstanding feature of the first phase is the variability in quantity and regularity of the total caloric intake within an unchanging dietary regime, while the second phase is characterized by the structural transformation of that diet. Here we have the industrialized Europe, where in the twentieth century country after country changed from a diet dominated by cereals of the wheat family to a diet in which most of the protein is furnished by products of animal origin.

Tracing this evolution on the level of national averages, J. C. Toutain's series of data suggests that the first phase, which occupied the entire nineteenth century and witnessed an increase in caloric intake from 1,800 to 3,200 calories, prepared the second phase; but this second phase, a mutation initiated in the years 1860-70 by a slight increase in the consumption of fats and animal products, was not really defined and realized until after 1890.[9] At that point, the caloric intake stopped rising, and even declined somewhat. It was the composition of the diet that changed in a straight linear evolution. In just over fifty years, France

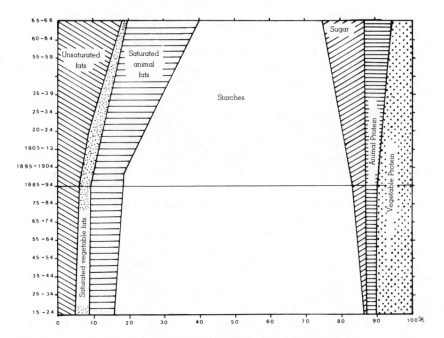

Figure 1.1. French Nutrition, 1815-1966: Carbohydrates, Fats, and Proteins

Source: J. C. Toutain, *La Consommation alimentaire en France de 1789 à 1964* (Geneva, 1971)

went from one end to the other of the road that still separates the developing countries from the world's industrialized areas today. Figure 1.1, the diachronic table established on the basis of Toutain's series shows essentially the same features as Figure 1.2, the synchronic table of the present-day nutritional situation of the world arranged according to per-capita income:

—The rapid decrease in the intake of carbohydrates, from 70 to 45 percent, is overshadowed by an even more spectular falling-off in the consumption of starches (cereals, tubers, legumes), which is partially compensated by a very marked rise in the consumption of sugars.

—The proportion of proteins in the diet remains stable at between 11 and 13 percent of the calories. But the positions are now reversed in favor of animal proteins, which are superior in quality to vegetable proteins. Proteins of animal origin represent two-thirds of the total protein intake, as compared to one-fourth until about 1880.

—After that of the sugars, the highest growth rate is that of the group of fats, which in the most highly developed countries are threatening to become the "basic foodstuff," or main source of calories. The decrease in the consumption of saturated plant fats contained in cereals, nuts, and oleaginous grains is offset by the increase in the consumption of both saturated and unsaturated fats from other sources. Unsaturated fats of plant and animal origin, such as butter, oil, and the various shortenings, are widely used in cooking, while the increased intake of saturated animal fats is related to the increased use of meat and dairy products. In this respect, however, nineteenth-century France, where the intake of animal products was already quite high as early as 1800, is an unusual case. Here the proportion of saturated vegetable fats was already quite small (below 20 percent), while the proportion of saturated animal fats remained stable at about 50 percent, so that the change amounted to no more than a relatively minor increase in unsaturated fats.

The structural stability of the dietary regime before 1880-90 should not surprise us. Until that time, in the England of the Industrial Revolution, wage gains are reflected in the increased consumption of liquor and beer, the only foodstuffs for which production could be adjusted to meet increased demand. Not before the end of the nineteenth century did a general transformation of food distribution take place. At that time, but only then, it became possible, due to the improvement of international trade and commercial channels of supply, to provide the urban masses with increased quantities of meat, milk, dairy products, fresh fruit, and vegetables.[10]

But this second stage, which by the end of the nineteenth century is reflected in the national averages, was reached earlier by certain privileged social groups, and even by certain cities, such as Rome, as Jacques Revel has shown,* or Lavoisier's Paris. Nonetheless, most of our quantitative series of data show that while persons of higher revenue could afford larger and more regular rations, the composition of their diet was identical to that of the ordinary consumer. This is true, for instance, for the copious menus of the archbishop of Arles in the fifteenth century,[11] which adhere to the dietary archetype of the average Provençal family and simply show vastly larger quantities, not only of bread, but of wine. On the other hand, the rations of the seventeenth-century Italian Jesuits, which were the same from the north to the south of the peninsula, already show the first sign of the mutation that was to occur in our own time: their bread ration, while still high, was lower than that of a field hand; the meat ration reached, and in some cases surpassed, 100 kilograms per year; two thirds of a still fairly low fat ration (50 grams) came from meat and cheese; but bread still supplied slightly over half of a more than adequate protein intake (115 grams), namely, 59 grams as against 56 grams from other sources.

Between these two extremes one could find, to be sure, an infinite number of intermediate examples. But for the most part, these would concern only a minority of the population, whose numerical importance would have to be established. As a general rule, differences in income were reflected, first and foremost, in the volume of the wheat ration. To be more accurate, I should say the ration of wheat and other grains, since outside of the Mediterranean Basin, high-quality wheat remained for a long time the cereal of the rich, while the masses had to be satisfied with the secondary cereals, barley, rye, sometimes oats, as well as spelt and the very wide variety of maslins [mixed cereals].[12] Here

*See chapter 2 in the present volume. — Trans.

again, it will be possible to distinguish several stages: the decreasing importance of barley (fourteenth-fifteenth centuries), the disappearance of the millets, and the advance of rye. These stages are highly significant in economic and human terms, and decisive aspects of the history of ways of life or of agriculture. But in terms of nutrition, they have very little or no significance, except in regions where maize, a cereal of poor protein content, was substituted for the other "minor" grains. Wheat is not superior to the other cereals, excepting maize and rice, either in caloric value or in protein, mineral, or vitamin content. This is also true, incidentally, of the color of bread, a matter of great human significance. White bread, of course, is more digestible and more completely assimilated. But the elimination of the outer shell of the grain in the bolting process involves the loss of part of the nutrients, a loss that was even more complete in the traditional milling techniques (which crushed the grain very coarsely and were unable to recover more than 60 percent of the pure flour) before the invention of the cylindrical mill. These losses were due to the fact that the aleuron cells, located under the pericarp, contain a very high percentage of the protein (18-24 percent) and minerals, and as much as 80 percent of the niacin and the other B_{12} vitamins. A population living exclusively on white bread would suffer, owing to the lack of thiamine, from the same beriberi that afflicted the populations of Asia who used to live exclusively on polished rice; and in fact this is exactly what happened in Newfoundland and Labrador in 1900-30.[13] Implying notions of social prestige, but also of luxury and waste, white bread—like white rice—makes sense only as part of a diet that can be balanced in other ways, by the intake of other nutritional elements.

Nor can whole grain bread, by itself, be sufficient. The protein of wheat, like that of the other cereals, is short of one essential amino acid, lysine. Lysine is thus the limiting factor in the protein of wheat, which improves when legumes and meat products, both of which are rich in lysine, supply from 22 to 25 percent of the total caloric intake. This minimum percentage is sufficient to raise the protein index of the limiting factor from 40 to 58. However, beyond that point, the protein index of the secondary limiting factors rises much more slowly. When legumes and meat products furnish from 22 to 60 percent of the total protein intake, the protein index rises by only five points, increasing from 58 to 63. This minimum figure of approximately 25 percent protein from supplementary sources is found in nineteenth-century France, as a national average, for proteins of animal origin alone. It explains the historical importance of legumes, which served as the meat of the poor and had long been recognized as such, so that the Church recommended their use during Lent. But legumes represent only 8 percent of the total amount of proteins consumed in the world, and they often elude our investigations. Therefore, one must use, as a complementary index, the percentage of calories furnished by cereals, starches, and sugars, keeping in mind that the critical threshold lies at about 80 percent. Whenever the percentage is higher, taking into account social inequalities of distribution, the diet of the masses becomes inadequate in quality, even if the caloric intake itself appears to be satisfactory. Significantly, many of the available figures lie in this borderline area, which is particularly dangerous when the caloric intake itself hovers close to the indispensable minimum. Thus, 79 percent of the 1,800 calories consumed in revolutionary France came from cereals, starches, and sugars, and 75 percent still came from the same source during the *Belle Epoque* [late nineteenth century], although this period was much better off, with its 3,200 calories and more than 100 grams of protein per person per day.

In this context, the meager food rations of the lower classes before 1800 warn us not to minimize the decisive role played by spirits and wine, which are often assumed to have supplied a maximum of 10 percent of all calories. This maximum is clearly underestimated, considering that a healthy, well-nourished adult oxidizes 2 grams of ethanol per kilogram of bodyweight per hour, with each gram of ethanol furnishing 7.1 calories. The maximum amount of energy derived from alcohol would thus be about 550 calories for a woman weighing 55 kilograms and 700 calories for a man weighing 65 kilograms. This would be a caloric value corresponding to one liter of 12° wine.[14] These figures have the advantage of tallying rather well with other historical data, such as the rations of soldiers, galley rowers, or agricultural day-laborers. In the insalubrious towns of early-modern Europe, wine was seen, as everyone knows, as the "hygienic" beverage, at least by comparison with the municipal fountains. But during the same period, wine may also have played a decisive role as a complementary source of energy for all categories of workers engaged in heavy physical labor, since a cereal ration that had not only fallen close to the minimum level but was also increasingly stripped of its complement in meat was no longer capable of fulfilling these needs. This brings us back to what we know about the history of agricultural production: while the medieval high point of meat consumption is linked to the advance of extensive livestock raising at the expense of the more intensive grain production, the cultivation of vineyards continued over long periods to be the only intensive culture, especially in Mediterranean Europe. Breweries and distilleries made it possible to absorb the surplus cereal, especially the minor grains, produced in years of plenty, as well as any surplus wine, for which better techniques of preservation had just been developed.

The meager diet of the lower classes and the tenuousness of a diet dominated by grain also raise, once again, the frequently thorny problem of dietary deficiencies, a problem that every historical study of nutrition is bound to encounter.

Deficiencies

1. VITAMINS AND MINERAL SALTS

Medical observation has isolated some thirty deficiency diseases directly related to an insufficient intake of vitamins or minerals. Some of these have had an undeniable historical impact and have occurred, or continue to occur, in a more or less disguised epidemic form. Only the most important of these can be treated here.[15]

Vitamin A: This vitamin is present in dairy products, egg yolk, fish liver oil, and also in the form of a provitamin (carotene) in certain fruits, in green leaves, and in certain roots. Its absence from the diet provokes, among other things, a variety of eye diseases. Unfortunately, the products containing it are particularly difficult to trace and quantify in the diets of the past, and this problem is especially acute in the case of fruits and vegetables. But in any case, it should be pointed out that this avitaminosis often occurs in conjunction with an insufficient intake of calories and proteins, whether it be permanent or temporary, and that its effects are particularly severe in young children whose intestinal walls, when weakened by infectious or parasitic disease, prove incapable of absorbing this vitamin.

Vitamin B₁ (Thiamine): The principal sources for this vitamin are cereal grains, legumes, and nuts, the basic foodstuffs of the traditional diet. It can therefore be assumed that historically beriberi was indeed related to the exclusive consumption of polished rice and white flour, and thus a consequence of industrialization.

Niacin, a vitamin of the B group: It too is present in whole-grain cereals, legumes, meat, and fish. Pellagra was identified in Spain as early as the eighteenth century as a disease of poor people living exclusively on maize. Its propagation in time and space closely followed the spread of maize in Europe from the Iberian Peninsula to southern Russia, and then to the United States. Paradoxically, it seems to have spared Latin America, thanks to a variety of complementary foodstuffs, such as beans or the chalk of the Mexican tortillas.

Vitamin C: Scurvy, which was known even in Antiquity and in the Middle Ages, was the disease par excellence of armies and sieges and, beginning in the seventeenth and eighteenth centuries, of long sea voyages. But it also almost invariably accompanied famine and became very prevalent in infants at the turn of the twentieth century, due to the changeover from breast feeding to artificial feeding with boiled cow's milk. Moreover, it remained latent wherever the cold of winter, the heat of summer, or any other cause regularly or intermittently brought about a prolonged interruption in the consumption of fresh fruit and vegetables.

Vitamin D and calcium: Rickets in young children, a disease related to an insufficient intake of milk, is also related to insufficient exposure to ultraviolet light and thus to living conditions (especially housing) and to climate. It appears in history by the Middle Ages and particularly from the eighteenth century onward as a disease of the European cities, and it is present even today in the cities of tropical countries. It is therefore a disease of urbanization in which dietary deficiencies do not play the major role.

Iodine: Iodine deficiency causes endemic goiter and, in its wake, a high incidence of deaf-mute and mentally deficient individuals. Described in these terms even in Antiquity, and today eradicated by the systematic addition of minerals to the water supply, goiter was found in certain enclaves in preindustrial Europe, especially in the poorest agricultural and mountain areas.

Diet-related anemias: Pernicious anemia (vitamin B_{12}) and chlorosis (iron) due to the lack of vitamins and iron, but also of proteins, are still endemic in a number of developing countries. Except for the classic nineteenth-century chlorosis, there is not much historical evidence about them or their incidence.

This list could be prolonged. But measuring the incidence of these deficiencies is a vexing problem for the historian, since the available sources are particularly imprecise, indeed often nonexistent, for all fresh products, fruit, vegetables, milk, and eggs. Moreover, while specific and objective standards do exist today, one wonders which ones—normal requirements, optimal requirements, recommended allowances—should be applied. They no doubt vary from individual to individual and from diet to diet. And finally, even assuming that deficiency diseases can be identified with relative assurance on the basis of historical medical observations, one is still only dealing with "privileged" cases, where it is possible to isolate the lack of one specific nutritive element because its deficiency was so pronounced and so overwhelming that it brought about a deficiency disease. But this does not tell us anything about partial and latent deficiencies. Nor do we know much more about the more complex but perhaps even more frequent deficiency diseases in which avitaminosis was only a side effect of a general deterioration of the diet as a whole, a phenomenon that is more easily measured in terms of calories and proteins.

In the majority of cases, I am afraid, the available sources will probably rule out an accurate appraisal of the incidence of avitaminosis. Only medical observations made at the time and the study of skeletons found in medieval or early-modern sites could furnish convincing evidence and lead us from possible to probable conclusions. There is no question that partial and localized deficiencies did exist, whether permanently or temporarily, of general or limited scope. If some of them, like endemic goiter, appear to be circumscribed in space at an early date, most resulted from disruptions in the traditional nutritional balance brought about by a new system of crops (pellagra), a temporary interruption of normal supplies (scurvy), or by urbanization and industrialization (scurvy of infants, rickets, beriberi, chlorosis). Hence their relatively recent history, at least in the European context, where these deficiency diseases were most prevalent in the period from the eighteenth to the twentieth century. (See figure 1.2.)

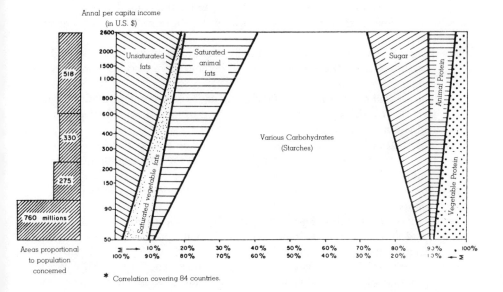

Figure 1.2. Calories supplied by Fats, Carbohydrates, and Proteins, as Percentage of the Total Caloric Intake, by Wealth of Country

Source: La Consommation, les perspectives nutritionelles . . . (Rome, 1969)

2. CALORIES AND PROTEINS

On the other hand, historians would seem to be in a much better position to observe the complex of deficiencies related to the temporary or permanent deterioration in the intake of calories and proteins. These deficiencies normally go together, since in all cereal-dominated diets the basic staple furnishes most of the proteins and since under those circumstances alternate sources of proteins are nonexistent. Added amounts of the limiting amino acid (lysine in the case of wheat) in the diet could, in theory at least, break this connection, but in practice the complements needed for a cereal diet are also in short supply whenever grain becomes too scarce or too expensive. In any case, the items most frequently listed in our sources are bread and wine, sometimes meat and cheese, but rarely anything else.

These deficiencies must be related, of course, to the minimum requirements in calories (for energy) and protein (for tissue replacement). The needs vary according to time and place. Factors to be taken into account include the following:

—The intensity of work, which becomes the main factor of adjustment in times of shortage;

—Climate, but to a lesser extent, since cold weather requires only 5 percent additional calories for every 10° C. drop in temperature (and even less today, when humans are better protected against variations in the outside temperature);

—Height and weight, to which the daily requirements are closely related. A person weighing 80 kilograms needs 60 percent more calories than a person weighing 50 kilograms;

—The sex and age distribution of the group under consideration, a factor that is too often overlooked when our sources force us to work with limited samples and youthful populations;

—The stages of life, since allowance must be made for increased needs during pregnancy, lactation, and periods of growth on the one hand and the simple maintenance of the body on the other;

—The composition of the diet, including such factors as the role played by alcohol.

In this manner, it has been found that today the impact of a more mature age pyramid, in conjunction with increased height and weight is such that the daily per-capita requirement of the industrialized countries is 15 percent higher than that of the developing countries, namely, 2,320 as opposed to 1,990 calories[16] for a moderately active individual. If J. C. Toutain's calculations for Napoleonic France (which adopt the highest possible figures for animal products and the lowest for vegetable products) are correct, the 1,800 calories of that period would already be close to the minimum requirement. Starting at this level, the slow but steady increase in caloric and protein intake over the nineteenth century could release an ample potential for growth in body size and resistence to disease, as well as an enormous reserve of human energy, thus making the majority of adult males capable of heavy physical labor.

Before the advent of this quantitative mutation, the unreliability of the harvests and the social and geographical inequalities in the distribution of available supplies exposed the human race permanently or intermittently to a series of pathological states. Some of these, such as marasmus or kwashiorkor, were the direct result of malnutrition. Much more frequent, however, were the diseases resulting from infection to which the poorly nourished individual becomes increasingly susceptible, especially the various forms of gastroenteritis and the respiratory infections that were rampant in Europe before 1800-1850 under a variety of names. No longer fatal today, these diseases had a high mortality rate in the past and still do in all countries living on the verge of scarcity. They also explain the time lag, frequently observed by historical demographers, between the peaks of mortality in the summer (a time when food supplies from the new harvest had become available) and the peaks in the price of grain in the spring (when supplies from the previous harvest were exhausted): most of the time people did not die directly of hunger, but indirectly of a disease for which malnutrition had cleared the way.

Certain age groups, particularly among children, are especially vulnerable to these diseases. Breastfed infants are relatively well protected by the breastmilk, whose protein content is maintained at the expense of the mother's reserves. Not so children between 9 months and 3 years, because this is the age of weaning and of the changeover from milk to an unsuitable adult diet based on cereals and starches. In the 1960s infant mortality (0-1 year) was 24.1 per thousand births in England and 186.9 in the Punjab, a difference of 1 to 9; while mortality between 1 and 2 years was 1.5 and 72.2 per thousand respectively, a difference of 1 to 48. Between 1901 and 1961 in England, the first rate declined sevenfold (from 151.3 to 21.4 per thousand), while the second rate declined thirtyfold (from 46.7 to 1.5 per thousand). For our purposes it should be noted that historical demography, a discipline that has learned to reconstitute families, and indeed entire censuses, has produced very accurate figures for infant mortality, thus providing us with an indispensable, albeit indirect source for the history of nutrition.[17]

Moreover, children are particularly vulnerable before birth, for we now know that malnutrition is responsible for as much as 40 percent of all premature births,[18] not to mention a high incidence of miscarriages. This fact, even more than the always temporary famine amenhorroea,* must have been responsible for the drastic decline in full-term pregnancies that has invariably been observed in times of famine.

The cyclical catastrophies with which the historian is familiar do not, of course, exclude chronic deficiencies like those noted by Abel Poitrineau in Limagne and by Guy Thuillier in Nivernais.[19] But such catastrophies serve to remind us that in our frequently approximate statistics, deviations from the average are at least as important as the averages themselves, especially when these hover close to the minimum limit of 1,800 to 2,000 calories. The history of nutrition must join forces with historical demography and the history of agricultural production, for their goal is the same as ours: measuring one aspect of the human past.

BIBLIOGRAPHY

Publications of the United Nations Food and Agriculture Organization (F.A.O., Rome) and of the World Health Organization (W.H.O., Rome)

1. F.A.O.
   Nutrition et travail, Etude de Base No. 5 (Rome, 1962)
   Troisième enquête mondiale sur l'alimentation, Etude de Base No. 11 (Rome, 1963)
   Malnutrition et maladie, Etude de Base No. 12 (Rome, 1963)
   Maize and Maize Diets (Rome, 1953)
   Les Graines de légumineuses dans l'alimentation humaine (Rome, 1964)
   Mesures à prendre en période de calamité pour faire face aux problèmes alimentaires (Rome, 1968)
   Le Blé dans l'alimentation humaine (Rome, 1970)
   From the *Plan indicatif mondial provisoire pour le développement de l'agriculture,* vol. 2, ch. 13:
   "La Consommation, les perspectives nutritionelles et les politiques alimentaires" (Rome, 1969)
2. W.H.O.
   L'Elimination des maladies de carence, Etude de Base No. 24 (Geneva, 1970)
3. F.A.O./W.H.O. (Reports by groups of experts from both organizations):
   Besoins en calcium (Rome, 1961)

*See Emmanuel Le Roy Ladurie, "Famine Amenorrhoea (Seventeenth-Twentieth Centuries)," in Robert Forster and Orest Ranum, eds., *Biology of Man in History* (Baltimore, 1975), pp. 163-78.—Trans.

Besoins en protéines (Rome, 1965)
Besoins en vitamines A, thiamine, riboflavine et niacine (Rome, 1967)
Besoins en acide ascorbique, vitamine D, vitamine B_{12}, acide folique, et fer (Rome, 1970)
Energy and Protein Requirements (Geneva, 1973)

NOTES

1. These pages owe a great deal to Mssrs. Lunven and Perissé, who received me with complete open-mindedness at the Food and Agriculture Organization's headquarters in Rome. They will find here the echo of their suggestions, their advice, and the bibliography to which they introduced me, as well as some inevitable errors of interpretation, for which I alone bear the responsibility.

2. L. Stouff, *Ravitaillement et alimentation en Provence aux XIVe et XVe siècles* (Paris, 1970), pp. 237-38.

3. J. C. Toutain, *La Consommation alimentaire en France de 1789 à 1964*, "Economies et Sociétés," Cahiers de l'I.S.E.A. (Geneva, 1971).

4. L. Randoin et al., *Tables de composition des aliments*, 5th ed. (Paris, 1973), pp. 12-13.

5. F.A.O., *Besoins en calcium* (Rome, 1961). All references in this paragraph are to this report.

6. F.A.O., *Mesures à prendre en période de calamité pour faire face aux problèmes alimentaires* (Rome, 1968), p. 74.

7. F.A.O., *Plan indicatif mondial provisoire pour le développement de l'agriculture* (Rome, 1969), pp. 549-54.

8. Ibid., p. 547.

9. Toutain, *La Consommation alimentaire*, table 47, p. 1982; table 50, p. 1987.

10. R. E. Dingle, "Drink and Working Class Living Standards in Britain, 1870-1914," *Economic History Review* (November 1972), 608-22.

11. Stouff, *Ravitaillement*, p. 237.

12. F.A.O., *Le Blé dans l'alimentation humaine* (Rome, 1970), pp. 24-32.

13. W.H.O., *L'Elimination des maladies de carence*, Etude de Base No. 24 (Geneva, 1970).

14. J. Trémolières and R. Lowy, "Physiology of ethanol metabolisms in alcohols and derivatives," *International Encyclopaedia of Pharmacology* (London, 1970), cited in F.A.O./W.H.O., *Energy and Protein Requirements* (Geneva, 1973), p. 39.

15. W.H.O., *L'Elimination des maladies de carence*.

16. F.A.O./W.H.O., *Energy and Protein Requirements*, table 27, p. 82.

17. W.H.O., *L'Elimination des maladies de carence*, table 2, p. 69.

18. F.A.O./W.H.O., *Besoins en protéines* (Rome, 1965), pp. 26-27.

19. *Pour une histoire de l'alimentation*, Cahiers des Annales 28 (Paris, 1970), pp. 152-53, 164-66.

2
The Potato in
the Eighteenth Century

Michel Morineau

Christian Vandenbroeke has written a fine article.[1] In a few pages he provides a number of welcome details concerning the introduction and expansion of a crop whose importance in the eighteenth century is often misunderstood for lack of information. He examines its impact on nutrition and demography and outlines a comparison that, although originally limited to two specific regions, the southern Netherlands [Belgium] and France, eventually encompasses all of Western Europe. In his conclusion the author advances a thesis that tends to establish a link among three facts by means of a consecutive causal relationship. These facts are the acceptance of the potato for mass consumption, the solution of the problem of subsistence, and the release of rapid population growth.

As the guiding thread of his study, Vandenbroeke uses lawcases involving the payment of a tithe. They have enabled him to date the appearance of the "American beauty" *as an open field crop*[2] from 1670 in western Flanders, and possibly even 1650 in the region of Tielt. The subsequent conquest of the Netherlands was slow, almost haphazard. According to Vandenbroeke, the potato spread in two major waves, one of which, starting perhaps in the garden of an English Carthusian monastery at Nieuport, moved from west to east, while the other, originating in the Vosges Mountains or even in Dauphiné—although one wonders whether the existence of the word really carries that much weight—flowed toward the northwest. Eventually both these waves met in the area of Liège around the year 1750.[3] The author claims that the potato reached eastern Flanders around 1720, Luxemburg province and the Namur area by 1730, and Hainaut after 1740. According to him, Hainaut was the last province to be touched, although it is not made clear in what way the Limbourg area can be considered an earlier incidence, since the potato was brought there from Maastricht, and since the first legal pleas [involving the potato] are dated 1762 and do not allude to a very long traditional use.

Annales, E.S.C. 25 (November-December 1970): 1767-84. Translated by Elborg Forster.

Vandenbroeke measures the increasing importance of the potato in the diet of the southern Netherlands by using contemporary estimates of the amount of grain needed to feed one person. He found an appreciable diminution of that amount over the course of the eighteenth century as a whole and claims that it decreased from 0.905 liters per day in 1710 to 0.617 liters per day in 1791. According to him, the difference was made up by the consumption of potatoes, which thus replaced 40 percent of the cereals. This became possible for three reasons: (1) The effectiveness of the new crop, which, given an equal surface of land, could feed five times as many people as wheat; (2) its consequent appeal for the poor, who were fortunate if they held a fraction of a *bonnier;** and (3) the remarkable extension of the surface devoted to its culture, even at the end of the Ancien Régime (9 percent of the arable land in the departments of Lys and Escaut by 1800).

In France, by contrast, only a few provinces had accepted the potato, and the dietary regime continued to favor bread. On the basis of this crosscheck, Vandenbroeke feels justified in moving from economics to demography. By correlating the unequal success of the tubers and the different rates of population growth in various places—the population increased by 100 percent in the Netherlands and in Germany, 80 percent in England, 50 percent in Sweden, 40 percent in Spain, and 31 percent in France—he makes it appear that these two phenomena went hand in hand.[4]

Actually, however, he does not make the nature of this connection altogether explicit. Forewarned, it would seem, by L. M. Cullen's recent article,[5] he drops the argument of younger marriages—despite indications to that effect in the prefects' reports[6]—an argument that has been at the core of the debate about Ireland. Vandenbroeke does not defend the thesis that the potato initiated or triggered the sudden rise in population but more cautiously believes that the new crop removed the obstacles that had curbed its long-term development. He thus basically agrees with the interpretation of the Ancien Régime crises that has become widely accepted in recent years. Yet the concatenation of developments he proposes does lead us back to the potato as the essential factor: increased planting of this crop, reduced dependence on cereal harvests for human consumption, less severe consequences when cereal harvests failed, marked rise in population. Four corollaries, which are only discreetly suggested by Vandenbroeke, follow from this sequence, but since they are in a sense obvious, no harm will be done by placing them in the full light of day. They are (1) the "progressive" connotation of the new crop; (2) the pioneering role and the advanced character of Belgian agriculture, which had already brought this crop close to its maximum potential by the end of the eighteenth century; (3) the shortcoming of French agriculture, which was incapable of accepting this beneficial disruption of agricultural and dietary habits; and (4) the demographic penalty paid by France for this shortcoming.

---

*1 *bonnier* = 1.3 hectares or 3.1 acres.

On first reading, one is carried along by the author's contagious enthusiasm, the logic of his reasoning, and the strength of his proofs. One is particularly happy and impressed with his constant efforts to call upon facts and figures for every problem; one admires him for finding the figures and for the way in which the conclusions flow from the source, so to speak. I would have liked to end my review with this well-deserved praise. But since I had just completed a study of French agriculture and its relation to the demography of the eighteenth century, the question he raised was of particular interest to me.

Following this natural interest, I began to use my own information to check Vandenbroeke's hypotheses in order to verify and perhaps even expand or strengthen them. By now the reader will have guessed that my conclusions do not entirely coincide with his, and that this is my reason for lengthening this text by a few pages. They were not written because I enjoy carping criticism, but in order to share certain new findings and to formulate the new perspectives that, in my opinion, are necessary. Needless to say, I am indebted to Christian Vandenbroeke for providing me with this opportunity; and I sincerely hope that in debating this matter with me he will not take offense at a critique that, whatever else it might do, recognizes from the outset the stimulative value, indeed the intrinsic value, of his work. It may not be amiss, moreover, that a French note be sounded in a discussion that has by now assumed international scope.

To begin with, one can readily grant Vandenbroeke the importance acquired by the potato in the southern Netherlands. Nonetheless, one might debate the exact extent of its progress and consider it arbitrary to apply to the entire country—*het ganse land*—the figures, down to the last decimal point, obtained in the departments of Lys and Escaut, which may well represent peak values. The information furnished by the prefects for the year IX [1801] is not uniform; while all of them mentioned the new crop, they did not attribute equal importance to it in every case.[7] In the department of Sambre-et-Meuse (administrative center: Namur), the local harvest provided no more than 500 grams of potatoes per day and per person, while in the department of Escaut that ration was 1 kilogram (or even 1.3 kilograms, according to the figure, based on a different calculation, adopted by Vandenbroeke). In the department of Dyle (Brussels), it is somewhat difficult to measure the importance of the new crop as long as only small farmers grew it; and in the department of Deux-Nèthes (Antwerp), we find obvious discrepancies between the arrondissement of Malines (where 9 percent of the arable land was planted in potatoes) and that of Turnhout (where the corresponding figure was 5.3 percent), although the average for the department was 7.3 percent. It is rather unfortunate that we do not have the detailed figures for the department of Lys, for it would be useful to know which of its arrondissements was most enthusiastically devoted to the potato. Was it that of Bruges, "naturally the poorest," or that of Courtrai, "Nature's spoiled child"? A keener perception of the nuances would thus be quite helpful; indeed it may be a necessity for a close analysis of the demographic figures.[8] But none of this can detract from the phenomenon as a whole in the southern Netherlands; and a juxtaposition of the corresponding English figures at the end of the eighteenth century (average ration, 400 grams in 1790; surface planted in Leicester, Worcester and Gloucester counties, 1.3 to 1.9 percent) establishes the proper order of magnitude.[9]

My second remark is more critical. All the precise quantitative data we are given concern the later period, that is, the last decade of the eighteenth century and the first decade of the nineteenth century. It is quite possible, however, that the popularity of the plant had its ups and downs, and that its actual development underwent considerable acceleration at a relatively late date; no one will question the impetus it received from the food shortages of 1740, 1770, 1793, and 1795. The case of Lorraine is a good example of this kind of diffusion. Thanks to the declarations of the parish priests in 1762, one can easily follow the geographic spread of the potato from the southern part of the province, the Vosges Mountains, to the northern part, adjoining Luxembourg. Not before 1740 or 1750 did it really begin to spread as an open field crop in the areas of Boulay, Sarregemines, and Bitche;[10] and yet, in the year IX [1801] prefect Colchen of the department of Moselle already assigned it a surface equal to 7.8 percent of the arable land, a figure roughly equivalent to what is found in Belgian Flanders. Other reference points include the English ration, which according to R. N. Salaman jumped from 250 to 400 grams between 1775 and 1795, and the fact that in the department of Rhin-et-Moselle (Koblenz), where the potato had become known barely thirty to forty years earlier, the daily per-capita ration already amounted to 800 grams in 1801.

It consequently becomes difficult to extrapolate any conclusions as to its importance for earlier dates, and the difficulties are even greater for the initial stages. It is understood, of course, that the mention of a tithe [to be paid in potatoes] in a lawsuit does indeed testify to the existence of a taxable base, in other words, to an appreciable amount of cultivation and a certain familiarity with the plant; but this does not mean that these two indications can be translated, respectively, into surface percentages and nutritional coefficients.[11]

The grain ration at Tielt in 1710, cited by Vandenbroeke himself, symptomatically illustrates this point: even though the peasants had been accustomed to the potato for the last fifty years and had been paying a tithe in potatoes for twenty, the per-capita grain ration remained as high as in the sixteenth century, namely, at 1,053 livres [Ancien Régime pounds] or approximately 750 grams. I do not doubt that the potato played a role, but I wonder just how important it was. I also feel that the application of this information to the issue of demography calls for a great deal of circumspection.

It is to this issue that I shall now address myself. But before proceeding any further and treating this subject in all of its dimensions, I feel it appropriate to provide some additional data for France, for it seems to me that Vandenbroeke's picture is rather too global. Some of his more audacious assertions, which he takes from sometimes questionable sources,[12] can be dismissed rather quickly. Thus, he tells us that by 1800 the potato had become known almost everywhere in France, although its introduction had taken place more or less recently and had been attended by varying degrees of success in cultivation and use. Yet it must be pointed out that in certain provinces its success was quite as great as in the Netherlands. In Lorraine, for instance, the figures for the department of Moselle testify to a history of more than a hundred years; Alsace also was converted (in the department of Haut-Rhin we find an assured daily per-capita ration of 575 grams in 1813), as was part of Franche-Comté. I do not have the figures for Dauphiné, but I feel that—with the usual caveats—the 1807 figures for the department of Mont-Blanc (Chambéry), where similar growing conditions prevailed, can be used for Dauphiné as well: 5 to 6 percent of the arable land was planted in potatoes. This order of magnitude is also plausible for some upper valleys in the Pyrennees and some of the slopes and basins of the Massif Central. Elsewhere, scattered enclaves could be cited, such as the department of Creuse, the department of Haute-Vienne (which produced roughly 175,000 metric *quintaux** in 1801 and devoted 2 to 3 percent of its arable land to potatoes), as well as the striking anomaly, especially by comparison with the former Austrian Netherlands, of the department of Nord, where [only] 1.2 percent of the arable land was planted in potatoes, even though prefect Dieudonné noted that potatoes formed a regular part of the peasants' diet.

Admittedly, the demographic growth of France in the eighteenth century was not, on the whole, much greater than 30 percent. But this percentage hides some enormous regional differences. I have had occasion to study these differences and to carry out a partial spot check of the available figures.[13] Table 2.1 shows that the demographic growth of the southern Netherlands was rivaled, indeed surpassed, in France, since Alsace had increased by 150 percent, Franche-Comté by 180 percent, and Lorraine by 200 percent. At first sight it is somewhat troubling to note that many of the prolific provinces had been early converts to the potato. Vandenbroeke's argument would be greatly strengthened if they could all be neatly lined up under the banner of the white-flowered potato stalk. This is not the case; moreover, Dauphiné, also among the long-standing devotees of the potato, lagged far behind.

Still, I have only half-elucidated the subject. Interregional comparisons are bound to be misleading unless they are weighted by an accurate evaluation of

Table 2.1—Demographic Growth of French Généralités in the Eighteenth Century

Growth	Généralité
Greater than 100%	Valenciennes, Nancy, Strasbourg, Franche-Comté, Roussillon(?)
Between 50 and 100%	Lille, Bourges, Moulins, Lyons, Montauban, Auch
Between 25 and 50%	Soissons, Paris, Caen, Brittany, Riom, Grenoble
Between 10 and 25%	Rouen, Champagne, Orleans, Tours, Poitiers, La Rochelle, Limoges, Languedoc, Provence
Less than 10%	Amiens, Alençon

Note: No conclusive figures are available for Metz, Burgundy, or Bordeaux.

*The metric *quintal* weighs 100 kilograms.

the initial levels on the one hand and an analysis of behavior between the two chronological reference points on the other. An outline of the first point will be found in note 14, below.[14] As for the second point, the following remarks are in order: The provinces that experienced run-away population growth were characterized by a steady progression throughout the century, while the others experienced frequently negative variations between 1697 and 1740 or 1745. Consequently, if the steep rise in population occurred in the second period, and if it was not slowed down in turn by a crisis, it was likely to be much more spectacular than expected and could go as high as 40 percent, as it did in Languedoc in a fifty-year period, compared to 15 percent in the preceeding one hundred years. Taking into account the negative cumulative effects of the first period on the "pool" of marriageable young people, we find that the discrepancy between the two groups in terms of their basic trend disappears at this point; Languedoc, with an annual growth rate of 5.5 percent, sometimes 7.5 percent, was growing almost as fast as French Hainaut (10-11 percent) and Franche-Comté and faster than Lorraine, which was running out of steam (4-5 percent) by the last decade. It is not difficult to see the analogy with the demographic evolution of the southern Netherlands.[15]

A clear and self-explanatory draft of the picture is thus emerging. For in considering the regions where population growth had taken hold after 1745, one cannot help but recognize that while some of them had adopted the potato, others (Languedoc, Ile-de-France) had not. It thus appears that in the second half of the century the potato was not required to promote or sustain a rapid rise in population. Now the question must be asked for the preceeding period: could it be that the *early* take-off of demographic growth coincided with an *early* introduction of the potato? As a first objection to this hypothesis one could point out that the effectiveness of a very new crop is bound to be uncertain and in any case undocumented in terms of nutrition. But there is no need to bring up this extra handicap,[16] because there is one case that very clearly does not fit this interpretation. This is the case of the *généralité* of Valenciennes. Here the potato was not grown at all until the last years of the Ancien Régime, and then only sporadically and in the outlying cantons of Condé-sur-Escaut and Avesnes. The population growth in this *généralité,* which is among those I was able to monitor most thoroughly, thus took place entirely within an unchanged agricultural system and on the immutable nutritional basis of a bread made with wheat flour. This pattern of development was by no means unusual; after all, this is what happened in England as well. But in the *généralité* of Valenciennes it happened very early and continued for a whole century. This example serves to eliminate the last privilege that might be assigned to the potato, that of supporting a continued demographic upswing beyond the point where it would normally have broken under the law of probability.

In short, the positive correlation postulated by Vandenbroeke cannot be shown to exist in every case. Not sufficient, by itself, to bring about the extraordinary demographic growth in eighteenth-century Dauphiné, the potato does not seem to have been necessary to trigger or accompany it anywhere else either. By breaking an admittedly tempting correlation in this manner, I do not mean to depreciate the very real help the American tubers brought to the populations of those regions where they had been adopted. I simply wish to stress that in a more complete panorama of Europe, we will miss the basic or sufficient cause of demographic growth as long as we concentrate all our efforts in searching for it in the economic circumstances of the time. This statement would make things very difficult if, while closing one approach that leads nowhere, it did not point to another, one that is just beginning to be explored, namely, the importance of biology itself. For this approach restores a measure of independence to the purely demographic phenomena; it is possible, after all, that a relaxation in the ceaseless struggle between man and his microbiological environment may have reactivated the equally permanent natural potential for growth.[17]

My incompetence in medical matters does not permit me to pursue this perspective, which has been placed on the agenda [of historical studies] in recent years. I will therefore have to leave it aside for the moment.[18] It should be obvious, however, that my last remarks, although arrived at in a different context, fit perfectly into this new approach. For the realization that there is no universal correlation between the spread of the potato and demographic growth naturally leads to another question: What was the real significance of this agricultural innovation in the eighteenth century? The partial answers to this question fall into two categories; some are general, and some apply only to Belgian Flanders.

Whatever the extent of its popularity, the potato was—and continued to be—a secondary, supplementary crop by comparison with the main crops, the major cereals, wheat and rye. Indeed, it was considered a crop for the poor, as can still be seen in geography textbooks on every educational level. It was neither the first nor the only one of such crops. Not to mention resources of a strictly local character such as millet (in the Vendée or in the region of Nantes) or chestnuts, France and Europe had earlier made good use of buckwheat—which in the department of Deux-Nèthes [Antwerp] still covered more surface than the potato in the year IX [1801]—and maize. These three plants are in the same category, and in its own time and place the potato was only the last innovation added to the list of groping and perpetually repeated attempts on the part of the peasants to deal with each successive problem of subsistence at their own level and with the means at their disposal.[19]

An equivalence between potatoes, maize, and buckwheat in terms of yields, corrected by nutritive value, is not easy to work out,[20] since every region, depending on its particular geographical conditions, had its own scale. It is not certain that the potato had an indisputable advantage everywhere. A. Dubuc has rightly called attention to the resistance against this crop in the western part of Normandy, where buckwheat was plentiful; and it is possible that the same plant also hindered the progress of its adjunct and competitor in Dauphiné.[21] A similar phenomenon can be observed in the Southwest of France, where in 1801 in the department of Haute-Garonne different crops were grown at different altitudes, maize on the plain and potatoes in the mountains.[22] Moreover, psychological obstacles also played their part, since people were no longer dealing with a cereal that could easily be made into flour, bread, or flatcakes—and here a brief smile is in order for Parmentier's baking trick, which has been described by J. J. Hémardinquer as a forerunner of the wartime *ersatz* bread of detestable memory. A whole new cuisine had to be invented for the potato, just as earlier it had been necessary to accustom cows to it *by taste,* since they were unable to recognize their new feed *by smell.*[23] The potato had served for so long as animal feed, especially for hogs, as Abbé Xaupi indicated in Cerdagne around 1770, that its adoption for human consumption could easily assume the stigma of a reduction in standard of living.[24]

Historically, this was certainly true. In all places and at all times the potato had always arrived in the baggage carts of distress, whether it was the English wars in Ireland, the thirty Years' War and Louis XIV's campaigns in Alsace and Lorraine, the War of the Spanish Succession in Flanders and Spain, or the catastrophic cereal failures of the eighteenth century, compounded in Saxony in 1770 by an armed conflict and in France by the civil disruption of the Revolution. Its favorite terrain was in poor regions, such as the desolate islands of the North Sea or the Hebrides, the mountains of Bohemia, the Vosges, or high Alpine valleys. From such areas it only spread when favored—not quite the word, perhaps—by shortages in neighboring regions, so that it was forever after associated with calamity, as it was in Lorraine, where it was considered a necessary evil, but an evil all the same.[25] This feeling that the potato represented at least a *qualitative* lowering of the standard of living was very real; it was a substitute, an *ersatz* for better food that was not available, and sometimes it was given up as soon as a plentiful supply of grain was restored.[26] This is confirmed by Vandenbroeke's description of the pattern of potato consumption in Belgium in the nineteenth and twentieth centuries. At times during that period consumption fell as low as 500 grams; and if indeed his figure for the late eighteenth century (1.3 kilograms per person and per day) could be proven, it would represent the high point of this consumption pattern. A quantitative diminution in caloric intake is less certain, but it would be a mistake to believe that the consumption of enough potatoes to replace bread had any meaning or reality except in the context of the self-sufficient farm. Calorie for calorie, this product was expensive in the market; one only has to consult the reports of the prefects for the year IX [1801] and the *mercuriales* [market quotations] of Bruges[27] to see that five hectoliters of potatoes cost more than one hectoliter of wheat, two of rye, or three of oats,[28] and that the availability of potatoes does not seem to have lowered the price of these cereals.

Pauperism and pauperization. What an unexpected and disconcerting new twist to a phenomenon that is usually considered the herald of an agricultural "revolution." One hesitates to apply this verdict to hard-working Flanders, a region that was technically ahead of the rest of Europe and held up as a model. Yet there are two arguments that must give us pause. Pursued to its logical conclusion, a mystique of the potato as the emblem of progress would lead to absurd claims, such as considering the agriculture of the Hebrides better than that of England, that of the Vosges better than that of the Brie and Beauce regions.* From this it follows that the presence and even the intensive cultivation of this crop cannot serve as the unique and infallible criterion of superiority in a comparison among several regions.

A different criterion was cited more frequently in the eighteenth century, and the mere reference to that loquacious agronomist, Arthur Young, will indicate that I mean the replacement of rye by wheat and the respective proportions in which these two cereals were sown. Let us adopt this criterion for a moment; it will lead us to another surprise. The information given by the prefects for the year IX [1801] is sufficient to construct a table for four departments: Nord [Lille], which, it will be recalled, was moderately involved with the potato, Lys [Bruges], Escaut [Ghent], and Deux-Nèthes [Antwerp]. (See tables 2.2 and 2.3)

Clearly, Deux-Nèthes, a department devoted to oats and buckwheat and visibly lagging behind in the race toward progress, was a special case. But one does note a kind of magic frontier, as clearly visible as that other famous frontier

Table 2.2—Proportion of Cereals Grown in Four Departments, Year IX [1801]

Cereals	Nord	Lys	Escaut	Deux-Nèthes
Wheat	51%	33%	29%	7%
Rye and Rye Mixtures	18	39	38	19
Barley and Barley				
Mixtures	8	10	14	7
Oats	23	18	19	53
Buckwheat	. . .	. . .	. . .	14
	100%	100%	100%	100%

Note: Buckwheat was distinguished in a manner suitable for the present purpose only in the department of Deux-Nèthes. In the department of Nord it was listed together with barley, just as spelt and maslin [a mixture of wheat and rye] were listed together with rye. To convey a general idea of the situation, I might say that the percentages for Belgian Flanders were similar to those of the departments in Brittany or mountainous areas, while in the rest of France—even in Lorraine, where certain *bailliages* (such as Bitche) had started to grow wheat relatively late (1740)—wheat was usually grown in greater quantities than rye.

Table 2.3—Proportion of Cereals Grown in Selected French Departments, Year IX [1801]

Crop	Finistère	Mont Blanc	Eure	Moselle	Dordogne
Wheat	20%	25%	63%	38.5%	39.5%
Rye	33	33	4.5	11.4	14
Barley	14	16	3.5	7.8	2.5
Oats	33	12	29	42.3	1.5
Buckwheat	no separate figures	9	. . .	. . .	1.5
Maize	. . .	5	. . .	. . .	4
	100%	100%	100%	100%	100%

*Considered to be the "bread baskets of France." [Trans.]

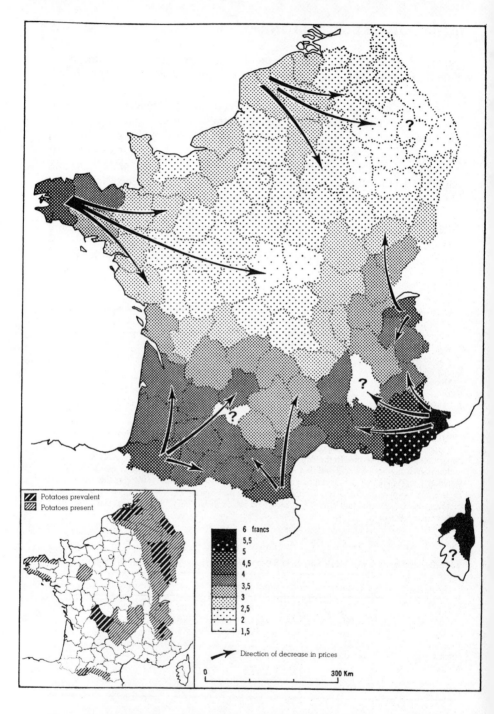

Figure 2.1. Wheat Prices and Potato-Growing Areas: Price of Wheat per Myriagram (10 Kilograms) in Francs and Centimes, Year IX [1801]

that was crossed by Arthur Young between Bouchain and Valenciennes, although it does not wind its way between tyranny and liberty[29] but between Brabant and Flanders. The question is whether certain methods could have been exported or whether physical conditions made this impossible. In Brabant the yields were "French," that is, average, varying between 9 *quintaux* (for wheat) and 11 *quintaux* (for oats). But one is struck by the fact that in Flanders itself the planting of rye continued to prevail over the planting of wheat, while the department of Nord was really interested only in the planting of wheat, the rich cereal that spelled white bread. Here, pure rye represented only 7.5 percent of the surface. This shows that such criteria must be handled with the greatest circumspection and that they must always be tested within their own context before they are used, for it would be only too easy to make assumptions about their importance in a national context. Not to anticipate, however, it will be sufficient to point out that the peasants on both sides of the frontier were engaged in parallel, but not necessarily incompatible pursuits: they grew wheat and rye or wheat and —potatoes.

If we now establish the nutritional quota of each department on the basis of its agricultural production, the preponderance of wheat in the department of Nord naturally makes for a higher wheat ration there, as can be seen in table 2.4.[30] It is true that in this table the department of Lys shows the highest overall figure and the department of Escaut comes very close; but since it is necessary to establish the averages for these two departments, where the supply of a major city like Antwerp had to come from the outside, one obtains much more uniform figures,

Table 2.4—Daily Per-Capita Consumption of Wheat and Rye in Four Departments [1801]

	Nord 137 inhabitants/km²	Lys 141 inhabitants/km²	Escaut 167 inhabitants/km²	Deux-Nèthes 160 inhabitants/km²	Belgian average
Wheat	450 gr.	350 gr.	240 gr.	40 gr.	210 gr.
Rye and Rye Mixtures	160 gr.	460 gr.	360 gr.	225 gr.	340 gr.
Total	610 gr.	810 gr.	600 gr.	265 gr.	550 gr.

and the department of Nord retains the advantage conferred by its superior flour.

The inclusion of potatoes in these calculations modifies the data. Table 2.5 converts them into their [nutritional] equivalent in grain and shows the new totals. This time, Belgium clearly comes out ahead. The inferiority of the department of Nord would be altogether glaring if one were to accept Vandenbroeke's claim that in an earlier period the grain ration had generally been higher and that the long-range decline in this ration was compensated by the development of the potato. It is Vandenbroeke's view that the French department experienced this decline, but without a corresponding rise in the consumption of potatoes, the result being a marked debilitation of the diet and

Table 2.5—Consumption of Grains and Their Nutritional Equivalents in Potatoes in Four Departments
[1801]

	Nord	Lys	Escaut	Deux-Nèthes	Belgian Average
Wheat, Rye, and Rye Mixtures	610 gr.	810 gr.	600 gr.	265 gr.	550 gr.
Potatoes	40 gr.	260 gr.	320 gr.	182 gr.	250 gr.
Total	650 gr.	1070 gr.	920 gr.	447 gr.	800 gr.

of the population. Unfortunately (or fortunately), the most exact calculations do not always bring out the whole truth. Three opposing arguments can be made: (1) Wheat rations comparable to those of the southern Netherlands are often found in France at the end of the eighteenth century in provinces that had adopted the potato (and here Vandenbroeke and his mentor, J. C. Toutain, were misled by their sources): in Alsace the wheat ration was 610 grams in the department of Haut-Rhin, in Lorraine it was 510 grams in the department of Vosges. Turgot's investigation of the supplies brought into Paris between 1764 and 1773[31] was summarized in a figure of 455 grams "per person of every age and sex." (2) Such wheat rations are not unthinkable for earlier periods, as has been shown by a number of studies published in the *Annales, E.S.C.* in recent years. The intake of wheat must be seen as one part of the diet as a whole, and it must be kept in mind that in the nutritional balance the *pot* counts as much as the bread, and that one pound of bread often proved to be an adequate, if not optimum, standard ration. (3) Even if one accepts the drastic decline [in the consumption of wheat] ascribed to Austrian Flanders, there is no evidence that a kind of Mariotte's Law came into play to raise the quantity of potatoes consumed by the population to a corresponding level. The reality was more complex than that. To mention only the department of Lys, the most conclusive and best known case, we do know that, on the one hand, it sold thousands of *quintaux* (900,000 according to prefect Viry) of its wheat to other areas and, on the other hand, that its consumption of bread had fallen far below the exemplary 810 grams: "In this department potatoes constitute the principal food of the inhabitants of town and country, and it can confidently be stated that the average inhabitant consumes barely 400 grams (3 *quarterons* [or three quarters of a pound]) of bread per day."

The available information thus pleads in favor of an intermediate position. It appears that the quantitative food intake of the Flemings was roughly the same on either side of the frontier, although on the Belgian side it was overwhelmingly (more than a third) composed of potatoes, while on the French side wheat furnished three-fourths of the total.[32] Under these circumstances, the verdict that Austrian Flanders was becoming pauperized no longer sounds quite so far-fetched. The prefects' reports testify to this phenomenon in terms of quality: "Even though the department of Lys produces an abundance of high-quality grain, the inhabitants consume very little bread and even in the towns they do not consume *as pure a kind of bread* as people in the interior of the Empire." It would seem that this was not essentially—or perhaps not at all—a matter of decline in general agricultural productivity or per-capita productivity (although this point is debatable) but rather a socially differentiated pauperization: "The farmers on large properties live well. Their homes show a certain amount of luxury, and so do their clothes. Small farmers have great difficulties in providing for their families by their labor and often must accept public charity. Their food is bad, and their dwellings, often poorly built, lack the most essential furnishings."[33] In its baldness and straightforwardness, this statement is eloquent indeed. In the department of Deux-Nèthes, the usual size of the farms was 10 to 12 *bonniers* (13 to 16 hectares); in the department of Escaut, most of them measured only 2 to 3 hectares. How, under these conditions, could the Flemish peasant, despite his admirable capacity for hard work and the almost prodigious yields he obtained, avoid difficulties in making ends meet, feeding his family, and paying his taxes, even if he owned his land? As for the wages of the day laborers, prefect Faipoult has given us the exact figures: in the year IX [1801] in rural areas the daily wage including meals was 0.80 francs for a man and 0.70 francs for a woman; excluding meals it was 1.40 francs for a man and 1.15 francs for a woman. The prefect estimated the sum needed for the basic necessities at 1.35 francs or, including a supplement of 0.15 for housing, at 1.50 francs in all. "The number of common laborers is very high," stated Viry, prefect of Lys, for his part, "they constitute almost the entire population of the countryside, not counting domestic servants." This statement is borne out by his statistics, in which common laborers account for almost four-fifths of the active population.

The official statements, then, paint a grim picture, and one wonders what happened in times of shortage. Was this, perhaps, the time when the potato exchanged its Cinderella rags for a fairy's gown? Its occasional role in mitigating the effects of grain shortages is undeniable. This can be illustrated by an example taken from the department of Jemmapes, canton of Lessines.[34] In 1811 the deficit in cereals by the standard of a normal year was about 25,000 hectoliters (15,000 hectoliters of wheat, 10,000 of rye); but an excellent potato harvest (65,412 hectoliters) almost cut the deficit in half (to 12,000 hectoliters). Proportionally, the departments of Lys and Escaut surely could do as well or better in a similar situation. The only trouble with calculations of this kind is the presupposition that in ordinary times the total potato harvest was not included in the daily nutritional quota of the population. And although potatoes were a very simple crop, their aid was not necessarily assured. The parish priests of Lorraine mentioned lean years between 1730 and 1761; one of Duhamel du Monceau's correspondents in Champagne reported that his potato crop was damaged by a drought in 1757; in the canton of Lessines potatoes were severely affected by bad weather in 1807 and 1808; diseases took their toll and, according to Vandenbroeke, the first blight appeared in the southern Netherlands as early as 1776.

In the case of a poor wheat harvest, the department of Nord was not automatically in critical straits, nor even worse off than its Belgian neighbors. I have thus far limited my comparative analysis to the two main cereals, wheat and rye, and the potato, but there is no reason why the so-called minor cereals should not be included in the total nutritional quota of the population. It would be very surprising if oats, for instance, although normally raised as animal feed (but this was, after all, partially true for the tubers as well), had not been mixed with wheat flour in times of shortage, especially since pure oat flour had been used in certain regions of Europe until very recently[35] and since it was a major resource in the department of Deux-Nèthes. I shall therefore take the minor cereals into consideration in drawing up my last table.

One immediately notices in table 2.6 that the figures for the various departments have become more uniform, except those for the department of Lys, where the quota was noticeably higher. The dietary balance of the department of Nord was based on a comfortable margin of reserves in oats; to be sure, this department would have suffered if this reserve had not been sufficient to stave off catastrophe when wheat failed, while the others would have managed more easily thanks to the potato. But at this point the discussion hinges on the evaluation of opposing alternatives originating in a series of momentary configurations. Such a discussion could go on and on, and there is no point in launching it.

On the other hand, it is worthwhile to investigate the possibility that the production of cereals may have been blocked by the increased production of potatoes. We know, for example, that the ample supply of oats in the department of Nord was due as much to the excellent yields obtained as to the amount of land devoted to this crop. Its yield was 40 hectoliters per hectare, almost twice as high as that of the department of Escaut and almost three times as high as that of Deux-Nèthes. In fact, at Quarouble and Onnaing, it was precisely oats that showed the first slight symptoms of a modest kind of "agricultural revolution" when their productivity, which had lagged behind during the Middle Ages, was brought up to the level of wheat, which was already quite good. Not considering any other factors,[36] one might therefore suppose that the potato, by using up an appreciable part of the available quantities of fertilizer and manure, curbed a corresponding development in Belgium. To be sure, this hypothesis calls for a certain number of correctives and for a more detailed investigation of the soil

Table 2.6—Total Daily Per-Capita Consumption of All Cereals in Four Departments [1801]

	Nord	Lys	Escaut	Deux-Nèthes	Belgian Average
Wheat, Rye, Rye Mixtures, and Potatoes	650 gr.	1,070 gr.	920 gr.	447 gr.	800 gr.
Barley and Barley Mixtures	107 gr.	175 gr.	100 gr.	62 gr.	110 gr.
Oats	360 gr.	274 gr.	130 gr.	470 gr.	290 gr.
Buckwheat	. . .	. . .	. . .	100 gr.	33 gr.
Total	1,117 gr.	1,519 gr.	1,150 gr.	1,079 gr.	1,233 gr.

conditions; for the line dividing high from low oat yields passed, not between the former Imperial States and France, but between the departments of Escaut and Lys (where the yield was 35 hectoliters per hectare); in fact it most probably cut right through the latter department. Another point that should be investigated at the same time is the tenacious resistance of rye against the advance of wheat, which may be another unfortunate side effect of potato farming.

Having stressed that "it is to this crop alone that the region owes the advantage of producing enough subsistence to feed its large population and also an abundance of grain for the distilleries and breweries, and sometimes even for export," Faipoult, the prefect of the department of Escaut, wondered whether the conquest of the potato should be carried even further in his department. He was hesitant: "Abundance is less constant in potatoes than in wheat and rye. Two months of drought can reduce the harvest of a potato field to almost nothing." He prophecied "frequent periods of distress for a population that would exclusively base its means of subsistence on an uncertain crop," a statement that was borne out, alas, only too well in Ireland. In short, he concluded: "I am inclined to believe that by comparison with other crops that should not be weakened too much, the cultivation of this crop has been carried about as far as sound judgment permits." These statements are custom-made for my purpose, and I unblushingly appropriate them for my argument, for they round out my initial diagnosis: As a secondary crop, a kind of stopgap, the potato may have contributed more or less effectively to the indispensable food supply of a population in the process of rapid growth; yet the limits of its effectiveness were already dimly perceived by 1800. Except in areas where sufficient heathland remained to be cleared, continued efforts to grow more potatoes in order to break the subsistence bottleneck would eventually have eaten into the land devoted to grain and, if we imagine the worst, to a complete substitution of the potato for grain, that is, to a mutation amounting to absolute pauperization.[37]

As far as I am concerned, the conclusions to be drawn from the present preliminary study are very simple.

My thinking is very close to Cullen's concerning the relationship between demographic growth and the cultivation of the potato.[38] I believe that the increased number of mouths to feed was the impetus for the development of potato planting. But I claim that this process was only *one* of the possible solutions to the bottleneck of the eighteenth century and that, for all kinds of reasons yet to be unraveled, many regions were able to find different ways of dealing with their difficulties. Yet in the nineteenth century, as the demographic growth assumed ever larger proportions, this choice probably tended to disappear. The potato, thanks in part to its very real advantages, became the only short-term solution everywhere in western Europe. This it remained, despite some periods of blight, as long as new granaries had not opened in other parts of the world and until in due course agricultural science was able to produce much higher grain yields than the traditional agriculture.

Secondly, I think that a certain relative pauperization was indeed linked to the spread of the potato in the eighteenth century. This may appear insulting to our Flemish friends in Belgium, but it is not meant to be so. If I had wanted, I could have slyly contrasted the description of the peasants' straitened existence in the departments of Lys and Escaut with the fabulous meals attributed to the inhabitants of the department of Nord by their prefect, Dieudonné.[39] But even the best sources must be used with reservations. Georges Lefebvre's thesis has taught us not to believe that the French provinces of Cambrésis, Flanders, and Hainaut were always and everywhere a fairyland of plenty. Here too the distribution of the products of labor was to some extent a function of the social spectrum and of the fragmented ownership of the land. Nor was day labor paid any better here than elsewhere.[40] But it is true that the people here almost always (except in periods of scarcity) enjoyed a bread that was, if not made of the finest wheat flour, then at least whiter than the bread eaten by their neighbors across the frontier. This was probably their only luxury, but it was a tangible one that they did not give up, even in the nineteenth century.[41]

In my portrayal of Belgian Flanders I have at this point done no more than to put forward contemporary evidence. Like the authors of my sources, indeed following them, I have noted a great wealth of production, the fruit of an extraordinary virtuosity on the part of the peasants—clearly symbolized by the fact that the department of Lys was far ahead of the others—and a lackluster human existence, sometimes bordering on outright poverty, in the countryside. The coexistence of sharply contrasting modes of life was not unusual in regions where small farms and mixed crops were prevalent; and one is often misled by such a situation into noting only one of these aspects, the fertility of the Alsation plain for example, or the rags and the bare feet seen in Brittany.[42] Yet in Flanders there was a very visible merging of these two aspects, owing both to the rapid increase in population and to changes in the *ratio* of the distribution of resources, in what one might call the social filter of the products of labor. And the new dietary dichotomy brought about by the potato, that food for and of poor people before Parmentier persuaded Louis XVI to taste it, only recalls, reproduces, or foreshadows other social discontinuities, which are equally apparent in dress, housing, city living, and so forth.

In conclusion, let us return to our Cinderella. Deprived of its good-fairy powers in demography, the potato has not recovered its magic wand in the rural economy either. Except, perhaps, in mountainous regions where it represented an absolute innovation, a net increase in the food supply, its benefits turned out to be a mixed blessing.[43] There is something ambiguous even in the attempts at speculation that its relatively high price occasionally spawned among the Flemish peasants, for such attempts could only develop on the basis of the increasing needs of a population whose diet was constantly deteriorating. Yes, all of this would seem to be true. Yet Christian Vandenbroeke was right to rehabilitate the Cinderella-like potato, to restore it to its rightful importance, which was immense in the southern Netherlands of the eighteenth century. One only has to weigh the services it rendered, the suffering it averted, to realize that the scales tip in its favor. Our Manichean way of thinking hates to see contrary principles joined and acting simultaneously in Nature, or indeed in society. And yet, a starving man who eats his fill of a blackbird pie is not likely to hanker after the taste of quail.

NOTES

1. Christian Vandenbroeke, "Aardappelteelt en aardappelverbruik in de 17e en 18e eeuw," *Tijdschrift voor Geschiedenis* 82 (1969): 49-68.
2. And no longer in botanical or kitchen gardens.
3. There is a rather puzzling geographical coincidence between the acknowledged centers from which the potato spread throughout continental Europe and the first experimental gardens of the sixteenth-century naturalists, Charles de l'Escluse at Antwerp and Gaspard Bauhin at Basel. Did science further agriculture even then?
4. Vandenbroek used the second edition of M. Reinhard and A. Armengaud, *Histoire générale de la population mondiale* (Paris, 1961).
5. L. M. Cullen, "Irish History without the Potato," *Past and Present* 40 (1968): 72-83.
6. C. Viry, *Mémoire statistique du département de la Lys* (Paris), p. 120.
7. Printed copies of the prefects' memoranda in the Bibliothèque Nationale (Paris): *Escaut*, by G. Faipoult (L₃₁ 10/3); *Lys*, by C. Viry (L₃₁ 10/6); *Rhin et Moselle*, by Boucqueau (L₃₁ 10/10); *Deux-Nèthes*, by d'Herbouville (L₃₁ 9/20); *Sambre et Meuse*, by Jardrinet (L₃₁ 9/26); and, in general, series L₃₁ 9 and 10. These memoranda have been used by Jacques Peuchet for his *Description topographique et statistique de la France* (Paris, 1809), a work that has the advantage of indicating where metric measurements were used (although this information is not always completely reliable), as well as supplementary data (see, for example, the data on the department of Mont-Blanc). The memorandum on the department of Escaut has recently been reedited by P. Deprez in Maatschappij voor Geschiedenis en Oudheidkunde, *Handelingen* 10 (1960).
8. Population density varied considerably from one *arrondissement* to the next: 108 inhabitants per square kilometer in that of Bruges, 73 in that of Furnes, 116 in that of Ypres, 198 in that of Courtrai.
9. In the year IX [1801] Estienne calculated, in a somewhat conventional manner, that the daily per capita consumption of potatoes was 275 grams (100 kg. per year) in the former United Provinces.
10. Archives Nationales, Paris, KK 1159-1178. I have used these documents in my forthcoming study *Les Faux-semblants d'un démarrage: agriculture et démographie en France au XVIIIe siècle.* [The book was since published (Paris, 1971)—Trans.]
11. Actually, several stages must be distinguished in the expansion of potato cultivation: (1) the discovery and first appearance of the potato; (2) its incorporation into the tithe, which did not necessarily take place at the same stage everywhere, given the differences in greed among the tithe owners (cf. Piat de la Broque, a parish priest who collected it as early as 1693 in the principality of Salm) and local resistance and customs (cf. Vandenbroeke, "Aardappelteelt," p. 52: in Belgian Hainaut, potato plantings destined for domestic consumption and not exceeding 0.35 hectares are exempt); (3) a stage of popular familiarity distinct from the preceeding stage; and (4) a stage of general use. In addition, one could also distinguish several nutritional or psychological stages (cf. below, n.24).
12. It was the prefect of Côtes-du-Nord, not the prefect of Nord, who brought Dr. Lavergne's work to the attention of his department, although the potato was known in certain parts of the latter department before 1789. In stating that no trace of potato cultivation in France can be found before 1700, Vandenbroeke neglects one choice testimony, that of Olivier de Serres for the Vivarais, even though he does tell us that he has read E. Roze, *Histoire de la pomme de terre* (Paris, 1898).
13. M. Morineau, *Les Faux-semblants d'un démarrage*, Annex V.
14. Alsace, Franche-Comté, and Lorraine had been devastated by the Thirty Years' War. A phenomenon of reconstruction (at times going hand in hand with immigration) was therefore the point of departure for the advance of these provinces, which, in comparison with others that had been spared, was bound to be more pronounced. The same was true in Germany. This kind of record does not constitute a basis for any real, absolute superiority in population growth. Nevertheless, the rapid increase in the population of these provinces is a fact that is graphically illustrated by their eventual population density. Moreover, there were very few regions that did not experience war and often equally murderous epidemics: the initial discrepancy between Brabant, badly shaken though it was by

the events connected with the League of Augsburg and by disease, and French Hainaut was probably negligible, so that a comparison of their growth rates is perfectly legitimate.

15. Global figures in J. A. Van Houtte, *Economische en Sociale Geschiedenis van de Lage Landen* (Zeist, 1964), pp. 205-15. The demographic figures for Flanders are taken from P. Deprez, "Development of Flanders in the Eighteenth Century," in D. V. Glass and D.E.C. Eversly, eds., *Population is History* (London, 1965), pp. 608-30.

16. In the scientific or athletic sense of the word: a real obstacle.

17. These potentialities were manifest throughout Europe in the sixteenth century, and in Flanders, Languedoc, and Provence in the seventeenth century. See M. Morineau, "Démographie ancienne: Monotonie ou variété des comportements?," *Annales, E.S.C.* 20 (November-December 1965): 1185-97. To make myself completely clear and to use a precise language comprehensible to everyone, I should say that I cannot assert that the intersection of the set of nutritional data and the set of demographic data represents an empty set; but I do claim that the content of this last set has not been sufficiently inventoried, and that, moreover, other sets overlap the set of demographic data. These are the set of biological data of which I am speaking here and the set of therapeutic data, the latter including one fact that may have been more important than the uncertain advances of medicine, namely, the more widespread use of the Indian pharmacopoea. Quinine, an excellent antipyretic (which, incidentally, may have been Madame de Sévigné's famous secret) was still imported in very small quantities in the seventeenth century, but by 1790 about 100 tons of it were available every year.

18. See the work of T. MacKeown and R. G. Brown, "Medical Evidence Related to English Population Changes in the Eighteenth Century," in Glass and Eversly, eds., *Population in History*, pp. 247-68, as well as the work of Jean-Noël Biraben and others. A convenient survey of the latest views concerning the plague and its retreat is to be found in C. Carrière, M. Courdurié, and F. Rebuffat, *Marseille, ville morte. La peste de 1720* (Marseilles, 1968), pp. 159-95. Note, in particular, that the great demographic catastrophes were not always caused by the plague. It appears that those of the last decade of the seventeenth century in Belgium and in France were due to dysentery rather than to the plague. The position taken above will be mitigated by the thought that in the eighteenth century more regular nutrition may have contributed to raising the biological threshold of resistance to disease.

19. This is in keeping with Marc Bloch's judgment on the slow progress accomplished over the generations by the peasants themselves.

20. Here are the figures cited by Vandenbroeke from C. Chatfield, *Tables de composition des aliments (Minéraux et vitamines)* (Rome, 1954): 100 grams of wheat flour: 350 calories; rye flour: 341; potatoes: 70.

21. A. Dubuc, "La Culture de la pomme de terre en Normandie avant et depuis Parmentier," *Annales de Normandie* (1953): 53-68.

22. See the corresponding memorandum by Peuchet [*Description topographique*]. Interestingly enough, it turns out that in 1840 those departments of southern France (Gironde, Hérault, Gard, etc.) where the potato was fairly important were also those where maize was not doing very well. The department of Haute-Garonne was in an intermediate position. Maize too has often been considered as a determining factor of economic growth, especially in Aquitaine. Yet its per-hectare yields were low and the area devoted to it was usually much smaller than that devoted to wheat. To my knowledge, maize was dominant in only three departments, Dordogne, Landes, and Basses-Pyrenées, all three of which were poor. Figures for the Mediterranean departments of the South in 1840: 1,703 hectares in maize in Gard, 599 in Hérault, compared to 6,000 and 7,000 respectively in potatoes!

23. *Corps d'observations de la Société d'Agriculture, de Commerce et des Arts, établie par les Etats de Bretagne (1759-1760)*, cited by Roze, *La Pomme de terre*.

24. Abbé Xaupi, *Description de Roussillon* (Bibliothèque Nationale, Paris, Fonds français, ms. 11,801). In this province, potatoes were called *truffes* [truffles]. A fence was put up when different varieties of potatoes were grown, some for human consumption and others for the feeding of pigs; the latter were set apart, like the carob fruit with which the prodigal son wanted to still his hunger in Biblical Palestine. Vandenbroeke has correctly observed certain psychological thresholds. The upper classes accepted the potato only after the common people were eating it, and after they had tried it out on their workers: "The habit of calculating the cost of the food for his domestic servants and his workmen made him [Sieur Rozaire, a Breton gentleman] realize that his expenses had become considerably lower since he had started giving them potatoes; now they prefer them to any other food." Cf. also Roze, *La Pomme de terre*. For all these questions, see Fernand Braudel, *Civilisation matérielle et capitalisme, XVe-XVIIIe siècle* (Paris, 1967), vol. 1.

25. Cf. the declarations of the parish priests of Champs, Girecourt, and other villages in Lorraine.

26. This happened in the departments of Marne and Indre, among others, according to the memoranda of the year IX [1801].

27. Published in the *Journal de la Lys* [1801].

28. Here is an example. Quotations of 15 September 1810: Wheat, 21.22 francs per hectoliter; rye, 10.88; barley, 9.73; dry beans, 9.52; oats, 7.34; potatoes, 4.89. In the year IX the potato was not appreciated as much as it is today; in the memorandum for the department of Escaut, prefect Faipoult established the following equation: 1 hectare of potatoes furnishes the same amount of subsistence as 3 hectares of wheat (rather than 5 hectares, as Vandenbroeke claims, following K. Sapper). This might explain the prices cited, but it does not in any way detract from the inordinately high price of potatoes in relation to the price of grain, especially rye. Conversely, the profitability of this crop adds an additional dimension to the discussion of an already very complex question.

29. The "tyranny" was French, according to Arthur Young.

30. Note applying to the last three tables: In the documents I have used, the quantities are expressed in *quintaux* ["hundredweights"] for the departments of Escaut and Lys. The use of the metric *quintal* [100 kilograms] was very rare at the time; Faipoult expressly referred to the *"poids de marc,"* which shows that he was using the old hundredweight (a fact that is borne out by the yields). Peuchet, in his *Description topographique,* thought that this measure was used by C. Viry for the department of Lys, but he was obviously mistaken, since the very low yields (13 hectoliters per hectare) arrived at in this manner are incompatible with the Flemish techniques and with the performance of the neighboring departments of Nord and Escaut (between 19 and 20 hectoliters per hectare). I have therefore concluded that in the department of Lys the metric *quintal* was indeed in use. This would make the wheat yields there (26 hectoliters per hectare) quite favorable, though still plausible. Two sets of figures are given for the departments of Lys and Escaut, one for the year IX [1801] and one for a good harvest year. Even though the difference is rather marked in the second department—768,006 (old) *quintaux* of wheat against 1,057,796 *quintaux;* 1,262,913 *quintaux* of rye against 1,624,487 *quintaux*—I have used the second set of figures, with the result that the comparison may be slightly unfavorable to the department of Nord, where the figures given by Dieudonné represent the averages of ten years (a decade of rather poor grain harvests). In the absence of any valid figures for potatoes in the department of Lys, I have arbitrarily substituted a figure based on the available per capita/per day ration of 1.3 kilograms, following the data furnished by Vandenbroeke. (The ration was 1.6 kilograms in Escaut).

31. Cited by Herbin, *Statistique générale et particulière de la France* (Paris, 1810), 7: 273. In the department of Nord, Dieudonné assumed that *in France as a whole* the daily bread ration was 734 grams, which led him to note an annual deficit of 33,000 hectoliters of wheat in his department.

32. According to Dieudonné, bread was made of pure wheat in the arrondissements of Bergues, Hazebrouck, and Cambrai; 2/3 wheat and 1/3 maslin in Lille; 3/4 wheat and 1/4 rye in Douai; 1/3 wheat and 2/3 spelt in Avesnes.

33. Viry, *Mémoire sur la Lys,* p. 55. See also p. 85: "There is today a larger number of beggars than ever before"; but this may be related to the poor state of the economy in the year IX [1801].

34. R. Darquenne, *Histoire économique du département de Jemmapes* (Mons, 1965), pp. 196-97.

35. *Mémoire statistique du Rhin-et-Moselle* in Peuchet, *Description topographique:* Rye had begun to replace oats in the Hohwald and the Eifel by the mid-eighteenth century.

36. The other circumstances being the quality of the newly cleared land (a great deal of acid heath in the arrondissement of Bruges); the breaking up of farms, which was an obstacle to large-scale investments; and so forth. Note that everywhere the use of fertilizer was felt to be a necessity, indeed a constraint, and that farmers dispensed with this practise as soon as they could reasonably do so, as in the Zeeland region of Flanders. In Lorraine it was estimated that, hectare for hectare, twice as much fertilizer was needed for potatoes as for wheat. A memorandum on the importance of the gin distilleries in Belgium, submitted to the government by the distillers of the department of Lys (see Peuchet's *Bibliothèque commerciale,* third issue, vol. 1) alleges the following facts: A gin distillery of three boilers, using 657,000 liters of flour to produce 76,500 *lots* [2,000 pints] of gin could use the residue to feed 150 oxen per year, or 50 at any given time, since the fattening took three to four months. The memorandum claims that in one month one ox provided one cartload of solid and 6 tons of liquid manure, enough to fertilize 302 measures of land (133 hectares 59 centiares) The fertilizer—altogether 600 cartloads of solid manure and 800 barrel-cartloads of liquid manure—was distributed as follows: The 600 cartloads of solid manure were spread over 35 measures of land planted in potatoes, where, in the next year, it was possible to grow a crop of rye without adding any more fertilizer; in the third year another crop of rye could be planted after the application of 6 barrel-cartloads of liquid manure; and in the fourth year the land yielded a crop of oats without any

additional fertilizer. Eighty-one measures were directly seeded with rye after the application of 7 barrel-cartloads of liquid manure, the next year they were seeded in oats without being fertilized again. In other words, it was felt that 17 to 18 loads of manure, probably weighing 5 tons each, were needed for each measure planted in potatoes, which is three times the amount needed for rye. These proportions must have been roughly the same in Flanders as in Lorraine. The absolute figures seem very high, even assuming that the cited tons were not metric tons.

37. G. Faipoult, *Mémoire sur l'Escaut,* p. 79. The cultivation of potatoes often led to a remarkable growth of hog raising, as in the Jura and in the Massif Central (I am indebted to Abel Poitrineau for this information). I have tried to find out whether in this respect the Belgian departments were more productive than the department of Nord. It turned out that this was true for Escaut, but not for Lys, so that the data are inconclusive.

38. See his conclusion, in "Irish History without the Potato": "The potato's role in Irish history is thus a passive rather than an active one. Its widening culture and consumption must be seen as fitting into a process of population growth already under way for reasons that are yet altogether obscure, and not as a cause of that growth."

39. In the countryside, a yearly consumption of 4 hectoliters of grain (for men), 45 and 35 kg. of butter, respectively, for large farmers and small householders, and 228 and 114 liters of beer, respectively. Milk, butter, tea, coffee, and sugar were widely used. And while potatoes were grown on a small scale, farmers sometimes raised enough to provide them with a comfortable ration. The farm near Lille described by Dieudonné devoted only 40 ares [about 1 English acre] to this crop, but the harvest of 73 hectoliters was sufficient to provide 2 kilograms per day to each of eight persons.

40. Average area per household: between 5.5 and 6 hectares. Wages in the countryside in 1789: men, including meals, 0.50 livres, not including meals, 1 livre. NB: wages were raised everywhere in the early stages of the Revolution.

41. The yearly per capita consumption was calculated as follows in 1828: 2 hectoliters of wheat, 20 liters of maslin, 20 liters of rye, 10 liters of legumes, 1.05 hectoliters of potatoes. This last figure, which is still close to that of the year IX [1801] (0.71 hectoliters), is indicative of the limited success of the tubers, while the figure for wheat indicates a desire to uphold dietary "standards."

42. For Alsace, I refer the reader to two well-known works: Paul Leuilliot, *L'Alsace au début du XIXe siècle,* 3 vols. (Paris, 1958), and Etienne Juillard, *L'Alsace: le sol, les hommes, et la vie régionale* (Strasbourg, 1963).

43. At Chamonix in 1782, potatoes represented almost half of the total volume of the harvest: 5,204 *coupes* out of a total of 12,347. At Salanches, they represented close to one third: 500 *octanes* out of a total of 1,793. The proportion was about one quarter for the whole of the Faucigny region in 1789: 52,536 *coupes* out of a total of 216,173. The deficit in food supplies remained high, however, amounting to from 70 to 100,000 *coupes.* See A. D. Haute-Savoie, IV, c. 90-92.

3
A Capital City's Privileges: Food Supplies in Early-Modern Rome

Jacques Revel

Even today, supplying food to a large city poses specific problems. Since the mid-nineteenth century, however, a series of technological transformations (the revolution in transportation, the development of food processing) and economic changes (the establishment of national or international networks of distribution) have tended progressively to standardize the way in which foodstuffs circulate between the various types of residential centers in the "developed" countries. Quite the opposite was the case in early-modern Europe, when the city constituted a domain that was both threatened and privileged: threatened because feeding the urban masses demanded enormous food supplies that in turn required, at a very early date, a concentration of production and distribution; privileged because the city generally wielded considerable authority over the countryside and also because the fear of food riots led civil authorities to subordinate everything to satisfying urban needs.

Since the end of the Middle Ages, the demographic burgeoning of the cities was accompanied by the creation of various institutions related to the *Annona*.[1] Under a variety of names and in a variety of ways, these institutions provided an entire gamut of services: supervision of production, sales, and prices; direct control of a part of the food supply; and estimates of the amount to be consumed. Chronologically, the phenomenon affected Mediterranean Europe first, where economic stagnation and political archaism subsequently permitted it to continue the longest.[2]

Rome can serve as an extreme example of this phenomenon. The tripling of its population during the sixteenth century (between roughly 1530 and 1600 the city grew from 30,000 to 100,000 inhabitants) was accompanied by acute food shortages during the second half of that century. This prompted the establishment, completed by about 1620, of separate Annonas for wheat, meat, and oil. During the seventeenth and eighteenth centuries the city's growth slowed considerably

Annales, E.S.C. 30 (March-June 1975): 563-74. Translated by Patricia M. Ranum.

(less than 140,000 inhabitants in 1700, and 166,000 in 1796). Yet, this relative stabilization did not cause the state to relax its intervention. The parasitic capital of a permanently depressed region, where the long stagnation of agricultural production aroused a concealed anxiety during the seventeenth and eighteenth centuries, Rome remained vulnerable to the usual accidents occurring in outdated economies. Indeed, when the great famine of 1764 indicated that the entire peninsula would experience a return of the grain shortages of the past (and, with them, the collapse of the fragile hopes of eighteenth-century Italy), a strengthening of the Annona's activities revealed this return to the past. At that point, under cover of what was falsely presented as liberalized legislation, the state's position in the urban market became so strong that it held a de facto monopoly.[3]

Organized food distribution of this sort had repercussions at both ends of the food cycle, since it affected production and market conditions alike. For the city was doubly privileged economically. On the one hand, the regularity and quality of its food supply was always assured, to the detriment of rural consumers. And on the other, Rome's needs and the amount of profit on the sale of essential products that was tolerated by public authorities determined the profitability of production, especially in the large capitalist estates that at an early date predominated in the Roman Campagna and the Latium. By the end of the seventeenth century, moreover, "liberal" opinion held the restrictions, requisitions, and "political" price fixing by the Annona responsible for the difficulties experienced by food producers and the impoverishment of the countryside. The study of long-term supply curves would undoubtedly clarify some of the issues in this debate.

These regulatory or interventionist institutions have left us rather varied documentation pertaining to fiscal matters (lists of controlled prices and taxes on retail sales), regulations (statements by retailers, market regulations), and even administrative practices (such as the extensive study commissioned during the early years of the eighteenth century by the congregation of the *Sollievo*).[4] The richness and usefulness of this documentation varies with the specific food item. Relatively complete for grain, meat, and wine, it is less so for other commodities. Yet in no case does it show us the actual amounts consumed, but only the average amount of that item available per person.

This type of data has been severely criticized by historians in recent years. First of all, and justifiably so, it is accused of failing to record, by definition, commodities smuggled into the city or the often sizable loss that can occur before a commodity is actually eaten, for example, during storage, during the various changes of hand as it moves from the wholesale to the retail level, during its preparation, and through wastefulness. These criticisms are, of course, pertinent, although it sometimes seems impossible to achieve the accuracy these historians seek. For how can one compute how much of all food supplies purchased was actually eaten at an aristocratic or bourgeois table or in a boarding school or hospital?

Above all, the notion of per-capita supply is criticized as being based upon the average consumer, unrelated to a demographic or social context. This objection is more serious; but then, it could be raised about other groups, for what social groups are represented in a given hospital? Indeed, we should not ask more questions of such data than they can answer, for all they can provide is an approximate standard of living within a given collectivity. It may be possible to make more effective use of such data. By taking into account, on the one hand, the "actual" amounts consumed by restricted, presumably representative groups, and, on the other, the entire socioeconomic distribution within the city, it should be possible to develop more effective criteria. It may be possible, for example, to calculate how much above the minimum dietary requirements the average food supply must be in order to meet the nutritional needs of the entire population. Until research models of this sort have been worked out, citywide averages, which certainly have no great intrinsic meaning, can be used in two ways. Compared geographically, they show the extent to which the cities were privileged. Followed over a long time span, they reveal changes, especially if, as in the case of Rome between 1600 and 1850, the social composition of the collectivity does not undergo a profound transformation.

From Wheat to Bread

The first indication of the city's insistence upon quality is the early predominance of wheat over all other grains. This predominance is indisputable after the second half of the sixteenth century and the triumph of the estate-based economy in the Roman Campagna. Records of grain entering the city, accounts of bakers, appraisals of the unprocessed product by the services of the Annona, and the account books of farms, permit me to measure the extent of this phenomenon. Excluding oats, which were kept for animals even during times of shortage, the minor grains accounted for less than five percent of the grains supplied to Rome and its nearby vicinity. The demands of the urban market, but also the diffusion of citified tastes, nonetheless influenced the spread of this eating habit far beyond the limited area in question. Even though the consumption of oats increased in such mountainous regions as the Reatin and the Tiburtin, it rarely exceeded twenty percent of the total grain production. In the Sabine region, where the slightest scarcity of wheat brought chestnut bread back into the diet, the virtual monoculture of wheat was never abandoned, despite the risks involved in growing such a fragile grain. The preeminence of wheat was well enough established to block any substantial development of rice or maize until the 1830s.

In most instances the wheat was soft wheat,[5] eaten in the form of bread. Even for the sixteenth century, the researcher finds very few references to gruel or semolina. In addition—in contrast to the situation in Naples, where by the mid-eighteenth century pasta accounted for between fifty and sixty percent of cereal foods—pasta remained a luxury item in Rome. Vermicelli cost three times more than an equal weight of ordinary bread in 1600; it still cost twice as much in 1700. Ministre, lasagne, or macaroni remained a Sunday dish on the tables of the well-to-do, and especially in boarding schools. These dishes never had a great effect upon eating habits, and Romans still describe them as *all' uso de' forastieri* [for use by "foreigners," that is, outsiders].

Eaten alone or with a *companatico* [something to eat on bread], or else used to thicken a soup, bread therefore was the basic food. Bakers regularly used 85 to 90 percent of the grain entering the city during the seventeenth and eighteenth centuries. Thus, they baked most of the city's bread and sold it at the retail level. Individuals only rarely bought their grain directly from the producer; when they did, they had to bring their dough to a public oven subject to official regulations. Except in large hospital complexes, almost no one baked bread at home. The intention of the authorities of the Annona are clear. By forcing distribution to pass through the market, they had more ways in which to supervise sales, both in terms of prices and the conditions of production. The public character of bread, evident even in villages, was a means of surveillance. At the same time, it made the consumer totally dependent upon the vicissitudes of the market. He bought his bread from day to day, as the meager amount of wheat in private homes shows (in contrast to what can be observed elsewhere). In compensation, all the efforts of the Annona were directed to giving the retail purchaser maximum protection from price fluctuations—chiefly seasonal variations, which were often the most deeply felt. Other historians have shown that the authorities were quite successful in their attempts.

Under the extremely unified control of these administrations, a luxury bakery was contrasted with an ordinary one, and white bread with brown bread, according to a clearly marked social hierarchy. Over a period of two centuries, and with little variation, brown bread—the typical food of the common people —accounted for four-fifths of all bread baked. During the eighteenth century this proportion even increased—an indication of declining social conditions in the city. Pope Pius VI's decree of 1782, which freed bakers from existing strict regulations concerning bread production and sale, did nothing to alter this trend. White bread, brown bread—both were, of course, wheat breads and differed from one another in the degree to which the flour used to make them had been bolted, that is, sifted. But this difference reveals a luxury or, if you will, a waste—in any case, a social privilege.

A numerical comparision of the two types of bread is a touchy matter, since it involves a relationship between a measure of grain usually expressed by volume and a loaf of bread sold by weight. In addition, for the same volume of wheat the weight can vary noticeably according to such factors as the quality of the harvest and atmospheric conditions. Fortunately for us, on several occasions the Annona carried out *scandagli,* that is, purity tests, and bakers noted the general results in their account books. According to these tests, grain yielded between 68 and 70 percent of its weight when transformed into white bread, and 90 to 95 percent when baked as brown bread. Only at the very end of the eighteenth century was a rate of almost 100 percent reached for brown bread.[6] The amount of wheat lost is shown to be even greater if one deducts from the weight of the bread the amount of water added to make the dough—about 20 percent of the bread's weight after baking. Then the amount lost would climb to 50 percent for white bread and 30 percent for brown bread. These percentages show that—just as white bread was a luxury item compared with brown bread, the very fact that urban dwellers chose to eat bread on the whole constituted a luxury compared with the gruels of the Middle Ages.

Now let us move on to the average amounts available. A group of parallel sources permits us to trace the Roman wheat supply over a considerable part of the seventeenth century and the entire eighteenth century.[7] Table 3.1 relates these figures to the urban population figures, which are well known for this period.

Two phenomena stand out clearly. First, the long-term erosion of the per-capita supply. It decreased by one-third during the seventeenth century and then, at a slower rate, dropped another fifteen percent during the eighteenth century. From then on it seems to have remained on a plateau until the years preceding the unification of Italy. Second, there was a remarkable stability in the overall supplies to the city. For over two centuries, the volume of grain tapped by Rome remained roughly constant, and it was the increase in the number of mouths to feed that provoked the drop in the average per-capita supply. It is as if in about 1600 an optimum supply had been reached, an optimum that would prove unsurpassable. Three hypotheses, none of them mutually exclusive, may explain this development:

1. By the end of the sixteenth century, a ceiling was reached, reflecting local conditions of wheat production and sale. This seems confirmed, at least as far as the existence of a ceiling is concerned, by the long stagnation in the curves of agricultural production.

2. The Annona's technical and financial mechanisms proved inelastic compared with market demands, at least once a certain threshold had been reached.

3. The stability of the wheat market could indicate urban pauperization and an accompanying decrease in individual buying power. This, to my mind, is the least likely hypothesis. First of all, it is given little confirmation in a comparative analysis of prices and urban wages, but these, I admit, are very inadequate indicators. And, in addition, if this hypothesis were true, bread would in all likelihood have been more stable and would not have followed the general decrease in supplies and consumption; the evidence does not indicate that this was the case.

Table 3.1—Per-Capita Grain Supply

Years	Grain Entering Rome (1 rubbio = 2.94 hectoliters)	Yearly Per-Capita Supply (in kilograms)
Late 16th century	140,000 rubbia	290 kg.
1605-8	134,600	266
1651-55	132,000	233
1695-1700	132,000	203
1751-55	130,300	178
1791-95	129,700	167
1864-66		182

In short, this decrease in the available per-capita food supply should be interpreted cautiously. The elevated figures of the seventeenth century are related to an available per-capita supply that was markedly higher than the amounts known for the other large Italian cities. The subsequent long-term decrease of the individual ration could in large part be interpreted as a sort of "reverse recovery," a return to an Italian norm. In actual fact, at the end of the eighteenth century Rome was merely catching up with the level of consumption allocated to each provincial "mouth to feed" by the administrator-statisticians in the Papal State (0.75 *rubbio,* or 163 kilograms per year). So this amounted to the loss of a privilege, which reduced the average diet in the capital to the poverty level. But the significance of this decrease should not be exaggerated. The statistics for food supplies year by year show that, after the early seventeenth century, the city's food supplies flowed smoothly. This regularity probably had more effect upon the diet of the common people than did the quantity of rations available. Besides, as we shall see, grain, which remained at an acceptable level, was far from playing the quasiexclusive role here that it played in the diets of other parts of Mediterranean Europe. The stubborn attachment to wheat bread shown by Rome and the surrounding countryside can therefore be considered a reassuring sign.

Meat and Other Sources of Protein

After the end of the fourteenth century, the urban demand for meat prompted the development of large, specialized stockfarms in the Latium and the adjacent portions of Umbria. The papal administration saw fit to requisition for its own use vast tracts of pasture land—the so-called *dogana*[8] for the cattle of Rome, the Campagna and Marittima, and above all the Patrimonio—and also to safeguard the herds along the route taken during transhumance.* In return, it very quickly claimed the right to control the sale of products being shipped to the city.

In response to the demands of the market, these stock farms became diversified at an early date, producing meat, dairy products, and wool. Sometimes this diversification ran counter to wise management; in addition, agricultural concerns were always subordinated to the demands made by Rome. The seeming modernity of these farms should not conceal the archaic methods of animal husbandry, which remained virtually unchanged until the late eighteenth century. Specialized pastures were rare; instead, the cattle were systematically pastured on fallow and uncultivated fields. They were not enclosed in stables at fixed times; instead, transhumance between the maremmas, Umbria, and the Abruzzi continued. The very low weight of the animals over the period under study —Werner Sombart commented upon it as late as the 1880s—reveals that practices had remained unchanged since the Middle Ages.[9]

*The periodic migration of herds of cattle, which are taken to graze in the mountains during the hot and dry summer months and only return to the low lands when winter approaches.—Trans.

For a few periods after 1550 and then uninterruptedly during the eighteenth century, it is possible to tally the number of animals butchered in Rome each year. Can we deduce, on the basis of these figures, the approximate weight of the meat thus made available for urban consumption? In theory, the tax of the *quattrino della carne*[10] was based upon the weight of meat sold in retail shops. In actual fact, by the early seventeenth century it had become the practice to assign an average weight to each type of animal. And so, even though the techniques of animal husbandry showed no improvement, we know that in at least one case—cows—the introduction of a new breed into the Latium could make such estimates quite inaccurate for the years following 1700.[11] For the eighteenth century I therefore propose an average between the rough data supplied by the old fiscal records and the data corrected in terms of other sources of information. In any case, I admit, the procedure remains rather crude. I therefore use these figures merely as a rough indication of quantity. (See table 3.2.)

Here again we encounter a long, two-century decline in the per-capita supply. The seventeenth century—and this is probably even more true for the mid-sixteenth century, but we have no statistics about the Roman population at that time—seems to have marked an optimum in the amount of meat eaten. Until then, the number of animals slaughtered easily kept up with the population growth of the city. During the entire seventeenth century (when the *Grascia,* that is, the government regulations of the Annona for meat, had been in force since 1620), the meat supply stabilized at the previously attained level, while the Roman population increased by approximately thirty percent. This inertia is strangely like that I have already mentioned for grains, and it gives rise to the same set of hypotheses.

But for the eighteenth century, there is no doubt about the existence of a crisis in stock breeding, and a well-documented crisis at that. Although it affected all livestock, it was most severe for sheep and pigs. The bankruptcies of animal breeders, the expansion of the supply area for Rome toward Umbria and the Marches, and the anxieties mirrored by public officials all attest to this crisis. In addition to explanations based on such specific circumstances as a recurrent series of epizootic diseases between 1705 and 1760, there surely was a structural cause. The long-term stagnation of meat prices on the urban market, which cetainly must reveal a lessened demand, could explain these difficulties, since it brought a long-term decrease in the profits of breeders and wholesalers.

And so, between 1600 and 1800 the average amount of meat available per

Table 3.2—Per-Capita Meat Supply

Years	Average Per-Capita Supply of Meat (in kilograms)
1600-1605	38.3
1655-60	31.4 (but includes a plague year)
1700-1704	29.4-32.3
1757-62	24.4-28.1
1785-89	21.5-24.7

capita was cut almost in half. It is true, as in the case of grain, that the decline began at an abnormally high level and bottomed out, after a spectacular drop, at what was an unusually favorable figure for Italy as a whole. But this was only the first phase of a decrease in food supplies, which would reach their lowest point during the second half of the nineteenth century. Moreover, the unusual stability of the Roman market for meat, year in and year out—excluding years with epizooty—proves that meat was always considered a basic component in the diet. Even a grain shortage as pronounced as that of 1764-65 did not change curves noticeably.

What more do we know about meat? The various types of meat were categorized according to a social hierarchy of taste. At the top was the milk-fed heifer (*vitella mongana*), costing two and a half to three times more than other meats and a luxury item purchased by only a small number of consumers. In the middle were mutton, fresh pork, and especially beef, which accounted for fifty percent of the total meat supplies by weight circa 1660 and sixty-five percent circa 1780. This category clearly was the largest and cost about twenty-five percent more than lamb. Lamb, which was strictly a seasonal dish available between Easter and Saint John's Day [June 24], seems to have been the standard food of the poor, who purchased meat irregularly. Lamb was also the meat for which demand dropped most sharply during the eighteenth century, despite the efforts of the *Grascia*. The deterioration of the Roman diet must have affected first and foremost the poorest segment of the population.

Was there partial compensation for this loss of animal protein? We have only hypotheses as far as the substitution of fish is concerned. The only statistics available to date are for fresh fish and *merluzzo* [whiting] coming into the city during the years 1697-99. There is no information about smoked fish or barrels of salted fish. More than eleven kilograms a year were available per person, making fish an important source of protein. Of this total, fresh fish—a commodity that was supplied according to age-old methods not easy to modernize—still constituted fifty-five percent, while *merluzzo francese e inglese* [French and English whiting] made up the remaining forty-five percent. Massive imports of fish from the Atlantic only began in the late sixteenth century and had not yet reached their peak a century later. We can assume that this new commerce in ordinary, cheap fish must have made its appearance in order to compensate for at least part of the meat eliminated from the diet of the common people.

On the other hand, the consumption of cheese and milk products seems to have decreased even more sharply than that of meat. Their production closely follows the general livestock trend. In addition, it was affected by the gradual disappearance between 1670 and 1720 of a breed of red-brown cows famed for their milk production; these were replaced by white cows more easily fattened for the market. At this point cheese had to be imported from Liguria or the Campagna, making it an expensive commodity. Meanwhile, the *pecorino* [sheep's milk cheese] became predominant in local cheese production, although it in turn must have been affected by the sheep shortage encountered during the eighteenth century. In any event, cheese with a high butterfat content remained a luxury, and its price, pound for pound, remained double that of average-grade meats.[12]

The Oscillations of Wine

Urban demand prompted the formation of a succession of wine-producing areas. In the early-modern period, these very differentiated regions coexisted and represented a very clearly marked social hierarchy of consumption. We can distinguish three categories of wine:

1. the oldest local wines: the *vino romanesco,* that is, wine from the Roman vineyards, a large unbroken belt surrounding the city that produced wine of uneven, but always mediocre quality. A multitude of little garden patches, usually rented, were cultivated during free hours by families who drank between forty and sixty percent of the wine they produced. This wine, often drunk as new wine and never kept for more than a year, was the wine of the poor; it "made them feel rich." Long exempt from all taxes, it was the only wine whose supply and sale was supervised by the municipal government.

2. important wines of long standing: the *vini navigati* that since the Middle Ages had been shipped in from the Campagna and, in increasing amounts as the seventeenth century wore on, from Sicily (Castelvetrano, Termini, Syracuse) and Corsica. These were expensive wines, high in alcohol and sugar, wines that traveled well and aged well. They were frequently drunk diluted with water. Although poorer quality imported wines, such as the so-called "Greek" wines of Ischia, were consumed by the common people, who diluted them with water, even such wines were basically luxury items.

3. recent plantings: the vineyards of the *castelli romani.* The production of these vineyards, which were developed during the sixteenth and seventeenth centuries as the Roman population increased, mirrors the vicissitudes of the local market. Medium-sized enterprises cultivated by hired workers, these vineyards produced light white wines of average and rather reliable quality, as indicated by a fairly restricted price range. This group of wines was by far the major source of supply for the capital.

With few exceptions, I have no direct information about Rome's wine supply, and indirect information, such as the taxes on retail wine sales, is generally difficult to use. But by checking one type of source against another, it is nonetheless possible to sketch out a long-term chronology of Roman wine consumption.

A first period is roughly the decades between 1600 and 1680. Consumption increased more rapidly than the urban population. No increase occurred for foreign wines, whose importation remained stable; the increased production affected the wines of the Roman vineyards (where rental agreements multiplied) and above all the wines of the *castelli* (which increased their production by fifty percent between 1630 and 1660 and doubled it between 1630 and 1710). The increased consumption was, therefore, chiefly due to increased consumption by the common people. For the poorest consumers it provided a form of cheap caloric compensation for the marked decline in the amount of meat and grain available, a decrease of which they must have been the principal victims.

Between approximately 1680 and 1760, a general stagnation of wine supplies is evident, but this apparent stability conceals noticeable shifts. The economic crisis in the suburban vineyards at the turn of the eighteenth century (these vineyards fell victim to both increased taxes and competition from the more standardized wines of the *castelli*) and the virtual unavailability of foreign wines (whose importation was restricted from then on) were somewhat compensated for by the creation of the vineyards of the Alban Hills [southeast of the city] until, by the 1720s, these vineyards supplied two-thirds of the city's wine. This substitution of one category of wine for another could indicate a homogenization of tastes through the adoption of one type of wine by the majority of consumers.

On the other hand, the late eighteenth century—roughly between 1760 and 1820—brought a sharp drop in overall consumption. This drop is reflected in a serious economic crisis in the vineyards of the *castelli*, which by 1770 were producing merely some two-thirds of the amount produced in 1710. One wonders why this decrease occurred, when the population of the city was still increasing slowly and steadily. One reason is, of course, the repercussions of the successive wheat shortages and the high cost of food characteristic of the final thirty years of the century. Bread, and to some extent meat, henceforth used up most of the buying power of the urban masses.

This pattern of development can help us to understand better the place of wine in the average Roman diet. If, keeping in mind the reservations I have already mentioned, one attempts to evaluate the average amount of wine available per capita over two centuries, one is struck by the large quantity drunk; for, despite the long-term fluctuations, the average per year always remained above two hectoliters [that is, 200 liters, or about 53 gallons]:[13] 2.10 hl. in 1636; 2.70 hl. (?) in 1660; 2.80 hl. in 1708-9; 2.50 hl. in 1750; 2.00 hl. in 1790; 2.12 hl. in 1812.

Of course, these were usually wines with a low alcohol content. Yet wine consumption in Rome remained considerable and was never really in jeopardy. Although the papal government was on the watch for intemperance, it never attempted to reduce the sizable annual and seasonal fluctuations of wine prices through a policy of importing and stocking wine, nor was it ever concerned about supervising quality or challenging vinification methods. This is adequate proof that in the seventeenth and eighteenth centuries wine was considered only a secondary food and that year in and year out, whatever difficulties arose, the supply met the demand. And the public, which, as I have shown, refused to give up meat during the serious grain shortages of the late eighteenth century (1764, 1772, 1779), seems to have been willing to accept without excessive complaint a reduction in its wine drinking.

Fats

Olive oil was unquestionably the predominant fat. From the tables of the wealthy to those of wage earners, it was omnipresent. However, despite the proximity of a number of major olive-growing districts (the Ciociarìa, the Sabini, the region of Viterbo, and the Umbrian borders), the supply never regularly met

Rome's demand and production was by nature irregular to boot. Even with the importation of oil from Genoa, Sicily, and Apulia, which was facilitated by the authorities, the chronic lack of oil persisted. The situation worsened with time, as evidenced by the very sharp yearly price oscillations, combined with the vigorous price increase throughout the eighteenth century. The municipal government was unable to set up an Annona for oil that could stabilize the market, nor was it able to convince the population to make do with vegetable oils instead. Under such conditions, is it possible to speak of an average supply? In any event, there is no doubt that the average per-capita supply decreased continually throughout the eighteenth century. Statisticians of the time estimated Rome's table oil needs at a stationary 36,000 kegs. Taking the city's growing population into account, this figure yields a yearly supply of 4.5 liters per person per year in about 1700 and 3.8 liters at the end of that century. These figures can at least be considered plausible indications of relative quantities.

Other fats clearly were used less frequently. Lard, which never appeared on the table of anyone living even a bit comfortably, replaced oil for the fried variety meats [that is, internal organs such as the liver], or the fried fish characteristic of lower-class cooking. Fatback remained very costly. And butter was a luxury item that became scarce during the dairy crisis at the end of the seventeenth century. It made a timid reappearance circa 1780, on the tables of seminaries and boarding schools, which always were in the vanguard of new luxury tastes. But until the unification of Italy, butter remained a somewhat exotic delicacy.

In 1641 *"tuttavia Roma consuma il doppio più carne et vino che consuma Napoli, benchè quella chittà sia il doppio più grande, "* [all Rome consumes twice as much meat and wine as Naples, although the latter city is twice as large].[14] People of the day clearly were aware of the privileged diet of the papal capital. As we have seen, the seventeenth and eighteenth centuries brought the increasing erosion of these favorable conditions. By 1800, the reduced average per-capita supply in Rome was nonetheless still one of the highest in Italy. For each type of product, an optimum seems to have been reached—in the late sixteenth century for wheat and meat, in the early eighteenth century for wine. It is as if the market had proved incapable of keeping up with the increasing pleas of the city. But did the city plead? The long-lasting economic recession in Rome, and the curtailment of commercial and banking activities, brought general poverty to a city experiencing a limited population growth. The increased number of mouths to feed does not seem to have made up for the decrease in individual income.

But this phenomenon is still more complex. Early in the seventeenth century the system of the Annona was able to assure the city a more than adequate supply, for the chief foodstuffs at least. It guaranteed the still wealthy population an abundance of wine and meat. But, as the population became more numerous and its buying power decreased, the authorities had to intervene more decisively in the market. They had to limit profits through price manipulation, reduce the opportunities to export foods, and, lastly, intervene and act as an economic partner (using the financial resources of the state) to determine the supply. By freezing the market in this way and by always giving top priority to a regular, annual supply of food rather than to the quantity of those supplies—and in doing so they surely were reflecting the feelings of the urban masses about their diet—they indisputably accentuated the tendency to inertia in an agricultural system of production that already was blocked technologically.

Yet, as far as the amount of food consumed and the quality of the available foods are concerned, even after the Roman diet had deteriorated, it retained some of the generally satisfactory characteristics that had made it so unique circa 1600. It would be pointless to present caloric and energy summaries based on the available documentation. Yet, it seems clear that, with the exception of milk, which was virtually absent, and cheese, which remained scarce, there was no major nutritional void in the Roman diet. In the "carnivorous Europe" described by Fernand Braudel, Rome was still in a good position, since its dietary level remained slightly higher than that of Paris during the last half of the eighteenth century. The drop in the amount of meat available reveals an increasing archaism of the system of production, even more than the decreased supply of grain does. But not until the mid-nineteenth century was the rupture complete, inaugurating the reign of bread and pasta.

But what is true for overall availability is not necessarily true for actual rations. At the moment of its greatest efficiency, the Annona attempted to make sure that each inhabitant received a minimum ration; and, in doing so, it attempted to restrict the range of consumption. The relative scarcity of certain foods on the Roman market must have, on the contrary, increased differences. During the seventeenth century in particular the social hierarchy of eating patterns became inflexible. Without including here a series of statistical tables that one day will appear in another article, I will limit myself to one example. Under the impetus of the reforms of the Council of Trent, the fare in boarding schools and seminaries was altered, toward the end of the sixteenth century. For the next two centuries a veritable dietary culture took shape, a culture that probably was more significant than the abundance—always doubtful—at aristocratic tables. At that time a prescribed order of courses was established (*antipasto, minestra,* meat or fish, dairy products and/or fruit) as well as a weekly cycle of menus insuring a pleasing rotation of flavors. But new quantitative privileges also appeared: five days a week these adolescents would receive approximately 340 grams of meat (71 kilograms per year in 1650-51, 78 kilograms in 1780-81, in the seminary of San Pietro). During the same period the orphans being raised by the proud hospital of Santo Spirito, cited as an example everywhere, received a daily ration of less than 160 grams. My example is, of course, a rather high-level one.[15] But it must be noted that, in an ensemble that was slowly sinking, the dietary privileges available to those who were well-off could only take firm root at the price of increased poverty for the majority of the population. The privileges that once had been those of all city dwellers became the privileges of the rich.

NOTES

1. Borrowing a term from antiquity, the governments of municipalities, provinces, or states created institutions called the *Annona* to regulate general problems involved in supplying food. In Rome it slowly took form between the second half of the sixteenth century and the early seventeenth century; it was concerned with all aspects of the capital city's food supply and with the status of food supplies throughout the Papal State, but it always kept the latter concern subordinate to the former. For the history of the institution, see Jacques Revel, "Le Grain de Rome et la crise de l'Annone dans la seconde moitié du XVIIIe siècle," *Mélanges de l'Ecole française de Rome (moyen age-temps modernes)* (1972), 1: 201-81.

2. Fernand Braudel, *La Méditerranée et le monde méditerranéen à l'époque de Philippe II,* 2nd ed. (Paris, 1966), 1: 301ff. For Italy there are a certain number of recent studies: Maurice Aymard, *Venise, Raguse et le commerce du blé pendant la seconde moitié du XVIe siècle* (Paris, 1966); Gian Luigi Basini, *L'uomo et il pane, Risorse, consumi e carenze alimentari della popolazione modenese nel cinque et seicento* (Milan, 1970); Gabriele Lombardini, *Pane e denaro a Bassano tra il 1501 e il 1799* (Venice, 1963); and Dante Zanetti, *Problemi alimentari di une economia preindustriale* (Pavia, 1964).

3. Cf. Jacques Delumeau, *Vie économique et sociale de Rome dans la seconde moitié du XVIe siècle,* 2 vols. (Paris, 1957 and 1959), especially 2: 251-649; and Revel, "Le Grain de Rome."

4. *Sollievo* was the official name for the congregation entrusted with carrying out inquiries about the way to relieve (*sollievo*) the Papal State's difficulties.

5. It is hard to pinpoint the exact time of the shift from hard wheat to soft wheat. It must have occurred during the sixteenth century, when the enormous demographic growth of Rome created, for producers, a nearby market where products could be sold rapidly. In the regions that continued to produce at least a sizable part of their grain for export, various types of hard wheat (which traveled and kept well) were still sometimes to be found well into the eighteenth century. Along the mountainous borders of the Latium they planted *meschiglie* [a mixture] of hard and soft wheat, intended for local storage. The predominance of soft weat was also clearly linked to the pressure of urban tastes, for it made a whiter bread and also produced more flour for a given measure of grain.

6. Niccolo Maria Nicolai, *Memorie, Leggi ed osservazioni sulle campagne et sull'Annona di Roma* (Rome, 1803), vol. 3, published a certain number of these *scandagli* for the eighteenth century. For the seventeenth century, see an essay dated 1648 in the Archivio di Stato di Stato di Roma [henceforth cited as A.S.R.], Camerale II, *Annona,* b. (*busta*) 1.

7. It is essentially a question of records of the grain entering the city and of the mill tax (*macinato*). For the sixteenth and seventeenth centuries, see the Vatican Library manuscripts, *Cod. Chigiani,* 1826; A.S.R., Congregazione economiche, *Sollievo,* b. 2. For the eighteenth century, see Nicolai, *Memorie,* 3: 142-45, corrected by Revel, "Le Grain de Rome," pp. 224-25, which contains a justification of the computations based on these data. I am saving the critical presentation of the sources used for a more expanded version of the article.

8. The *dogana* was a very complex system that preserved for the Apostolic Chamber (that is, the state) a monopoly over the administration of large pasture areas, for which users had to pay a tax. Thus, the *dogana* was both a unit of territory supervised by the *dogana* and a "fiscal" unit. For further information, see Peter Partner, *The Papal State under Martin V* (London, 1958).

9. Werner Sombart, *La campagna romana* (Rome, 1892), pp. 51ff., an Italian translation of his *Die Römische Campagna* (Leipzig, 1888).

10. On the retail level meat was subject to a tax on the amount theoretically sold. The *quattrino* is a small monetary unit.

11. A criticism of the estimates of weight accepted by the *Grascia* is to be found in A.S.R., Camerale II, *Dogane,* b. 140 (1765-87). Moreover, the essential points of the sources in this chart are to be found in A.S.R., Camerale II, *Grascia,* b. 1-6 (Precettazione degli agnelli), and b. 15-25 (Gabella della scannatura); ibid., *Dogane,* b. 227; Vatican Library manuscripts, *Cod. Chigiani,* 1926. For the sixteenth century, cf. Delumeau, *Vie économique,* 1: 123-24. The weights indicated are, theoretically at least, weights for retail sales.

12. See A.S.R., Congregazione economiche, *Sollievo,* b. 2.

13. A.S.R., Camerale II, *Dogane,* b. 49 and 111; ibid., *Grascia,* b. 9; ibid., *Sollievo,* b. 2; Camille, comte de Tournon, *Etudes statistiques sur Rome et les départements romains* (Paris, 1831), 2: 66.

14. Vatican Library manuscripts, *Vaticani Latini,* 8354, fol. 187 verso.

15. On seminary reform, cf., for example, the "Relazione latina dei Visitatori Apostolici al Papa Sisto Quinto," concerning the Roman seminary, Vatican Library manuscripts, *Cod. Ferraioli,* 154. For the *putti* of Santo Spirito, see *Vaticani Latini,* 7941, fol. 187 recto.

4
The Family Pig of the Ancien Régime: Myth or Fact?

Jean-Jacques Hémardinquer

In *De la cochonnerie,* his brief treatise on pig raising—a set of calculations worthy of La Fontaine's milkmaid*—Sébastien Le Prestre de Vauban wrote: "This animal is so easy to nourish that everyone can raise one, there being no peasant, poor as he be, who cannot produce one home-grown pig per year."[1] This reassuring opinion is still generally held. Pig raising seems a national tradition that has continued uninterrupted since the forests of the ancient Gauls.[2]

But even in Vauban's day there was a distinction between the possible and the actual. Today historians are stressing this from various regional points of view. Pierre Goubert, historian of Picardy, writes: "Half the peasants [1600-1750] had neither cows, nor pigs, nor hens."[3] "How could poor folk who mixed barley flour and maslin flour when baking bread really have fattened pigs? How could they have saved for the pigs the by-products of a virtually nonexistent dairy?"[4] Abel Poitrineau, historian of Lower Auvergne, agrees.[5] Raymond Delatouche, writing of Lower Maine, does not exclude the possibility of a family pig but notes the same "characteristically" small number of pigs being raised before the arrival of the potato.[6]

Relating his own statistical research for the seventeenth and eighteenth centuries at Grenoble to Goubert's work, which had served as his model from the beginning, the late Edmond Esmonin (d. 1965) wanted to call attention to this question. Prevented from doing so by illness, he passed his notes on to me when

---

*Perrette, the milkmaid in La Fontaine's fable about the milkmaid and the jug of milk, imagines as she walks to market what she will do with the profit on the milk she plans to sell. She will buy a hundred eggs; she will raise a pig, which she will sell at a profit for a cow and a calf; and so forth—until the jug slips from her head and breaks.—Trans.

Annales, E.S.C. 25 (November-December 1970): 1745-66. Translated by Patricia M. Ranum.

the *Annales, E.S.C.* began to prepare its issue on food (which he "applauded enthusiastically").[7] I am, therefore, duty bound to ask the same question of researchers that I have already asked of people with whom I correspond: Was the family pig a myth or a fact?[8] Nor did Jean Meuvret avoid this question in the course he gave at the Ecole des Hautes Etudes.

Finding regions where pigs were scarce, determining the dates of such scarcities, and drawing a distinction between the respective situations of city and country—these are the first steps in the research plan outlined here.

The City Pig

Cities are doubly interesting, for they were outlets and consumer centers, as well as centers of independent animal raising. Did the urban market shrink during the sixteenth and seventeenth centuries? There is some evidence that the pig was both prized (by the rich) and expensive (for the poor) in Paris, and even in Bordeaux.[9] Coming from a country of cold cuts, the Venetian ambassador to the court of Henry III observed that with the exception of ham from Mainz, cold cuts were eaten only by the poor; shopkeepers and artisans, even small-scale ones, wanted to eat leg of mutton (*membro di montone*), capon, and partridge.[10] At the end of the reign of Louis XIV, Nicolas Delamare echoed virtually the same thing.[11] According to him, Parisian pork-butchers sold less than 15,000 pigs per year (compared with 30,000 at the end of the fourteenth century and again at the end of the eighteenth?).[12]

Certain documents of a nonquantifiable nature only partly belie these impressions. "The poverty of *procureur's* clerks" in 1628 consisted of a constant diet at their master's table of beef or cod (although, in season, the roast at supper might be "pork, either fresh or salted"); to which one *procureur's* wife retorted that the clerks had lost their appetites because they had been given treats by clients:

Wherever it be matters little, as long as
There is good wine and they are sure to be served
An array of pork, pigs' feet, mustard,
Tongue, sheep's feet, some sausages
Crushed to a pulp, chitterlings, and slices of ham. . . .
When it comes time to serve mutton and beef
They find that to their mind the meat is not good. . . .
To hear them talk, although a sirloin of beef,
A shoulder, a leg of mutton, or a piece of veal
Is prepared for supper, they will eat no more. . . . [13]

Roast sirloin of beef was the "eight o'clock morsel,"[14] and it was considered odd if a marquise lunched on cold cuts.[15]

This is how meals were served in Cardinal Mazarin's palace: a whole pig was placed, if not on the cardinal's table, at least on the table closest to him, and on that of his pages (there were sixteen or seventeen of them), and two pig's ears on the table of his valets de chambre.[16] In other stately households, standing orders with purveyors assured a regular supply of fresh pork. Not only was the stipulated price higher than that of beef (some twenty percent higher between 1648 and 1657), but by 1624 it also cost more than veal or mutton.[17] After 1670 the standing order for the royal household no longer included much pork, beyond suckling pigs and ham, but it still almost always included white lard [that is, fatback],* fatback for soup, and often lard as well. Peas with fatback, as a sixteenth-century saying went, do not disgrace the finest banquet.[18] A century later this must still have been true.

It should be added, however, that Paris—and Versailles—were atypical, because the "fat fairs"† skimmed off the best produce of far-distant farms.[19] As early as the fifteenth century, one dealer in the province of Périgord sent north a shipment of four hundred pigs, all at the same time, via Orléans. This commerce remained one of Périgord's major sources of income.[20] Many other examples could be cited to confirm the truth of one of the terms of the hypothesis: there was no shortage of outlets but pork was fairly expensive. In Nîmes—a city fond of blood sausages, fricandeaux [forcemeat balls made of chopped pluck], and cervelat, but a bit short of them from April to December ("d'abriou cabre morte et porc viou," in April a dead goat and a live pig)—it did not hurt if a girl's dowry included an annuity of three fine slabs of fatback.[21] And if, by definition, the bourgeois is a man who keeps something to fall back on, the bourgeois in the province of Languedoc during the seventeenth century made sure that he had at least a chest full of fatback.[22] A strange story told in Marseilles to Monsieur de Monconys bears proof of a craving for pork.[23]

The persistence of urban animal raising appears most significant. At Alençon, during the early seventeenth century, a certain Guillaume Cochon, who owned land both inside and outside the walls, rented out pigsties.[24] In Laval, during the succeeding century, the bourgeois bought acorns to fatten their porte-lard [literally, "fatback bearer"].[25] Statistics compiled for Franche-Comté in 1688 revealed few pigs (about thirty in the city of Besançon), but those for the province of Dauphiné in 1730 showed no less than eighty in Grenoble and about a hundred in Montélimar.[26] The difficulty in finding food during the Revolution can only have stimulated activities of this sort. In Paris—where virtually the only mention of pigs was as family pets (!) once the edict of 1539 had banished them

---

*The French word lard is by no means equivalent to the English word "lard," but instead designates the "fatback"—that is, the layer of fat over the pig's spine—which is preserved by salting and some degree of air drying. Some translators mistakenly equate lard with "bacon," which is cut from the leaner underbelly of the pig and then salted and cured by smoking. In the past the word lard was often applied to pork in general, more particularly salt pork and fatback, the forms most frequently appearing on the average person's plate. Therefore, although I consistently translate lard as "fatback," the reader should be aware that the item described may range from salt pork to fatty bacon, and even to pork roast or chops.—Trans.

†Established by royal charter in 1222, the foires grasses—also called the foires aux jambons (ham fairs) or the foires au lard (fatback fairs)—specialized in the sale and purchase of fatback, grease, and pork meat. Originally held the three days preceding Good Friday in the square before the cathedral of Notre Dame, the Parisian foire aux jambons was moved in 1899 to the vicinity of the place de la Bastille, where it is still held today.—Trans.

from the streets—a wholesaler from Ghent proposed a way to have always an abundance of "this meat cherished by the sans-culottes." Each year, he claimed, twenty thousand pigs could be raised in the capital if the age at weaning were lowered and the sows were allowed a shorter rest between litters.[27] A few days earlier, in Privas, an ordinance had been passed forbidding hogs to run free "untended and after nine in the morning."[28] In view of this text and the scarcity or total lack of statistics for rural areas, Elie Reynier wondered whether more pigs were raised in cities than in the countryside; and Esmonin asked the same question about the Rhône Valley in 1730.[29]

Pigs in Fields and Woods

Distinctions must be drawn between the different sorts of rural areas. First of all, the vineyards form a category all their own. Sometimes hogs were present; and while they created problems in town, their instinctive rooting about could be useful in other situations.[30] But how could one feed them? And so almost all pigs eaten in Aude or Médoc [vinegrowing regions] had been purchased far away.[31] For the province of Saintonge, M. R. Delafosse, who was then director of the departmental archives of Charente-Maritime, pointed out to me the existence of a "production report" that may be typical.[32]

I am referring to statements of indebtedness signed between 6 April and 8 May 1542 by plowmen of parishes near La Rochelle in favor of the dealers of that city. These "plowmen" must have been vineyard workers or at least peasants whose main crop was grapes, for the area around La Rochelle was vineyard country and the due date of the debt—when that date was given—was the coming vintage. The dealers of La Rochelle, therefore, were making sure they would receive a part of the harvest they exported. It was spring, a difficult time, and the plowmen were borrowing in order to make it through the harvest. Of thirty-six statements, usually for small sums (under ten livres and often less than five) fourteen mention that the money due is all or in part to compensate for the "selling of fatback" or the "cost of fatback." (Today in that region the word "fatback" still refers to pork in general, hence they say a "fatback roast.") The rest of the debts were incurred for "money lent," linen cloth, woolen cloth, or barrels. According to Delafosse, their discoverer, these sample documents show that the peasants—or to be more accurate the vine-growers—around La Rochelle bought pork during that season. Where did the pork come from? The four or five principal dealers lending money carried out various activities; it is not impossible that they bought this pork in Périgord, a practice for which we have several seventeenth-century examples. Were it not for the wrong seasons, these dealings at La Rochelle would fit a Portuguese proverb: "A pig on credit makes a good winter, but a bad spring."[33]

On the other hand, in regions with fallow fields and unsown plowed lands, the practice of letting pigs run loose, as the ancient Gauls had done, persisted, at least from March to October. "The pigs graze like sheep."[34] Like sheep—more thoroughly than sheep, to the astonishment of Bernardin de Saint-Pierre. They devoured bitter grasses, horsetail rushes, and henbane.[35] But they did not get very fat on that diet. To complement and complete it, the kernels produced by the oak and beech forest were needed. Just as pigs are being raised today in the suburbs of Seville, this raising of pigs in forests is still practiced in southern Spain, especially in Andalusia and Estremadura.[36] There the family's black pig gains only one kilogram for every ten kilograms of sweet acorns it eats, as much as it would gain on three kilograms of modern hog feed or four kilograms of grain. It is not slaughtered for two years, at which point it weighs 160 kilograms. (Modern breeds gain more than half that weight in one-fourth of the time, and they are better shaped.)[37] Still, regions with oak forests could consider themselves fortunate. This was the case for the Pyrenees, the Capcir region, and French Cerdagne, in 1730.[38] In thirty small communities of Cerdagne, every head of a household raised at least one pig and often three or four, even the perpetual leaseholders or hired hands who had no other livestock.[39]

But this margin of safety was only apparent. There were years with acorn crops and years without.[40] Vauban noted that, in his own region of Morvan, semiwild fruits were becoming scarce and pig raising had begun a corresponding decline, doubtlessly aggravating the food shortage of 1694. In the fifty-six parishes of the *élection* of Vézelay, an average of only one pig for every four families remained in 1696; there were five pigs for sixty families in Voutenay and none in Provency or Vauclaix.[41]

Last, the potential acorn crop was not always available to everyone. Thus, in the region around Agen the commandery of Nomdieu closed the woods of Pourqueyrat to the inhabitants of the village of Francescas. During the period when acorns were being collected (24 August to 1 January) the individual leasing exclusive rights to the acorn crop could kill any pigs he found in the woods.[42] In the fifteenth century the "acorning" of Birac had been rented out for three years by an innkeeper from Marmande, and a swineherd from Béarn had come there to pasture his "urban" herd of pigs, while a large number of pigs belonging to the inhabitants of the nearby seigneury were being confiscated.[43] In 1552 few pigs in the region of Agen were fattened on the spot,[44] and in the early eighteenth century pigs being sold in the fairs of the subdelegation of Agen had not been fattened.[45] And this despite the fact that there were chestnuts to complement the acorn diet. Indeed, the famous hogs of Périgord ate chiefly chestnuts and turnips.[46] The pigs of the mountains of Béarn even ate dried beans; but their fat was considered less firm than that of acorn-fed hogs, for it would melt in summer.[47]

From that time on, pigs and men competed for virtually the same foods. "The nourishment given to these animals," says a description of a large community near Limoges in 1782, "is taken from the victuals eaten by men, and especially here, where there are no oak trees."[48] Disregarding the occasional damage to crops,[49] in "open," that is, unwooded, regions, it was necessary to "give bran to the fatback-bearing piglets,"[50] and even more than bran. In the region of Beauvais, "only big cultivators can raise them because of the variety of grains available in their farmyards."[51] Big farmers, and millers too. For in the county of Montbéliard the list of livestock on 21 January 1771 reveals that there were forty-nine hogs for thirty-eight families, but eight of these belonged to the miller (as well as five horses, two oxen, one cow, and four ewes), and eight families, or twenty-one percent, raised no pig or had slaughtered it by then.[52] The same was true for the Vivarais region, where very fat pigs under a year old (weighing between 440 and 460 pounds of the Ancien Régime, that is, between 215 and 230 kilograms) were purchased from the miller or the baker.[53]

Olive pulp left after pressing out the oil in Languedoc,[54] and whey in the mountains of Franche-Compté and Auvergne[55] (or whole milk in Normandy)[56] merely supplemented acorns and wheat.

Under such conditions, there had to be many regions where there was not enough pork to go around, where a pig for each family was impossible (see statistical table in appendix). At Exincourt, in the region of Montbéliard, in 1771, there were fifty-three heads of households, including the regent or schoolmaster.[57] Nineteen (36 percent) had no livestock; thirty-one (60 percent) had cows (ranging from one to a maximum of four per household); fifteen had oxen (from one to six); and only three had ewes (there were ten in all). Nineteen families (36 percent) had at least one pig, and three families even had three apiece. (One was a "plowman" and another was a relative of mayor Rigoulet, the offspring of a *coq de village,* or village "big-shot".) But only one family had a pig as its only livestock, while seven had only a cow. Even in Brittany, in the diocese of Quimper, toward 1750, subdelegations other than that of Corlay kept only one pig for every two families.[58] In the region of Boulogne-sur-Mer,[59] in Poitou,[60] and in Bresse,[61] during the eighteenth century only the most well-to-do had a pig to kill each year, although traditionally Poitou and Bresse were regions producing hogs for market. The daylaborers of Mayenne ate "a little piece of fatback" only a few Sundays a year,[62] and laborers in the part of Champagne bordering on the province of Berry never ate any meat at all, according to documents dealing with salt-tax trials.[63]

On the whole, a fundamental dichotomy persisted between raising pigs "in the woods," that is, in "covered" regions, and raising them on the grain-growing plains where "people die of cold every winter"[64]—of cold and undernourishment. This dualism appears, for example, in the *élection* of Niort in 1716 (only five parishes near forests had a few pits), and it is clearly there in 1744.[65] Alleged by many medical topographical maps drawn up in terms of antitheses, this dichotomy is obvious in Auvergne, where the man of the Limagne region was the "real Tantalus of the fable."[66]

The world of the forest retained a wild aura about it. Since the rural pig generally could not be fed "at home,"[67] selective breeding—as known and taught by such men as Olivier de Serres[68]—had little effect upon an animal still closely related to the wild boar (a black or white pig, with clearly visible tusks, like the sow described by Vauban). It could not be prevented from mating with the "black beast" [the wild boar].[69] Even better, how many times, as in Issy in 1747, were full-blooded wild boars raised domestically?[70]

Surely this panorama did not go through the centuries unchanged. In all probability (a theory or a hypothesis?) pig raising declined increasingly until the agricultural revolution, that is, until the introduction of new high-yield crops, such as the potato,[71] and until a general increase in productivity.

Over the long run, pork's fall from favor with luxury consumers, evoked by Etienne and Liébaut, and then by Delamare,[72] is not a myth. Going even further back in time, into the accounts of the domain of the Count of Flanders for 1187, we find beef represented only by a few aged cows; the head of the list, just ahead of eels, was occupied by the pig, more often fat than lean.[73] Although the first "animal-feed revolution" improved sheep and cattle raising, deforestation made it difficult to raise pigs. The driving force for both phenomena was the demographic upsurge of the fifteenth and sixteenth centuries. Emmanuel Le Roy Ladurie proposed as much about Languedoc, located at the opposite end of France, although the spread of "oil trees" [olive trees] across the plains corresponded to the chestnut "plantations" of the Cévennes Mountains.[74] On a more local scale, René Baehrel has traced throughout the seventeenth century the progressive decrease in the size of the herds of pigs in Provence compared with flocks of sheep.[75] In Auvergne, the price of a pig rose twice as fast between 1508 and 1735 as that of a fattened sheep.[76]

Commercial and "industrial" pig raising (for salt pork) was also adversely affected by the increase in grain and salt prices.[77] According to the recorded market quotations of Castelnaudary, in Languedoc, the price of salt increased by 180 percent between 1639 and 1680, as a result of the *gabelles* [that is, salt taxes].[78] This burden was even heavier in the regions of the *grande gabelle*.* The French Revolution removed this obstacle, but, on the other hand, it hastened deforestation.[79]

A knowledge of how pigs were raised for family use by small landowners or holders of quitrents would require an unbroken series of documents, such as a series of inventories after death. Colonel Ligeron is diligently scouring the middle valley of the Saône River for such records. His work seems to indicate that the end of the eighteenth century witnessed a low level of pork consumption:

Pork was only raised for family use; I even find it among common laborers, but not all of them. There are plowmen who seem to have been well enough off, yet have no pig. In the nine inventories at La Bruyère, I found no mention of a pig; at Le Châtelet, in two out of eight; at Pagny-la-Ville, one out of ten; at Pagny-le-Château, despite the existence of one hundred and fifty hectares [roughly three hundred and seventy acres] of woods, only nine out of eighteen inventories refer to a pig. Those fortunate enough to be among the owners had only one or two of the animals; only one had five, two others had four. For earlier periods, we only know that circa 1530 there was a swineherd at Le Châtelet, indicating that these animals must have been numerous enough to constitute a herd.[80]

---

*In the twelve provinces subject to the *grande gabelle,* not only was there an excise tax upon salt, but for every fourteen inhabitants over eight years of age the population was obliged to purchase a minimum of seventy-two liters of salt each year. This did not include the special salt used for preserving food, subject to an additional tax. In the regions of the *petite gabelle,* the "little gabelle" — one of which was Languedoc — salt was less severely taxed and hence the consumption per person was higher. — Trans.

Still, even earlier, during the fourteenth and fifteenth centuries, when the population was less dense and the pig supposedly had more room, a search through the archives of Burgundy being carried out by the Ecole pratique des hautes études (VIe section) thus far shows a rather similar situation: little meat was being preserved by salting; and although herds of pigs existed, they belonged to nobles and bourgeois.[81]

The Role of the Potato

During the eighteenth century the pattern of development may well not have been a one-way street. Of course, there were regions where pig raising was on the increase: Aquitaine, with its maize, where salt pork was no rarity, although such food was held suspect by people concerned with public health;[82] and above all, the regions that pioneered in raising potatoes. This tuber was thought to produce mediocre fatback,[83] but at least it freed Scotland of the Biblical prejudices against the unclean animal.[84] In a few instances in France, the new crop was introduced to feed pigs: in the region of Angoulême, near La Rochefoucauld, circa 1760,[85] and in the arrondissement of Baugé (Maine-et-Loire).[86] According to Abbé de Voyon, and later Abbé Expilly, "The only reasonable objection to the introduction of the potato into Limousin was that the pigs of that province did not like them. Yet since then [that is, before 1765] people have come to agree that [the pigs] were beginning to like them," even raw.[87] The success in Limousin was dazzling, according to administrators under Napoleon I! Raising one or two pigs was no longer too costly for "the smallest household," with the exception of "a few families."[88] At least this was true for the southern parts of the department of Haute-Vienne, that is, the region of the Vienne River, but not the Châtaigneraie [a region of chestnut forests]. Thus, the traditional imbalance seems to have been reversed, but this text should be checked on the spot.

Limousin was merely following the example of the Vosges Mountains, for which, with the exception of the high Chaumes region with its dairies, the agricultural inquiry of 1761 reveals many nuances.[89] Livestock raising was even more difficult than usual after the shortages of 1740. Where the potato was not grown or did not do well, the number of livestock decreased. And so, on the limestone plain to the southwest of the plateau of Lorraine, in the towns of Loro and Montzey (in the arrondissement of Lunéville), "in the past our poor freemen almost all had a pig, today few do; the well-to-do had sows, our plowmen frequently do not." Even in potato-growing villages, near Domrémy, it was the parish priest who supplied the male. He gave up, or would have been glad to give up, his tithe in piglets in order to be free of that obligation. One last example: in Foug, a town in the canton of Toul, the old competition between man and pig reappeared, for "the well-to-do fattened their pigs with potatoes when grain is scarce," but "the people" were reduced to eating the pig's potatoes. (In the Vôge region potatoes were "the bread and meat of many folk.")

The same *social limitation* of progress occurred elsewhere, or later, for example, in Poitou and in the department of Hautes-Alpes, where the production region expanded.[90] But production is not consumption. The people living near Nevers in 1820 ate meat only on major religious holidays or at harvest meals.[91]

Did the separation between the diets of the rich and the poor continue or even worsen during the first half of the nineteenth century? The case of Flanders indicates that it became more pronounced. My friend Jean-Paul Desaive told me about the series of letters published by Dr. Wachter of Rusbroeck. In rural areas, this physician noted, "the difference between the food of the well-to-do and the poorest class has no criterion more valid than the *habitual use or habitual lack* of fatback. . . . This difference in diet by itself summarizes almost all the differences in other living conditions."[92]

Usual Food, Drink, and Condiments

Well-to-do Class	Poor Class
Rye bread	Rye bread
Potatoes	Potatoes
Salt	Salt
Fat back	
Buttermilk	
Vinegar	Vinegar
Coffee	Coffee

Indeed, only rarely did the indigent person find himself in a position to use fatback daily, with the possible exception of a few Belgian provinces, such as Luxembourg. According to Dr. Ceuleneer-Van Bouwel, the Walloon provinces were less compelled to remain vegetarian.[93]

Breakfast of fried fatback and slices of rye bread greased with fatback accompanied coffee; or else potatoes with fatback increasingly took the place of the buckwheat soup made with buttermilk still being eaten in the Campine.[94] But "gone are the days when people running small farms had their cellars stocked with beer and salt pork."[95] "Before the potato was added to the diet of the proletarian class, legumes formed the basic food. That is to say, a diet rich in nitrogen was gradually replaced by one containing only a few traces of it."[96]

Too unsystematic and too rapid for a problem that should properly be studied "serially," this introduction may nonetheless be sufficient indication that the family pig is just like the "chicken in every pot" supposedly promised by King Henry IV of France,[97] the self-same chicken that has been "plucked for the last two centuries,"[98] and even longer. Many proverbs express the feelings of safety symbolized by a store of fatback:

He who has barley bread
And fatback for his gullet
Can say that he is happy.
He will not be troubled by a bad year
Who has millet bread and enough fatback at home.[99]

Beyond this, we can only see the picture on the local level. The predominant meat in the province of Limousin,[100] pork was even rarer than "Christmas meat" from an old cow in the Revermont region.[101] France is diversity itself, like all of Europe, including the British Isles.

Indeed, the question of whether or not the pig was "done in" by deforestation is part of the larger question of the "depecoration," [that is, the increasing meatlessness] of early-modern times, as posed for Germany by Schmöller and Abel.[102] The antithesis between the "covered" countryside and the wheat plain was noted by William Cobbett, in *Rural Rides*. The fact that bacon was served in a little house in the forest confirmed for him the "great comfort" of people living in the woods and the impossibility of their ever being reduced to the same famine level as the inhabitants of the grain-growing part of the realm.[103]

Any future studies of this subject should, therefore, be carried out on an international scale.

NOTES

1. Sébastien Le Prestre de Vauban, "De la cochonnerie, ou calcul estimatif pour connaître jusqu'où peut aller la production d'une truie pendant dix années de temps" [On pigs, or an estimated calculation to find out just how many piglets a sow can have in ten years' time], in Albert de Rochas d'Aiglun, *Vauban, sa famille et ses écrits. . . analyses et extraits* (Paris, 1910), 1: 404-9. The computations ended with 6,434,338 descendents in the tenth female generation, or 6,000,000 clear, taking into account the wolf and illness—"which is as many [pigs] as there are in France," and as were tallied by government statisticians during the Revolution. Cf. the observations of Gilbert White:

The natural term of an hog's life is little known, and the reason is plain—because it is neither profitable nor convenient to keep that turbulent animal to the full extent of its time: however, my neighbor, a man of substance, who had no occasion to study every little advantage to a nicety, kept an half-brèd Bantam sow, who was as thick as she was long, and whose belly swept on the ground, till she was advanced to her seventeenth year; at which period she showed some tokens of age by the decay of her teeth and the decline of her fertility.

For about ten years this prolific mother produced two litters in the year of about ten at a time, and once above twenty at a litter; but, as there were near double the number of pigs to that of teats many died. . . . At a moderate computation she was allowed to have been the fruitful parent of three hundred pigs: a prodigious instance of fecundity in so large a quadruped! She was killed in spring, 1775.

The Natural History of Selborne (first published London, 1789, with numerous editions into the twentieth century), letter 33 of the "Letters addressed to The Honourable Daines Barrington."

In France, the sow was probably the only female domestic animal neutered. See Jacques-Joseph Juge Saint-Martin, *Changemens survenus dans les moeurs des habitants. . .* (Limoges, 1808); and Olivier de Serres, *Théâtre d'agriculture,* ed. Huzard (Paris, 1804), editor's note. In Dordogne in year II [1793-4], Representative Romme requisitioned "altered [*coupée*] female pigs," ten for each one hundred workers (Camille Richard, *Le Comité de salut public et les fabrications d'armament* [Paris, 1922], p. 305).

2. Strabo, *Geography,* book 4, 4, 5. Edmond Esmonin thought that the pig appeared less often in classical literature than other animals, but examples of its place in nineteenth-century folklore are not difficult to find. Cf. the introduction to the statistical appendix to this article.

3. Pierre Goubert, paper delivered at the International Congress of Historical Sciences, Rome, 1955, in *Congrès international des sciences historiques, Riassunti delle Communicazioni* 7 (Rome, 1955): 285.

4. Pierre Goubert, *Beauvais et le Beauvaisis de 1600 à 1730* (Paris, 1958), pp. 106-7, statistical tables, pp. 191-96, and p. 770, where he refers to the small number of pigsties. As for the dairy products available for fattening pigs, the situation at any rate had changed in the region of Clermont (Oise) by the late eighteenth century; cf. Octave Festy, *Les Animaux ruraux en l'an III* (Paris, 1965), 2: 156.

5. Abel Poitrineau, *La Vie rurale en Basse-Auvergne au XVIIIe siècle (1726-1789)* (Paris, 1965), p. 297, a publication of the Faculté des Lettres et Sciences humaines of the University of Clermont-Ferrand, series 2, part 23.

6. Raymond Delatouche, "Quelques particularités du métayage et de la vie rurale dans le Bas-Maine aux XVIIe et XVIIIe siècles," *Les Etudes sociales* 3-4 (1952), page 13 of the offprint. See also Delatouche's "Le Livre de raison de Guillaume de Chevigny, président des élus d'Alençon, 1591-1605," *Bulletin de la Commission historique et archéologique de la Mayenne* 44 (1954): 18, for confirmation of the moderate fertility of sows: a maximum of between five and seven piglets at the most per litter. These figures were used by Vauban, but the people of Limousin, compatriots of Juge Saint-Martin (*Changemens survenus,* p. 143), paid for the services of the boar in liards, in hope of obtaining that many "young boars," that is, twelve.

7. In his letter to me of 7 December 1960.

8. Some of the information they provided appears further on in this article. The academies in the various provinces had already been asked that question in the eighteenth century. Cf. François Quesnay, "Questions intéressantes," in *Oeuvres,* ed. August Onchen (Frankfurt, 1888), pp. 275-76; and Victor Riquetti, marquis de Mirabeau, who wrote: "Is a quantity of pigs raised, are they fattened in the area, is it with acorns or with chestnuts, beech seeds, roots, grasses, or grains . . . are these pigs eaten in the region or are they exported either alive or salted?" (*L'Ami des hommes* [n.p., 1760], vol. 4, pt. 2, art. 18, p. 280).

9. "Anyone who takes from a child a certain peculiar and obstinate fondness for dark bread with *fatback* or with garlic is taking a delicacy away from him. There are some who act put-upon and long-suffering at not having beef and *ham,* along with partridge" (my italics). Michel de Montaigne, *Essays,* bk. 3, chap. 13.

10. J. Lippomano, "Voyage en France en 1577," in *Relations des ambassadeurs vénitiens,* ed. Niccolò Tommaseo (1838), 2: 573-74; which also appears in partial translation in Father Pierre-Jean-Baptiste d'Aussy, *Histoire de la vie privée des Français* (Paris, 1782), and in Alfred Franklin, *La Vie privée d'autrefois. . . des Parisiens,* vol. 3, *La Cuisine* (Paris, 1888), p. 107, where *capone* is translated as "roebuck." As for the fondness for ham during the seventeenth century, see Joseph Pitton de Tournefort, *Voyage du Levant* (Paris, 1717), 2: 302. It was ham that the city of Troyes, despite its reputation for chitterlings, offered to Louis XIV's entourage in 1650 (and earlier to the leaders of political factions in 1576 and 1586). See also the claims by paper workers in 1775 in Pierre Léon, *La Naissance de la grande industrie en Dauphiné* (Paris, 1954), p. 308.

11. "With the exception of hams and a few other more delicate portions, today only the lower classes are nourished with it," Nicolas Delamare, *Traité de la police* (Paris, 1710), 2: 310.

12. Ibid. According to the anonymous *Ménagier de Paris* (written circa 1393, published in Paris, 1846), 30,800 pigs compared with 30,000 beefs, 19,600 calves, or 108,500 sheep. According to Guillebert de Metz, *Description de la ville de Paris au XVe siècle,* ed. Le Roux de Lincy (Paris, 1855), 31,500 pigs compared with 12,500 beefs, 26,000 calves, or 208,000 sheep (a suspicious similarity between 208,000 and 108,000!); Antoine-Laurent Lavoisier, *De la richesse territoriale de la France,* ed. Daire, Collection des principaux économistes (Paris, 1847), 14: 597, tallied 35,000 pigs, comprising 7,000,000 pounds of meat, compared with 88,000 steers and cows, 120,000 calves, and 350,000 sheep. For other cities, in the eighteenth century, see the list of food items drawn up in 1761 by Intendant La Michodière, Archives départementales [hereafter cited as A.D.], Hérault, C 28. In Lyons, there were 7,527 pigs, compared to 14,091 beefs, 28,741 calves, and 123,144 sheep, which apparently was a lower proportion of pigs than the number given by Armand Husson for 1850, cited by Robert Mandrou, "Consommations en viande des villes françaises au milieu du XIXe siècle," *Annales, E.S.C.* 16 (July-August 1961): 744; and also his article "Les consommations des villes françaises (viandes et boissons) au milieu du XIXe siècle," *Pour une histoire de l'alimentation,* Cahiers des Annales 28 (Paris, 1970): 71-78. At Clermont-Ferrand there were 1,674 pigs, compared with 1,905 beefs, 4,732 calves, and 16,362 sheep, a much higher proportion. This trend toward geographic differences—between large and small cities—is probable, even though the figures are not reliable.

13. En quelque lieu qu'il soit il n'importe, pourveu
    Qu'il y ait du bon vin, et ne soit depourveu
    D'un pannache de porc, des bas de soye, moutarde,
    Langues, pieds de mouton, quelque capilotade
    De saucisses, d'andouilles, et tranches de jambon. . . .
    Quant on vient à servir du mouton et du boeuf,
    Ils trouvent qu'à leur goust la viande n'est pas bonne. . . .
    A leur ouyr parler, quoy que d'un alloyeau,
    D'une espaule, ou gigot, ou d'un morceau de veau,
    On apreste à soupper, ils ne mangent davantage. . . .
Madame Choiselet, *La Response à la misère des clercs des procureurs* (Paris, 1628), p. 11, Bibliothèque nationale call number Y 4,938, pièce; this volume seems to be an important document concerning

daily life. It reveals that pork was a meat eaten in "bars," just as today we eat sandwiches and franks; it was the meat of the "riff-raff" and not of the bourgeoisie. Dietary concerns may have also played a part; see the reservations expressed in *La Cuisinière bourgeoise* of 1680: "I will not talk much about it, for its flesh is nourishing, difficult to digest, and slackens the stomach." See also the opinions of Sanctorius [Santori de' Santori, the seventeenth-century author of *Medicina statica*], and later of Sir John Pringle in his writings about feeding armies.

14. Antoine Furetière, *Dictionnaire* (Paris, 1690), s.v. "Aloyau." Emile Magne, *La Vie quotidienne sous Louis XIII* (Paris, 1942), quotes a poem about the sirloin of beef. He could also have quoted Guillaume Colletet:

Mais ho! du boudin blanc peau délicate et tendre,
Hachis emprisonné, qui se pourrait défendre
De s'enfler la bedaine et de vous avaler?
C'est un excellent mets dont je veux me souler.
Délices des fricats, andouilles, et saulcisses,
Je vous voy, je vous gouste, et gouste autant d'espices.

[But oh! white pudding, with your delicate and tender skin,/Imprisoning minced meat, who could prevent himself/From swelling his paunch and swallowing you?/'Tis an excellent dish with which I shall stuff myself./Oh voluptuous pâtés, chitterlings, and sausages,/I see you, I taste you, and taste as many spices.]

15. Louis de Rouvroy, duc de Saint-Simon, *Mémoires*, ed. Gonzague Truc, Bibliothèque de la Pléiade (Paris, 1948-61), 6: 579.

16. P. Couperie, "Régimes alimentaires dans la France du XVIIᵉ siècle," *Annales, E.S.C.* 19 (November-December 1964): 1135-38.

17. Ibid. For the period of the Fronde a few texts provide examples of how "common" or abundant beef was (but this abundance was in comparison with veal; see Baehrel's reference to the Provençal's reticence about "heavy meat"). Mademoiselle de Montpensier served a five-course meal in 1652 where nothing but beef was served (Jean Loret, *La Muze historique ou recueil de lettres en vers...écrite à S.A. Mademoiselle de Longueville [1650-1665]*, ed. J. Ravenel and E. V. de La Pelouze [Paris, 1857], vol. 1). Jacques Charpentier de Marigny wrote a satirical song about "Poor Monsieur d'Elbeuf who had no resources and ate only beef" (Gabriel-Jules de Cosnac, *Souvenirs du règne de Louis XIV* [Paris, 1866-82], 1: 212).

18. Jacques Dalechamps, *Histoire générale des plantes..., puis faite française par Maître Jehan des Moulins* (Lyons, 1615), vol. 1.

19. Delamare, *Traité de la police*, p. 1345; Jacques Savary des Bruslons, *Dictionnaire universel du commerce* (Paris, 1759), p. 672 (based on the *Almanach royal* of 1719); Huzard, in editor's note to the 1804 edition of Serres, *Théâtre d'agriculture.*

20. A. Thomas, "Note sur l'élevage et le commerce des porcs au XVᵉ siècle," *Annales du Midi,* 1908, pp. 61-64. Cf. the letter of the bishop of Périgueux of 23 March 1708, in *Correspondance des contrôleurs généraux*, ed. Arthur de Boislisle (Paris, 1874-97), 3: 20.

21. I cannot possibly cite the many examples available. But we should also keep in mind Abbé Delille's line concerning the pig: "The unfortunate martyr to the *luxury* of the table." One certainly could purchase second-quality pork, from pigs mildly afflicted with porcine leprosy; for instance, the tripe sellers of Chalon-sur-Saône in the twelfth century held the pork monopoly as well as the monopoly for he- and she-goats, and they retained the monopoly of "stippled pork" after 1657.

22. Albert Puech, *Une Ville à la fin du XVIᵉ siècle* (Nîmes, 1896), p. 428.

23. "Peyssonel told me that a woman had advised him how to cure his mother by serving a supper at which there was neither salt nor pork, and that those who were willing to eat supper, without salt or pork, would be removing a pork bone that she had in her thigh, which was causing her illness." Balthasar de Monconys, *Journal des voyages de M. de Monconys* (Lyons, 1665), 1: 92. This is a tall tale typical of Marseilles. According to A. Husson, in the nineteenth century Marseilles was the least pork-eating of all the cities with customs barriers (Mandrou, "Consommations en viande").

24. Delatouche, "Le Livre de raison," p. 18.

25. Jules-Marie Richard, "Thierry d'Hireçon, agriculteur artésien, (13..-1328)," *Bibliothèque de l'Ecole des Chartes* 53 (1892): 128, used by Delatouche, "Le Livre de raison."

26. See statistics in appendix, F and G.

27. Archives nationales, F 10,500, memorandum about a new system by Schwarts (who sometimes called himself "artist and cultivator," and at others "wholesaler at Ghent"), dated vendémiaire, year VII [1798]. Cf. A. Leclercz, "Saint Antoine, les pourceaux et le vieux Paris," *La Cité Bulletin de la Société historique de Paris*, 1938-39, pp. 257-68. Is it not also significant that the pig was included among the family pets living in Parisian apartments? Although Mathieu-François Pidansat de Mairobert,

Mémoires secrets (London, 1777-89), 29: 331-33, shows no *grande dame* suckling a piglet Papuan-style, he does reveal that Bertier de Sauvigny, first president of the Maupeou Parlement, raised one in his official mansion (addition of 10 January 1775), prompting the song, "The Allegoric Pig":

Du corps amovible un de nos Présidens...
Dans son hôtel avoit depuis quatre ans,
Petit cochon dont parfois le bon homme
Se récréoit, quand travaux importants
Avoient parfois fatigué sa cervelle....
Tous les reliefs il lui portoit,
Partant le drôle profitoit,
Etoit gras comme père et mère.
En animal reconnoissant,
En bon cochon, il caressoit son maître;
Puis se vautrant en l'abordant,
Sitôt qu'il le voyoit paroître,
Sans cesse il lui disoit *hon, hon,"* etc.

[One of our presidents of the unresigning body.../Kept for four years in his mansion/A piglet, with which at times the good man/Played, when important work/Had at times fatigued his brain..../All the leftovers he brought to it;/Consequently the funny thing flourished,/Was as fat as its father and mother./As a grateful animal should,/As a good pig should, it caressed its master;/Then sprawling about when he came near,/As soon as it saw him appear,/It continually called out, *oink, oink.*]

In the end the animal, "stubborn like all its breed," was even less willing than its master to vacate the premises. For quite some time one of its fellow pigs is supposed to have been one of the dinner guests at the famous gourmet meals of Grimod de la Reynière, where it would lie on a bed. Cf. Jean Vartier, *Les Procès d'animaux* (Paris, 1970). Alexandre Dumas told in his memoirs of having presented the actor Harel with a little pig that the man had expressed a desire to possess and with whom he shared his bed—until the day he had it butchered.

28. E. Reynier, *Histoire de Privas* (Privas, 1941), 2: 300.

29. Ibid. See also the statistics, table F, in the appendix, for Montélimar. Many texts should be cited. For the seventeenth century, for example, there is the episcopal visit to Paray-le-Monial in 1697, in A. D., Saône-et-Loire, G 934, no. 60: "The cemetery has no wall around it and the pigs continually enter." Robert Mandrou, chairman of the session at which this paper was originally presented, confirmed that police regulations were the same everywhere, with the possible exception of the South. For the South in the late eighteenth century, J. Vidalenc confirms this for La Ciotat, citing Boucher de Perthes (although Festy referred only to raising pigs for their manure) and also for Gars (in Alpes-Maritimes) between 1790 and 1806. Outside France, Hippolyte Taine saw "filthy pigs wandering in the streets" of Pouzzoles in 1854 (*Voyage en Italie* [Paris, 1866], 1: 47). Delatouche writes: "Even today in the suburbs of Seville, in front of the huts of poor people, one sees the family pig, a recycling machine" ("Le Livre de raison," pp. 8-9).

30. In oak forests, and in regions with apple trees, where they took over the job of cultivating around the roots of old trees (Juge Saint-Martin, *Changements survenus*, p. 147). The customary laws of Bazas forbade allowing pigs in vineyards; R. Georlette, "Les coutumes des pays de l'ancienne France," *Revue des sciences économiques*, Liège, December 1956.

31. Abbé Bouet, "Mémoires statistiques," 1730, ed. E. Caraman, *Archives historiques de la Gironde*, vol. 48: 11, 18. Baron Claude-Joseph Trouvé, *Description du Département de l'Aude* (Paris, 1818), p. 551.

32. A.D., Charente-Maritime, uncatalogued notarial archives (Notary Macainy). Another sample, from the archives of Notary Roy, revealed only one debt of this sort out of ten.

33. Elian-J. Finbert, *Dictionnaire des proverbes du monde* (Paris, 1961).

34. Polybius, *History,* II, 15.

35. Jacques-Henri Bernardin de Saint-Pierre, *Harmonies de la nature* (Paris, 1783), study 11; cf. the version edited by L. A. Martin (Paris, 1840), 1: 379. In Franche-Comté they ate wild apples and pears, and in the Gâtine region of the Vendée, elm leaves stripped from hedges; E. Longin, "Une Statistique inédite de Franche-Comté, 1636," *Mémoire de la Société d'émulation du Jura*, 11th series, 1925, p. 37.

36. J. D. Parsons, "La economia de las montañeras en los encinares del S. O. de España," *Estudios geográficos* 17 (May 1966): 322, and earlier, cf. Pierre Birot and Jean Dresch, *La Méditerranée*, collection Orbis (Paris, 1953-56), 1: 215.

37. Parsons, "La economia," p. 322; and C. Clark, "The Tropics as a World Food Source," *New Scientist*, 1962, p. 314.

38. A. D., Pyrénées-Orientales, C 1902, statistics of Capcir for only six parishes: 371 heads of

households owned 348 work horses and 474 pigs.

39. A. D., Pyrénées-Orientales, C 2045.

40. Jacques Savary des Bruslons, *Dictionnaire universel du commerce* (Paris, 1742), vol. 1, pt. 1, col. 178, "Bourbonnais." Boislisle, *Contrôleurs généraux,* 2: 963, for the summary of a letter from Oloron, 7 July 1691, and also p. 991 for Bordeaux. See also "Essai sur le commerce de la Franche-Comté," dated 1775, published by Charles Godard, *Bulletin de la Société grayloise d'émulation,* 1906; and J. A. Demian, *Description du royaume de Hongrie* (Paris, 1809), 2: 159.

41. Sébastien Le Prestre de Vauban, "Statistique de l'élection de Vézelay," ed. Arthur de Boislisle, *Mémoire de l'intendant de Poitiers* (Paris), pp. 739-47; and E. Coornaert, ed., *Projet d'une dixme royale* (Paris, 1933), p. 288.

42. J. Benabon, *La Commanderie de Nomdieu et ses annexes* (Toulouse, 1914), pp. 305-9.

43. A. D., Lot-et-Garonne, records of the bishopric, series G, subseries H, bundle 58, parish of Birac. I owe this reference to Mademoiselle Lucile Bourrachot.

44. On the difficulties in the region of Agen in 1552: "And as for feeding pigs, it is said that for lack of acorns and chestnuts in the said country, there being none at all, even so little, and they are forced to obtain pigs fed and fattened in the country of Limousin and other circumscriptions." A. D. Lot-et-Garonne, CC 54. I owe this reference to Claude Martin, of Clairac.

45. Abbé Bellet [Bouet?], "Mémoires statistiques," ibid., p. 27.

46. A. D. Gironde, C 316, a report on production in the *élection* of Périgueux circa 1730. P. Decandolle (sic), "Rapport sur un voyage botanique et agronomique dans les départements du Centre," *Mémoires de la société d'agriculture de la Seine* 15 (1812): 224, which discusses how chestnuts were kept through the winter.

47. Memorandum of Intendant Lebret about Béarn in 1704, Louis Soulice, *Mémoires des intendants* (Paris, 1906), p. 91. "The fatback obtained in this manner is less firm than that of pigs fed on acorns and even melts in summer."

48. A. D., Haute-Vienne, C 121, a monograph dated 1782 about Hautefages, in the *élection* of Tulle. There were 988 inhabitants, and 150 pigs were fed for eleven months of the year. See also Boislisle, *Contrôleurs généraux,* 1: 991.

49. Robert Latouche, *La Vie en Bas-Quercy du XIVe siècle* (Toulouse, 1923), pp. 146-48.

50. Claude Gauchet, *Le Plaisir des champs* (n.p., 1604), verse 3, 442, which provides a description of a small property along the borders of the modern departments of Oise, Val-d'Oise, and Seine-et-Marne, where the yearly pig was more than a myth.

51. At Arsonvilliers (Festy, *Les Animaux ruraux,* 2: 150-51).

52. A. D., Doubs, E 844, record of all flour...and list of cattle on hand, 21 January 1771. Cf. the situation at Pontlieue (today a part of the course over which the twenty-four hour race of Le Mans is run): No pig is found in inventories for day workers or artisans of the town, but there were three at Massu's mill in November 1692 and two in an inn in Arnage, according to Marcel Mémin, the author of a monograph on Pontlieue, whom I wish to thank for this information. Even in Hungary there is written evidence that pigs had been fattened with "mill dust," as early as the fourteenth century, M. Belenyesy, "Viehzucht...im 14 u. 15 Jahrhundert," *Viehzucht und Hirtenleben* (Budapest, 1961), p. 23.

53. P. d'Albigny, "Le Prix des denrées de 1732 à 1736 (livre de raison de Ballioud des Granges, de Bourg-Argental)," *Revue du Vivarais,* 1898, p. 518.

54. In Bayeux (Festy, *Les Animaux ruraux,* 1: 145).

55. François-Louis, comte de Lubersac de Livron, *Vues politiques et patriotiques sur l'administration des finances* (Paris, 1787), p. 155. On exports, cf. the memorandum of the intendant of Franche-Comté in 1698; in 1777, Servien Vesoul (Godard, "Essai sur le commerce du Franche-Comté") wrote: "This d__n Ethis [the subdelegate] made a fortune through selling the right to drive herds of pigs to Switzerland, at a cost of three livres per pig;" and Lucien Gachon, *Les Limagnes du Sud et leurs bordures montagneuses* (Tours, 1939), pp. 53-55. See also P. Ruwet, *L'Agriculture et les classes rurales dans le pays de Herve au XVIIIe siècle,* a publication by the Faculty of Letters of Liège, 1943, no. 100; this had been a grazing region since at least the sixteenth century.

56. In Bayeux, see Festy, *Les Animaux ruraux,* 1: 145.

57. A.D., Doubs, E 645, January 1771 (for Exicourt, east of Monbéliard, at 585 meters altitude). There, as in Raynans, we could compare this document with other lists for years less trying than 1719 (for example, E 646). In the statistics drawn up for 1688, (see appendix, F), the column "pigs" is missing.

58. Statistical summary for the bishopric of Quimper, n. d. (mid-eighteenth century), tallied by Edmond Esmonin.

59. J. T. Desmars, *De l'air, de la terre et des eaux de Boulougne-sur-Mer et des environs,* new

edition (Paris, 1761), p. 47; and cf. Ernest-Théodore Hamy, *La Vie rurale au XVIIIe siècle dans le pays reconquis* (Boulogne, 1865). During the Napoleonic Empire, "the little properties belonging to unskilled laborers can raise only hens and turkeys."

60. Jacques Peuchet and P.-G. Chanlaire, *Description de la Vienne* (Paris, 1911), p. 11, to be compared with Charles Cochon de Lapparent, *Description générale* (Paris, year X [that is, 1801-2]; and Jacques Peuchet and P.-G. Chanlaire, *Description des Deux-Sèvres* (Paris, 1911), p. 32, and C.F.E. Dupin, *Mémoire statistique* (Paris, year XII [that is 1803-4]). See also, for the regions of Loudun and Mirebeau, "Statistique de la Vienne," Archives nationales [hereafter cited as A. N.], F²⁰ 270.

61. Lucien Guillemaut, *Histoire de la Bresse louhannaise . . . jusqu'en 1789* (Bourg, 1896), 2: 661. On the Bourg region of Bresse, cf. Charles-J. Bossi, *Statistique du département de l'Ain* (Paris, 1808), p. 310, who wrote that "the pig least suitable for sale is the pig the local man saves for his own table," but "the meat or fatback are saved for feast days or for visits by relatives or friends."

62. A. N., F²⁰ 219, summary of the situation in Mayenne, year XI [1802-3].

63. E. Salle, *Revue de l'Académie du Centre,* 1939, p. 83.

64. Archives of the bishopric of Orléans, memorandum of the prior of Sennely (1701), cited in Christianne Marcilhacy, *Revue d'histoire moderne* 6 (1949): 6. The dichotomy between the cereal-growing plains and the wooded regions where pigs lived goes back to the iron age and to Caesar's *Commentaries* (?) [sic], according to L. Champier, *Annales Universitatis Saraviensis,* 1952, no. 2. See also the conclusion of this chapter, below. For a "wooded country," cf. Georges Lefebvre, *Les Paysans du Nord* (Bari, 1959), p. 359.

65. List for the élection of Niort in 1716, published in L. Desaive, *Mémoires de la société de statistique des Deux-Sèvres,* 1886, pp. 9 ff. (cited in Lefebvre, *Les Paysans du Nord,* p. 239), who describes the plains as "having no woods, . . . few vegetables, having no pastures, no milk, no income from animals," while in the "covered" regions there are few who cannot raise one or two hogs, a cow. . . ."

66. D.G.F. (Defourt) de Pradt, *Voyage agronomique en Auvergne,* 2nd ed. (Paris, 1828), vol. 1, used by Poitrineau, *La Vie rurale en Basse-Auvergne.*

67. Wandering pigs caused destruction to the harvest in Quercy, see Latouche, *La Vie en Bas-Quercy,* p. 146, for the year 1785.

68. Cf. Olivier de Serres, *La Maison rustique* (1675), 1: 103, chap. 23, "Swineherds." I am referring to cross-breeding carried out circa 1775, as described in Bossi, *Statistique de l'Ain;* this cross-breeding produced pigs that were easier to fatten.

69. Madame de la Getière, *Mémoires d'agriculture,* Autumn 1789, pp. 151-66, dealing with Lower Poitou. This still occurs, for example in New Guinea.
Note that in the province of Maine, among other unusual breeds of animals, Messieurs Guerrier raised "the wild-boar-pig; it has the head and pelt of a wild boar; it is the size of our fattest pigs, . . . lives among our pigs, and eats the same food; they say its flesh is better and more delicate" ("Rapport fait au Bureau d'agriculture du Mans sur l'établissement de S. Martin au canton de Bellême," *Gazette du commerce, de l'agriculture et des finances,* 10 February 1767).

70. Pierre Guyot, *Répertoire de jurisprudence* (Paris, 1784), 6: 6, s.v. "disme." For the consequences of a hard winter, cf. Pierre de Vaissière, *Curés de campagne de l'ancienne France* (Paris, 1932), pp. 88-89.

71. On this question we must wait for the results of M. Morineau's computations.

72. Delamare, *Traité de la police* (ed. of Paris, 1770), 2: 1340; P.-A. de La Mésangère, *Le Voyageur à Paris* (Paris, 1797), 1: 102-3; A.-B.-L. Grimod de la Reynière, *Almanach des gourmands* (Paris, 1803), pp. 63-64.

73. Raymond Delatouche, "Le Poisson d'eau douce dans l'alimentation médievale," *Procès-verbaux des séances de l'Académie d'agriculture de France,* especially p. 796.

74. Emmanuel Le Roy Ladurie, *Les Paysans de Languedoc* (Paris, 1967), 1: 213. The author espouses Salvador de Madariaga's theory about the Moorish origin of oil-based cooking.

75. René Baehrel, *Une Croissance: La Basse-Provence rurale* (Paris, 1963), pp. 119-20, summarizes the changes in the sizes of herds of pigs, sheep, and goats. At Auriol the number of pigs compared to each sheep fell from 3.37 in 1604 to 2 in 1647, and 1.15 in 1672. Some acts of sale for piglets are still extant, but they are for the succeeding century. There is little useful information in the Marquis Donatien de Sade's Provençal "Président mystifié," in *Oeuvres complètes* (Paris: Cercle du livre précieux, 1967), 14: 124, except that a château in Brie had a pigsty directly under the bedchambers.

76. Dutot, *Réflexions politiques sur les finances et le commerce* (Paris, 1735). The sale price for sheep increased from 10 sous to 25 and 35 livres; the price of pigs increased from 7 sous to 10 livres.

77. Archives of the Affaires Etrangères, Paris, Mémoires et documents, France, 1401, folio 99 recto," Avis de Mr [le comte d'Artois, brother of the king] présenté le 23 mars 1787 à son bureau de l'assemblé des notables," which was trying to replace the gabelle [a tax on salt consumption] by a tax on all subjects proportionate to what the gabelle had been costing them. "The countries of the 'little gabelle'—Languedoc, the banks of the Garonne River—will become more able to preserve their food with salt, which is the object of an important commerce for these provinces, at much less cost; they will even increase this commerce because the owner, who thinks twice about raising pigs owing to the high price of salt, no longer being impeded by this obstacle, will devote himself more fully to this useful speculation." I was told about this position taken by the Comte d'Artois by Marc Perrichet, whom I thank warmly. Cf. the report on commerce in the *élection* of Aurillac in 1788 in Gabriel Esquer, *La Haute Auvergne* (Paris, 1911), p. 297, where we find: "The commerce in pigs is essentially carried on for exportation in the region of Maurs and can only be expanded by establishing a *salage* [a curing by salt]." For Béarn, Edmond Esmonin was convinced that the trade in so-called Bayonne hams reflected the low cost of salt from Salies. In Brie, under Louis XIV, E. Mireaux explains the small number of pigs being raised by the cost of salt in those regions of the "grande gabelle," *Revue de Paris,* November 1958, p. 84. However, during year III [1794-95], the only remaining concern was a lack of bran, although the supply at the time was adequate, according to Festy, *Les Animaux ruraux,* 2: 217-18. Giorgio Doria, *Uomini e terre di un borgo collinare dal XVI al XVIII secolo* (Milan, 1968), also shows how unprofitable it was to fatten a pig; this doubtlessly is why sharecroppers often were given that task.

78. Le Roy Ladurie, *Les Paysans de Languedoc,* 1: 481.

79. Jean-Antoine Huguet, *Statistique du département de l'Allier* (Paris, year X [that is, 1801-2]), p. 14; and, later, Sonnini in P.-Etienne Herbin, *Statistique générale et particulière de la France* (Paris, 1803), 1: 296-98. The price of wood increased greatly during the eighteenth century, except the firewood for heating Parisian homes, which was price-controlled. But even so, in Alsace the sale of the right to collect acorns from the forest of the domain of Haguenau brought in more than all the wood cut during the year (P. Fromont, *Problèmes d'économie rurale* [Paris, 1964], p. 361, citing Guinier; cf. H. Hanauer and Ney, *Geschichte des heiligen Forstes bei Haguenau* [Strasbourg, 1890]).

80. L. Ligeron, "Monographie de Pagny," unpublished, to be consulted in A. D., Côte-d'Or, which I summarize here. The same is true for the region of Le Mans, already referred to several times, using information provided by Marcel Mémin. At Pontlieue there was "a devouring, sandy soil, the poorest in the canton," according to a report submitted to the intendant of Tours in 1748, to be found in the Archives communales of Le Mans, 19, statistique. Seven times out of ten, the number of pigs and sows tallied on the large sharecropping farms in 1650, 1662, or, more frequently, in the last quarter of the seventeenth century—up to four, plus the "nurslings of the summer"—is not to be found during the eighteenth century. In fact, in regions with good soil the number even fell to zero. As for very small sharecropping farms [*bordages*], references to pigs are always the exception (five out of sixty), but in Le Buisson, which had four pigs and sows in 1683, there were only two "nurslings" to sell during the year 1762; in another town, a shelter for pigs existed in 1780, but it was classified as "out of service." In Moncé en Belin, a nearby parish, a notary from Le Mans, who owned one of these *bordages,* refused the parish priest his old right to the "second pig fed on the spot," for he was raising no pigs at all (notarial act, Morin archives, 28 October 1780).

81. I wish to thank Mademoiselle Françoise Piponnier for this information.

82. This was discussed in a paper by J.-P. Desaive at the National Congress of Learned Societies held at Tours in 1968. Cf. A.D., Gironde, C 1,310, for a statement from the parish priest at Salères, subdelegation of Ax, attached to the census of 1782: "bad salted meat."

83. Cf. Decandolle, "Rapport sur un voyage agronomique," p. 273, about the use of the melon-like plant called "clams" (*palourdes*) in the region of Angers; and earlier, the memorandum of the intendant of Béarn in 1704 about the results obtained by dried beans.

84. R. N. Salaman, *A Social History of the Potato* (London, 1949), pp. 392-93.

85. Festy, *Les Animaux ruraux,* 2: 128, 132.

86. *Statistique agricole de 1814,* p. 333.

87. Jean-Joseph Expilly, *Dictionnaire historique, géographique et critique des Gaules et de la France* (Paris, 1766), 4: 258-60. For the department of Tarn, see Octave Festy, *L'Agriculture pendant la Révolution française, l'utilisation des jachères* (Paris, 1950), p. 131.

88. Louis Texier-Olivier, *Statistique du département de la Haute-Vienne* (Paris, 1807), p. 263; ibid., pp. 86-87. In the Vivarais, estimates for the extremely poor stratum of the population that was excluded from such computations would be made in 1828 by the subprefect at Largentière: at the

most, one-fourtieth raised pigs. See my appendix on Flanders.
  89. A. N., KK 1164-1170, available on microfilm.
  90. "If the least bit of extra money comes into a household, they eat the pig that they have been feeding during the year." Pierre-Antoine Farnaud, *Exposé des améliorations introduites depuis environ cinquante ans dans l'économie rurale des Hautes-Alpes* (Gap, 1811), p. 53. It was only later that pig raising spread to the hills, "where formerly not one was to be seen," Barthélemy Chaix, *Préoccupations statistiques . . . des Hautes-Alpes* (Grenoble, 1845), p. 827.
  91. Guy Thuillier, "L'Alimentation traditionnelle," *Aspects de l'économie nivernaise au XIXe siècle* (Paris, 1966), p. 50, no. 1, based on a rather late (1878) source of Montalivet's. Cf. Sébastien Guyétant, *Essai sur l'état actuel de l'agriculture du Jura* (Lons-le-Saunier, 1822), p. 94, who wrote that "the poor sometimes fatten pigs, but in order to sell them."
  92. Dr. Wachter, "Du lard et ses auxiliaires dans l'alimentation des campagnes," *Annales de la Société de médecine d'Anvers* 20 (1859): 172 and 184. In the department of Maine, they still say that the price received for the pig "should somersault three times."
  93. Ibid., citing page 503 of Dr. de Ceuleneer-Van Bouwel.
  94. Ibid., p. 185.
  95. Ibid., p. 505 of the same doctor's text.
  96. Ibid., p. 186.
  97. A. N., F^{10} 500, Py to the deputies of the Committee of Public Safety. Is this the Michel Py de Cauterets, 1744-1831, mentioned in René Cuzacq, *L'Ours des Pyrénées* (Bayonne, 1961), p. 19? "A piece of fatback in a pot," wrote Py, "is worth Henry IV's chicken in the pot. Each household should be enabled to kill a fatback" (sic).
  98. Pidansat de Mairobert, *Mémoires secrets.*
  99. Arnaud Oihenart, *Proverbes basques,* ed. Francisque Michel (Bordeaux, 1847), p. 78, no. 78. (This book first was published in 1657.) Today they say, "A pig for the winter and a tourist for the summer."
  100. Texier-Olivier, *Statistique de la Haute-Vienne,* p. 361. Cf. Margaret Cussler and Mary L. de Give, *Twixt the Cup and the Lip, a Story of American Food Habits* (New York, 1952), p. 55, for the diets of the blacks in Georgia and Carolina.
  101. P. Carru, "La Nourriture des campagnards de la Bresse burgensienne dans la première moitié du XIXe siècle," *Bulletin de la Société des naturalistes de l'Ain* 1 (1909): 28, where we find: "No one raises pigs." Cf. the earlier Dr. Ignace Druhen the elder, *De la pellagre en Franche-Comté* (Besançon, 1868), p. 24, who wrote: "In the mountains of the departments of Doubs and Jura, instead of pork, beef and cow meat are eaten salted, going by the name of 'brazil.'" This remark doubtlessly is too much of a generalization, for it contradicts the observation made a century earlier, before 1758, in the memorandum on the county of Burgundy found in A. N., KK 1106, that states that the people in those mountains ate "a little fatback, for they also feed many pigs. . . ." For Savoy, cf. Jean-Joseph de Verneilh-Puyraseau, *Statistique du département du Mont-Blanc* (Paris, 1807), which studied the lower valley separately.
  102. Robert Mandrou, "Théorie ou hypothèse de travail?," *Annales, E.S.C.* 16 (September-October 1961): 965-71. Cf. W. Abel, "Wandlungen des Fleischverbrauchs und der Fleischversorgung in Deutschland seit dem ausgehenden Mittal-alter," *Berichte über Landwirtschaft,* Neue Folge, vol. 12, no. 3 (1937).
  103. William Cobbett, *Rural Rides* (London, 1830), entry of 13 November 1825.

STATISTICAL APPENDIX

Edmond Esmonin considered inventories after death "far preferable" to statistics such as those provided by a quantitative source (letter to me dated January 1962). Nonetheless, he had copied a certain number of such statistical sources and had given them "a rough meaning" (letter of November 1961), despite the combined factors of fiscal dissimulation by the taxpayer and administrative negligence.

The argument based on silence can certainly not be used as proof (letter dated November 1962), especially in the case of pigs. Jacques Peuchet gave up including them in his *Statistique élémentaire de la France* (Paris, 1805) because of the "lack of bases for computation" (p. 343).

As A. Ramus or Georges Dupeux noted for the nineteenth century (*Aspects de l'histoire sociale et politique de Loire-et-Cher* [Paris, 1962], p. 237), it is particularly difficult to tally the number of hogs because they were so widely scattered and above all because of the slaughtering and rapid renewing of the stock— before they were a year old and, therefore, during the course of the year. This is (or at least used to be) the most "flexible" form of animal raising.

The statistics that follow provide only background data from which to proceed. They chiefly reveal the relationship between the number of pigs and the number of families; comparisons with the number of other animals are less informative, chiefly because hog raising did not produce several products, as was the case with other animals (cf. Jean de La Fontaine's fable, "The Pig, the Goat, and the Sheep"; and Olivier de Serres, who commented "How does it happen that for one hog there are thirty [sheep and goats]?")[1]

A. ILE-DE-FRANCE

Reform of the Forest of Fontainebleau (1528)

Parishes Using Forest	Number of Households	Pigs	Ovines*	Bovines
Samois (fewer pigs than people)	184	119	1,449	351
Avon	201	279	1,503	497
Bois-le-Roi	238	400	2,322	524

Source: Archives nationales, Z le 1135, folio 43; Michel Devèze, La Vie de la forêt française au XVIe siècle (Paris, 1961), 2: 17, 124.
*Includes a small number of goats.

The general average is just over one hog per household. The grand master of the waters and forests, Pierre de Warty, who was personally carrying out his duties, did, however, take one precaution for the future when he limited the use of the forest to six hogs "to be raised by each householder" and forbade access to the occupants of any houses that subsequently might be built. A stricter series of decrees by supreme judges was issued in 1549 for the forests of Compiègne and Laigue (Valois).[2] These decrees set a maximum of two pigs,[3] as well as two horned animals, per peasant household in houses constructed during the previous forty years.

A century later, the mature forest at Laigue was totally razed.[4] The liberal "reform" of the forest of Orléans, however, was carried out on a different note.[5]

B. BRIE

Inquiry of 1717 Involving Twenty Parishes in the Tax District (Election) of Melun

Horses & Donkeys	Cows & Bulls	Ewes & Sheep	Hogs
1,482	2,649	16,202	667

Source: Archives nationales, K 901; analyzed in Emile Mireau, Une Province française au temps du Grand Roi, La Brie (Paris, 1958), p. 132.

One independent farmer (laboureur) at La Grande Barusse cultivated between one hundred and fifty and one hundred and eighty hectares; upon his death in December 1684 he left to his heirs fourteen pigs and fourteen cows.

C. HAINAUT

Statistics for the prévôté and county of Valenciennes in 1700, drawn up by Baldi Magalotti, published in Henri Caffiaux, Essai sur le régime économique . . . du Hainaut (Valenciennes, 1873), p. 435, show that in the twenty-seven villages of the prévôté there were only 669 hogs for 1,668 families, compared with 3,515 cows, 2,134 goats, and 7,825 sheep.

R. CHAMPAGNE

Tally of Farm Animals (1732)

Subdelegations	Horses, Mares & Colts	Steers	Cows	Sheep	Hogs
Troyes	17,294	1,824	25,615	98,677	9,029
Châlons	11,416	916	17,245	59,215	8,752
Reims	20,776	380	28,152	147,530	15,111
Rethel	20,501	1,630	15,783	70,650	9,835
Mézières	10,353	292	4,614	21,932	1,792
Vaucouleurs	3,021	246	2,221	6,819	1,699
Ste.-Menehould	3,548	2,992	10,581	36,961	8,195
Vitry	10,185	878	16,265	39,215	7,638
St.-Dizier	9,938	682	1,567	6,500	1,610
Joinville	2,845	3,261	7,859	27,966	5,244
Bar-sur-Aube	11,383	3,747	13,735	54,386	6,750
Chaumont	6,905	5,699	5,428	29,450	4,539
Langres	16,446	12,360	20,620	58,864	10,766
Sézanne	4,321	464	4,354	36,999	2,274
Epernay	4,734	2,414	1,659	17,851	3,611
Total per species	153,666	37,778*	175,698	713,015	92,884†

213,476

Source: Memorandum of the intendant of the province to the trade council, in Library of Châlons, ms. 239.

*This total seems slightly inaccurate (instead of 37,782), as does the next total.
†This total clearly is too low; it should be 96,845.

Comment on folio 159 verso: "No matter how many pains we took to learn the total number of animals in the province as requested by the trade council, we cannot delude ourselves that the memoranda supplied us were as accurate as we might have wished, for most parishes tried to make the true situation less favorable." (These lists are dated late September 1731.)

D. LORRAINE

Statistics for the duchy in 1706 (Archives départementales, Meurthe-et-Moselle, B 11,920-11,926): the number of hogs, in column 30 of the tables, seems relatively low; cf. R. Schmitt, Le Barrois mouvant, pp. 405-6. For 1708, see A.D., Meurthe-et-Moselle, B 11,720-11,727; cf. F. Vivien, in Annales de l'Est (1952), p. 171.

F. FRANCHE-COMTE

List and general enumeration of houses, households, men, women, and children, male and female servants, and cattle in the county of Burgundy, made in the year 1688 (Bibliothèque nationale, Ms. fr. 2793).

Total for the County of Burgundy (Folio 46)

Houses	Households	Men	Women	Children	Male Servants	Female Servants
60,242	63,375	77,900	79,811	152,598	10,173	11,417

Horses & Colts	Steers	Cows & Calves	Sheep	Goats	Pigs
50,208	60,293	143,068	112,523	37,145	54,152

Bailliages Apparently Having Fewer Pigs than Inhabitants

Towns & Bailliages	Houses	Households	Men	Women	Children	Pigs
Salins	2,099	2,790	3,763			934
Baume	5,439	5,832	5,930			2,407
Ornans	2,097	3,840	5,282	5,459	6,059	1,467
Pontarlier*	3,406	3,895	5,853	6,227	9,981	312
Arbois†	1,005	1,508	1,573	1,614	3,752	154
			5,278			(125 + 29)
Poligny	2,818	3,353				1,437
Lons-le-Saunier‡	3,344	3,882	5,926	5,217	8,382	1,767
Orgelet**	3,536	3,589	3,566	3,974	10,197	150**
St.-Claude	2,827	2,792	3,647	3,254	7,160	#

*Pontarlier: none in town (329 cows, 465 households, 351 houses); numberous blanks (for steers also).

†In the town of Arbois (folio 32 v°): 29 hogs for 462 houses and 763 men; numerous blanks for nearby villages.

‡Within the market town (291 houses): 79 cows, but no pigs. No figures for Augisey, Beaufort, Bletterans (only horses?), Blye, Bourgeau, Briord, Châtillon, Longeverne, etc. Coulaou had 40 houses and households, 60 men, and 120 hogs, or 3 per household (compared to 120 steers and 100 cows).

**Dubious: for the town of Orgelet and the first three villages listed the column is blank; after that the column "pigs" is missing, and with it the total. There are 11,286 bovine animals.

#No entry for hogs at Saint-Claude, folio 41 v°-42 v°.

Bailliages with a Rather Large Number of Pigs

Besançon: almost 1 per house (5,042 households, 3,241 hogs); within the city there were only 31 for 1,350 houses (65 cows)

Dole: more than 1 per house (5,373 houses, 5,851 households, 19,623 pigs)

Vesoul and the prévôté of Jussey (17,544 houses, 13,485 households, 19,623 hogs)

Gray: over 2, the record (6,157 houses, 13,567 hogs, although a few villages had none at all)

G. DAUPHINE

Localities with Few or No Pigs

		Inhabitants	Pigs
Election of Grenoble	Biviers	483	0
	Les Infernets	77	0
	Livet-et-Gavet	252	3
	Ornon	324	9
	Oulles	188	0
	St.-Christophe-en-Oisans		3
	St.-Ferjus	743	0
	St.-Ismier	726	2
	St.-Martin-le-Vinoux	505	3
"How to explain the	St.-Vincent	88	2
difference?"	Vaulnaveys-le-Bas	532	6
(Esmonin)	Vaulnaveys-le-Haut	902	98
	St.-Pierre-d'Allevard	1,463	113
	St.-Maximin-Grignon		136
	Les Adrets		81
	Uriage	1,528	393
	Voiron		357
	Varces		88
	St.-Bonnet		150
	Orcières		150
	Grenoble		80

Total: 7,801 for 143,931 inhabitants (sheep: 153,460)

Election of Vienne	St.-Clair-de-la-Tour	0
	St-Clair-près-Condrieu	0
	Vornes	0
	Vernioz	0
	Vertrieu	0
	Vessilieux	0
	Vignieu	0
	Villeneuve-de-Marc	0
	Ville-sous-Anjou	0
	Bourgoin	350
	Châteauvillain and Quinsonnas	
	(2,719 inhabitants)	600

Total: 14,446 for 240,639 inhabitants (sheep: 199,826)

Election of Romans	Anjou	0
	Cras	0
	Fay	0
	Lans-Lestang	0
	Moras (1,585 inhabitants)	600

Total: 7,628 pigs for 78,870 inhabitants (sheep: 95,727)

Election of Valence   Pigs everywhere except at Saint-Quentin.
Total: 5,461 pigs for 56,224 inhabitants (sheep: 76,322)

Election of Montélimar   No pigs in 47 communities, and many others had only between 2 and
6. The record-holder is the city of Montélimar, with 99 (Sauzet was
runner-up, with 95).
Total: 2,730 for 104,658 inhabitants (but sheep: 165,680)

Election of Gap   No pigs in 18 localities.
Total: 1,864 for 60,339 inhabitants (but sheep: 87,811)

No count of pigs was made for the region of Briançon.*
Population: 23,153 inhabitants, 14,314 sheep.

Totals for the entire province (excluding the vicinity of Briançon): 39,930 pigs† for 560,270 inhabitants,
that is, one for each 15 people; there were 778,826 sheep, 141,749 steers and cows, and 48,373 horses
and mules.

Source: *Statistics for Fontanieu circa 1730* (Bibliothèque nationale, Ms. fr. 8361).
*No mention is made of pigs in the very detailed memorandum about the subdelegation of
Briançon by subdelegate Bonnot, dated 1762 (Municipal library of Grenoble, ms. R 7464).
†In G. Dubois, pp. 34-35: 39,912 pigs and 782,140 sheep, 128,127 bovines, and 50,542 horses. See
the list for the period of the Revolution, to be found in Archives départementales, Isère, L 304.

Revolutionary Period

Tally of Livestock in the Canton of Barraux, Year IV [1795-96]

Pigs	240
Horses and mares	331
Steers	548
Cows	1,245
Calves and heifers	308
Mules (male and female)	3
Donkeys	35
Sheep	1,414
Goats	232

Canton of Bourg d'Oisans, Undated

Pigs	749
Goats	3,740
Sheep	7,017
Cows	3,987
Calves	1,179

Canton of Corps

Pigs   218
(4,009 sheep, 687 goats, 2,094 steers and cows)

City of Grenoble

Pigs: none were being raised
(267 sheep, 10 goats, 491 steers and cows, 45 calves, 211 horses,
13 mules, and 2 donkeys)

Canton of Goncelin

Pigs: 452   452
(3,551 sheep, 687 goats, 2,094 steers and cows)

Canton of Lans

Pigs: the column is blank
(2,592 sheep, 250 goats, 2,335 steers and cows, 645 horses)

Canton of Meylan

Pigs   36
(1,329 sheep, 129 horses, 971 steers and cows, etc)
For the full listing, see Archives départementales, Isère, L 304.

Animals in the Countryside in Year III [1784-95]

District of Briançon (dated 24 frimaire, year III)
            9,106 cows (small, used for plowing)
            1,117 heifers
              596 calves
           23,558 ewes, 5,837 lambs
            5,131 goats
                3 hogs and sows
Serres (dated 18 pluviôse, year III)
            2,879 hogs and sows
            3,016 steers, only 79 cows, 15 heifers
           30,629 ewes, 10,895 lambs

This information is taken from Octave Festy, *Les Animaux ruraux de l'an III* (Paris, 1965), p. 88. The original text gives the breakdown by canton.

Consulate and First Empire

There were in all 7,049 pigs, compared to 22,500 ewes, 14,600 goats, and 2,500 horses. But the distribution by arrondissement reveals that almost all these pigs (6,404) were in the arrondissement of Gap; there were only 19 in the arrondissement of Embrun and 626 in that of Briançon.

The population was estimated at 118,100 inhabitants. This means that there was one pig for every sixteen or seventeen residents (However, the prefect admitted that the totals for the various species were too low.)

Source: Prefect Rouvaire, *Statistique des Hautes-Alpes* (year IX [1800-1801]).

Statistique agricole de 1814 (published in *Notices et extraits de documents* [Paris, 1914], vol. 2) states:

p. 14. Arrondissement of Barcelonnette: "Few pigs are raised in the arrondissement. Although a few individuals fatten them, it is for their own personal use, and they buy them in Piedmont or in the Hautes-Alpes."

p. 23. Arrondissement of Castellane: approximately 1,500 pigs

p. 29. City of Digne: 80 pigs

p. 38. Arrondissement of Forcalquier: 26,250 pigs

p. 49. Arrondissement of Sisteron: 6,000 pigs (estimated)

p. 59. Arrondissement of Briançon: no reference to pigs

H. HAUTE-SAVOIE

Few pigs

Canton of La Chambre

Mongellafrey: 737 inhabitants, 49 pigs, 300 cows, 425 sheep, and 157 goats
La Chambre: 318 inhabitants, 1 pig, 124 cows, 128 sheep, and 46 goats
Grésy-sur-Isère (month of prairial): 4,231 inhabitants, 694 pigs, 541 cows, 1,111 sheep

Canton of Evian (month of floréal)

7,394 inhabitants, 932 hogs, 1,247 cows, and 1,432 sheep

Source: Statistique du Mont-Blanc, year V [1796-97] (Archives nationales, F²² 224-25).

POSTSCRIPT

An estimate made by the agronomist Jacques Bujault (circa 1840, in a favored region [the former province of Poitou], permits some conclusions about the difficulties involved in determining the level of consumption during the so-called "statistical era" ("Des races porcines cranaises dans le Poitou," in Oeuvres [Niort, 1845], p. 338).

Half the people do not know how the other half lives. They nonetheless suspect that in this department there are 270,000 individuals [out of 580,000] who eat neither beef, veal, nor mutton, and that a small amount of pork meets the needs of this immense segment of the population. How much does it consume? I do not believe that, in the cities, market towns, and the countryside, one could find 36,000 pigs [note that this would average 101 per township. They certainly were not slaughtered].

Giving each of these 36,000 implausible pigs an average weight of 160 pounds— which is too low, because the butchers were striving to produce very fat animals, and very expensive ones— "this would mean less than six-sixteenths of a pound per week, per person [31 grams per day for six days].... Rounding it off, a quarter pound (125 grams) per week.... You will note that they render out all they possibly can, and that the grease is used as a condiment."[6]

NOTES

1. Cf. Edmond Pognon, in Histoire du peuple française, ed. L.-H. Parias (Paris, 1952), 2: 254-55, a volume covering the years 1380 to 1715. "Olivier de Serres clearly held the hog in low esteem.... Its skin was just good enough 'to make sieves and cover buffets, which one can do without in times of scarcity.'"
2. Cf. Michel Devèze, La Vie de la forêt française au XVIe siècle (Paris, 1961), 1: 98-100.
3. Compared with ibid., 2: 126, where the law of 1550-51 states: four pigs "with their offspring a half year old and under" (found in Louis de Sainctyon, Les Edicts...des eaues et forests [Paris, 1610], p. 1042). Unfortunately the declarations themselves are missing.
4. Michel Devèze, La Grande Réformation des forêts sous Colbert (Paris, 1954), p. 181.
5. Ibid., p. 178.
6. Indeed, this is the essential nutrient to be considered. As for proteins, a strange cannibalistic "model" provides a comparison: a man weighing 50 kilograms [110 pounds— trans.] would, if properly cooked, provide 30 kilograms of muscled meat, including 4 kilograms of protein. Each cannibal would therefore be inadequately nourished unless he could eat an entire man per year. (S. M. Garn and W. D. Block, "The Limited Value of Cannibalism," American Anthropologist 72 [1970]: 106.) On the seasonal psychological importance of cold cuts, see R. J. Bernard, "L'Alimentation paysanne en Gévaudan au XVIIIe siècle," Annales, E.S.C. 24 (November-December 1969): 1461.

5
The Diet in Boarding Schools at the End of the Ancien Régime

Willem Frijhoff and Dominique Julia

$\mathbf{F}$rom Mathurin Cordier to Restif de la Bretonne, via Charles Sorel and Jean-François Marmontel, there is no lack of literary evidence about the food served to boarding students during the Ancien Régime. Although these students lived under various boarding systems—ranging from Marmontel's bed in a private home to Sorel's room and board with a schoolmaster and on to being a live-in boarder at the school—the various comments about the diet seem to have two points in common. The amount of food was *insufficient.* "Oh, God, what pitiful fare, like that only the pigherds of our village would eat!" exclaimed Francion shortly after his arrival at the home of Hortensias, a schoolmaster in the Collège de Lisieux in Paris.[1] And it was of *low quality.* In his memoirs the Count of Vaublanc recalled a general student riot at the Military School of Paris during the academic year 1770/71, provoked by the poor quality of the dishes being served.[2] Although we are reduced to recording the groans concerning this second complaint and are unable either to exonerate or condemn the cook, in the case of the first complaint it is possible to measure quite accurately the amount of food served to boarders, at least at the end of the Ancien Régime.

The Sources of Information

Indeed, the account books of eighteenth-century *collèges** are not lacking. Yet we must simultaneously keep in mind both the presence of students and the

Annales, E.S.C. 30 (March-June 1975): 491-504. Translated by Patricia M. Ranum.

*In contrast to its English cognate, college, the French *collège* was—and still is—a secondary school, rather than a university.

The four institutions studied in this article are representative of the regional diversity of France. The royal Military School was located on the outskirts of the capital. Molsheim is a small town near changes in the expenditures for their upkeep. This double requirement—a requirement for any study of food rations—led us to focus our attention in this study upon the secondary boarding schools at Auch and Molsheim, the Military School of Paris, and the Collège des Bernardins at Toulouse, a sort of seminary school within the Cistercian order.

At the Military School the bursar recorded the amount of bread and wine consumed daily, showing for each of the four meals (breakfast, noon-hour dinner, afternoon snack, and evening supper) the number of pupils "in prison," [that is, confined to their quarters for disciplinary reasons]. The same attention to details was applied to professors and masters, to the domestic staff, and to the kitchen help. The only extant account book is the one for 1767.[3]

At Auch the records of the income of the boarding school provide the names of boarders for each trimester (although their parents paid quarterly) from 1 November 1773 to 31 October 1779. In addition, three books of expenditures for the same period show, month by month, the purchases made for the boarding school.[4] For Toulouse, we have the account books for the collège for the year 1754-55.[5]

The boarding school at Molsheim kept better accounts than the other three institutions.[6] On the one hand we have for each academic year from 1767/68 to 1787/88 a "general accounting," which summarized under main headings the institution's income (from fees paid by pupils for private rooms and for board, with precise notations of entrance and exit dates) and expenditures. Expenditures were broken down into two subgroups, "domestic expenses," that is, cash purchases, and "commodities and their monetary equivalent," that is, supplies produced and consumed by the collège. In addition, for each academic year between 1768/69 and 1789/90 there is a register, with a page for each pupil, of the credits and debits, "paid in part with the cash deposited by the boarders and in part the money spent for them by the collège." These accounts specify the geographic origin and the class of the paying or scholarship student. In addition, there is an account book of expenditures made between 1 November 1767 and 30 April 1791, which shows for each month the purchases made by the institution (even when these are fictitious purchases corresponding to articles produced at the school). These purchases are divided into various categories: bread and flour, wine, fish, butter and cheese, eggs and milk, fruits and vegetables, épicerie [sugar, jam, rice, salt, and so forth], candles and oil, heat, furniture, upkeep, and miscellaneous expenditures.

The Student Body

As a first point, the high cost of board limited the gamut of social groups represented by the parents sending their children to the collèges studied here.

Strasbourg in the Germanic province of Alsace, annexed to France in 1648. Auch (a major city in the Armagnac region, or Gascony) and Toulouse (capital of the province of Languedoc) were part of the southern regions speaking the *langue d'oc,* where the agriculture was basically Mediterranean.—Trans.

Board cost 360 *livres tournois* a year at Molsheim, and 420 *livres tournois* at Auch (but, since most pupils only attended school for ten months, the respective costs would be 300 and 350 *livres tournois*). We know that admission to the Military School was reserved for the sons of "poor" nobles who could prove four quarters of nobility.

Enrollment in the boarding school at Auch, which began its first school year in October 1773, was largely regional, limited specifically to the confines of the *généralité* of Auch. All the evidence we have been able to find about its student body reveals a large proportion of young nobles. The boarding school of Molsheim, which, like that of Auch, was run by secular priests, first opened its doors in the fall of 1767.[7] Twenty places were reserved for scholarship students, with ten places for boys born in the city of Haguenau and ten for boys from Sélestat, to compensate for the elimination of the institutions in those cities after the expulsion of the Jesuits. Although these scholarships were awarded, as the letters patent of 5 July 1766 specified, to children from the "largest families," the clause reserving them for the "least opulent" families does not seem to have been respected.[8] Family dynasties of local notables shared these scholarships, which were awarded and supervised by the municipal oligarchy. The other boarders, with the rare exception of a few important French or German lords (such as the Welsers) came from the Alsatian upper middle class. All four *collèges* therefore drew students from a restricted circle of privileged families.

The Methodology Used

In order to obtain the results presented here, we had to work our way through the registers and establish for each type of food a table of quantities and prices, month by month. Calculating the days/meals at the Military School posed no problem, since the number of diners was recorded for each meal. For Molsheim and Auch we made cards for each student, showing the dates of his arrival and departure (for vacation or because of illness). Then we calculated the numbers of days actually spent in the *collège,* month by month, including the arrival day but excluding the day of departure.

For domestic and administrative staff, the impossibility (except at Beaumont) of determining absences forced us to count them present throughout the year but with their total number reduced; besides, if they were not actually present that many days, it would merely increase the average ration that we have calculated. Last, at the Bernardins of Toulouse, the school year ran from 2 November to 20 August, so we based our days/meals upon those dates but assumed that at least four staff members would remain during vacation.

That left only the daily ration to calculate. The often touchy metrologic questions involved in converting pre-Revolutionary measures to the metric system were solved with the help of tables published during the Revolution and the Napoleonic Empire. The overall results were obtained by determining an average for the six years available for Auch, for the twenty years at Molsheim, and two averages based on decades (1767/68 to 1776/77 and

1777/78 to 1786/87). We believe that this procedure has eliminated errors based on pure conjecture.

The Food Budget for Molsheim

During the twenty years in question [fall 1767 to spring 1788] the food portion of the total budget of the boarding school showed almost no variation, the low being 77 percent in 1771/72 and the high 86 percent in 1767/68.[9] Bread, wine, and meat always accounted for over two-thirds of the food budget, but after 1770 there was a clear drop in the amount spent for wine (from 30 percent down to 22 percent). The amount spent for meat showed much less fluctuation (between 25 and 30 percent), while fish decreased from 8 percent to 6 percent. All other categories showed a clear increase: butter and eggs rose from 7 to 11 percent, *épicerie* and sugar from 3 to 5 percent, cooking oils from 1.3 percent to 3.5 percent, and fruits and vegetables remained between 3 and 9 percent, with marked fluctuations reflecting economic conditions. The cost of bread poses a problem. After having constituted 16 percent of the food budget during the initial three years, it climbed to 23 percent in 1770/71 and then suddenly jumped to 27 percent in 1771/72, after which it remained permanently at about 20 percent, in other words, slightly higher than at the beginning of the twenty-year period.

The Wheat Shortage of 1771

There is no doubt that in Alsace the increased expenditures for bread must be blamed upon the Alsatian wheat shortage of 1771. But we must also try to determine whether this increase corresponds to a similar increase in the amount of bread eaten. The account books tallied the bread (chiefly brown bread) by the large round loaf, whose price between 1767 and 1791 remained stable at four sous [for a small loaf] and eight sous [for a large one]. These increased expenditures therefore suggest an increased consumption of bread. Strasbourg can serve as an example of how this worked: the highs and the lows are not based upon the *price* but upon the *weight* of the loaves. So, in 1770, the local officials undertook a reform of the bakeries and established new official prices. From then on the loaves would have a *fixed weight:* three pounds or six pounds for brown bread. The price per pound of the loaf changed when the *rézal* of wheat increased or dropped twenty sous on two successive market days.[10]

Using those data we calculated a daily ration of bread loaves for each month between November 1769 and March 1772, and then a theoretical ration in kilograms, assuming that the weight of a small loaf remained at three pounds throughout the shortage. (See fig. 5.1.) The absurdity of such computations is immediately evident, since for February 1771 we came up with the aberrant ration of 1.424 kilograms. On the other hand, since we know the price per *rézal*

Price index

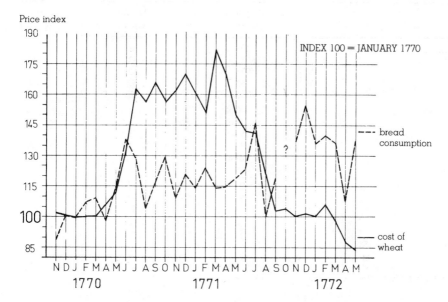

Figure 5.1. Bread Consumption and the Cost of Wheat at Molsheim during the Shortage of 1770 71

of wheat for each month and we also know the corrective factor established by the price control office at Strasbourg, we were able to calculate the monthly cost in sous of a pound of brown bread, and then the number of pounds that a four-sous loaf weighed each month. After that we multiplied this number by the daily ration of loaves and converted the weight in pounds into kilograms. We finally came up with two hypothetical bread rations, one calculated in terms of the price of wheat during that month and a second calculated in terms of the price of wheat during the preceding month. This produced plausible figures, with the second hypothesis seeming the more valid: the daily ration fluctuated within reasonable limits (between roughly 600 and 900 grams). In view of these results, there is reason to wonder whether the term "wheat shortage" is valid here, for even at the time of the greatest price increases, daily bread consumption never fell below 660 grams per person. Indeed, the boarding school at Molsheim was one of those protected milieus in which the word "hunger" did not exist.

Average Daily Rations

In each of the schools for which we have computed rations (see table 5.1), *bread* was the basic component of the diet. Alone it provided more than half the calories and most of the B and E vitamins, iron, calcium, and phosphorus. Indeed, although during the two final decades of our study of Molsheim the proportion of the total calories obtained from bread decreased slightly, the

Table 5.1–Average Daily Rations

Food Item		Daily Ration (grams)	Calories	Protein (grams)	Fat (grams)	Starch (grams)
Bread and baked goods	A	1,103	2,640	88	13	541
	T	1,033	2,468	83	12	506
	M I	775	1,858	62	10	380
	M II	868	2,087	69	11	427
	P	721	1,723	58	9	353
Wine and brandy	A	60 cl	393	. . .	. . .	1
	T	71 cl	459	. . .	. . .	1
	M I	88 cl	690	1	. . .	35
	M II	99 cl	778	1	. . .	39
	P	27 cl	362	. . .	. . .	. . .
Meat (beef, veal, mutton, pork)	A	221	542	29	41	1
	T	173	498	29	37	. . .
	M I	295	667	49	48	1
	M II	271	680	44	53	1
Poultry	A	96	208	19	14	. . .
	T	276	754	51	59	. . .
	M I	9	14	2	1	. . .
	M II	14	26	3	2	. . .
Furred and feathered game	A	4	5	1	. . .	. . .
	T	3	3	1	. . .	. . .
	M I	6	7	2	. . .	. . .
	M II	20	23	5	. . .	. . .
Fish	A	18	38	7	1	. . .
	T	35	47	7	4	. . .
	M I	39	61	11	2	. . .
	M II	31	50	9	1	. . .
Dairy products	A	6	20	1	2	. . .
	T	24	108	3	10	1
	M I	77	227	4	22	3
	M II	79	256	4	26	3
Eggs	A	75	113	9	9	1
	T	86	140	11	11	1
	M I	40	61	5	5	. . .
	M II	50	76	6	6	. . .
Fresh and dried vegetables	A	27	80	5	. . .	14
	M I	184	233	12	1	44
	M II	268	297	14	1	58
Vegetables and fruits (estimated at 5%)	T	119	244	9	8	27
Fresh and dried fruits	A	59	141	3	7	16
	M I	95	61	. . .	1	3
	M II	150	102	1	2	6
Epicerie (sugar and jam, rice and salt)	A	21	16	. . .	. . .	4
	T	4	15	1	1	4
	M I	10	34	1	. . .	8
	M II	12	42	. . .	. . .	10
Olive and walnut oil	A	30	272	. . .	30	. . .
	T	15	138	. . .	15	. . .
	M I	10	95	. . .	10	. . .
	M II	15	137	. . .	15	. . .
Total	A	2,260	4,468	162	117	578
	T	2,478	4,874	195	157	540
	M I	2,420	4,008	149	100	474
	M II	2.768	4,554	156	117	544

A = Auch; T = Toulouse; M I = Molsheim 1767/68 to 1776/77; M II = Molsheim 1777/78 to 1786/87; P = Paris (Military School).

amount of bread on the table increased by one-tenth. Moreover, the account books of the Military School of Paris clearly show that it would be incorrect to try to draw a distinction between a "poor," basically bread-oriented diet for the pupils and a "rich," higher quality diet for the masters. The amount of bread was almost equal for all categories (721 grams per day for pupils, 649 grams for students "in prison," 725 grams for domestic staff, 688 grams for supervisors, and 787 grams for teachers).

On the other hand, it is at the Military School that the difference in the amount of *wine* drunk is most noticeable. While the students on the average drank only a quarter liter (27.3 centiliters),[11] servants (with a set ration) drank a half liter (46.6 centiliters), supervisors were allocated 1.291 liters, and teachers drank up to 1.221 liters! Although this wine was probably of low alcoholic content, the quantity drunk was nonetheless considerable.

The amount of *butchered meat* in the diet keeps within the quantities one would expect of the type of boarding schools being studied, but the proportion of beef, veal, and mutton differed quite a bit from one *collège* to another. At Auch, beef predominated, accounting for 96 of the total 221 grams of meat. At Toulouse, mutton came first, with 73 of the total 173 grams. At Molsheim beef and veal initially were almost equal (110 grams of beef and 98 grams of veal out of an average 283 grams), but beef gradually won out over veal and mutton. Pork was chiefly eaten as ham, fatback, sausages, or blood pudding, but it was a minor item, even at Molsheim.[12]

In addition, we must take *seasonal variations* in the diet into account. Veal was eaten chiefly in the spring and mutton in the fall. Although the amount of beef eaten remained quite stable, there was a pronounced decrease during Lent. But Lent was not observed in the same manner everywhere, for although meat virtually disappeared from the menu at Auch (with the exception of a few pounds intended for the sick), the decrease was a relative one at Molsheim and corresponded to Lenten fast days—Wednesday, Friday, Saturday, and Holy Week. At the same time, the number of *eggs* eaten—which was always sizable, with one egg a day at Molsheim and one and a half at Auch and Toulouse —increased sharply. From Ash Wednesday to Easter Sunday, each person at Auch ate between two and three eggs per day.

The difference between the two curves of overall meat consumption at Auch and Molsheim (fig. 5.2) is in a large part compensated for by the consumption of *poultry,* which was considerable at Auch and even more so at Toulouse, where it was twenty-five times greater than the ration calculated for Molsheim. Turkey with chestnut stuffing seems to have been a common menu in the Armagnac region [of Auch, a region of chestnut forests] during the fall and winter months. On the other hand, at Molsheim one is struck by the sudden, fourfold increase from one decade to the next in the amount of *game* eaten. Does this mean a modification in the diet? In general, expensive items or foods considered luxury items were purchased in increasing quantities, while traditional commodities such as veal or mutton or inexpensive ones such as fish became less and less frequent in the account books.

Very little *fish* was eaten, and most of it during Lent at that. Air-dried cod

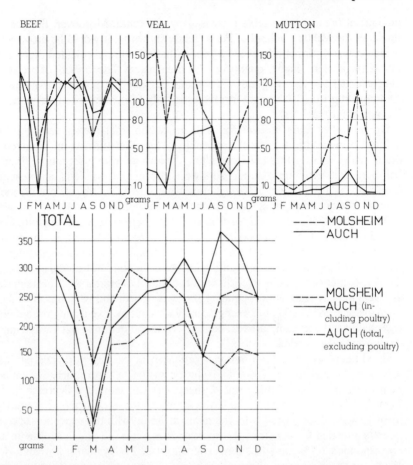

Figure 5.2. Average Daily Consumption of Meat, by Month, in the *Collèges* of Auch and Molsheim

(*stockfish*) or salt cod, and the vague category "white fish" accounted for most fish purchased in all the schools we studied. Molsheim was, however, an exception, for the diet included 4.6 grams of frogs' legs per day. Considering the volume that represents, they must have appeared on the menu relatively often!

One of the basic differences between the diets at Molsheim and Auch is the very small role played by *dairy products,* which are rich in vitamin A and calcium. The same disparity can be noted for the amount of oil consumed, this time to the advantage of Auch. Have we grounds to view this as indicative of two types of cooking, cooking done with butter and cooking done with oil? In eighteenth-century Alsace, butter-based cooking was thought to be reserved for the rich.[13]

Since *fruits and vegatables* generally came from the schools' own gardens, the account books usually refer to a total volume of fictitious "purchases," without specifying the exact amounts of the foods they list. Only in the case of Auch are they recorded daily, with a degree of precision that enables us to calculate the amount eaten. Now, even under these circumstances, the amount of fruits and vegetables seems very low and, in addition, is subject to the obvious seasonal fluctuations that threaten the well-balanced diet, especially during winter months. Yet, we can draw three conclusions. First of all, the ration shows that the menus of *collèges* were very *regional:* an abundance of cabbage for sauerkraut at Molsheim (60 grams per day), and of white beans (17 grams) for *cassoulet* [a regional baked-bean dish] and chestnuts (20 grams) for the turkeys at Auch. Second, a pronounced increase in the use of the *potato* is evident at Molsheim; its consumption doubled from one decade to the next (from 89 to 158 grams per day),[14] while the potato did not put in an appearance at Auch until the early nineteenth century. The same is true for *apples;* consumption increased from 91 to 142 grams at Molsheim—that is, an apple a day—and included chiefly those varieties that were rich in vitamin C (calvilles and pippins). These two foods show that important steps were being taken toward a well-balanced diet.

But we must point out a few *missing foods:* beer, even at Molsheim [Alsace is a beer-drinking province]; coffee (less than 1.5 kilograms per year for the entire *collège* of Auch) and tea; chocolate, which apparently was never served; honey; and lemons and oranges, which doubtlessly were still too costly and too exotic for everyday use, for at Auch the ration was less than one per year per student, while at Molsheim they were served only to the sick, as medicine.

Overall Nutritional Content

First we wish to point out that these overall figures are estimates of the ration *supplied.* We know nothing about any possible resale by the bursar between the time the purchase was recorded and the time it could be eaten; and we know nothing about how much food was left over or what was done with it. One thing is sure: most of the food eaten by the servants at Molsheim consisted of leftovers from the tables of the boarders, which justifies—if justification is needed—their inclusion in our calculations. Doubtlessly we will never know the difference between the amount of food available and the amount actually eaten. Moreover, we must be cautious when analyzing the caloric needs and the vitamins and minerals required by children and adolescents. Recent research by the Food and Agricultural Organization concluded that the norms accepted by modern dietitians are far in excess of minimum requirements.[15] The "deficiencies" we have found often are merely poorly balanced diets, and most of these imbalances are minor.

Even in the absence of sure and complete data about the amount of fruits and vegetables eaten, the *caloric intake* (table 5.2) seems more than adequate, if not abundant, in each of the three cases we studied. All schools exceeded the figure of 3,800 calories desirable for the proper growth of boys between the ages of twelve and eighteen. The same is true for *protein* and *fat* (table 5.3).

Table 5.2—Sources of Calories

	School			Years	
Food Item	Auch	Toulouse	Molsheim Average	1767/68 to 1776/77	1777/78 to 1786/87
Cereals	59.2%	50.7%	46.5%	46.9%	46.2%
Meat, poultry, game	16.9	25.7	16.6	17.2	16.0
Fish	0.9	1.0	1.3	1.5	1.1
Eggs	2.5	2.8	1.6	1.5	1.7
Dairy products	0.5	2.2	5.6	5.7	5.6
Fruits, vegetables	4.9	(estimated at 5.0)	8.1	7.3	8.8
Oil	6.1	2.9	2.7	2.4	3.0
Sugar and jam	0.2	0.3	0.4	0.3	0.5
Wine	8.8	9.4	17.2	17.2	17.1
Total	100.0%	100.0%	100.0%	100.0%	100.0%
Total available calories	4,468	4,874	4,285	4,008	4,554

Incidentally, the latter increased markedly at Molsheim over the twenty-year period. The substantial amount of bread in the daily diet did, however, lead to a certain imbalance between animal and vegetable protein, and this imbalance surely was increased by the fruits and vegetables omitted from the account books. It is likewise impossible to calculate precisely the nutrition obtained from variety meats, which often are mentioned only infrequently in the accounts. Hence, there is an appreciable margin of error as far as the total amount of phospholipids is concerned. Thanks to a more than abundant supply of poultry, the collège at Toulouse came close to the ideal ratio between animal protein and vegetable protein. The amount of carbohydrates in the diet was roughly average, but in no case did it exceed the maximum suggested amount.

In the rations we calculated, most *vitamins* were quite well, if not abundantly represented (see table 5.4), especially vitamins E and PP, owing to the great amount of bread and olive oil in the diet. The amounts of vitamin B_1 and vitamin B_2 seem almost excessive, again owing to the superabundance of grains. Nowhere was vitamin A lacking, but at Auch it seems to have been touch-and-go, especially during periods when egg consumption dropped. This near deficiency resulted from the virtually total absence of dairy products. The deficiencies in provitamin A (carotene) revealed by our calculations may have been compensated for by fruits and vegetables; but in the case of Auch, for which we have the most complete data, the suspected deficiency remains plausible. This fact is especially significant, since vitamin A plays an important role in growth. A similar deficiency is suspected for vitamin B_6, which is of comparable importance. On the other hand, vitamin D, which prevents rickets, was more than adequate in each case.

The case of vitamin C is complicated. It seems to have been adequately, although not excessively, represented in the diet at Molsheim: 56 milligrams, or even 68 milligrams if, as the records suggest, the main varieties of apples were

Table 5.3—Chemical Composition of Rations

School	Protein (%)	Fat (%)	Starch (%)	Ratio of Animal Protein/ Vegetable Protein	Ratio of Protein/ Starch
Auch	18.9	13.7	67.4	0.66	0.28
Toulouse	21.8	17.7	60.5	1.16	0.36
Molsheim Average	19.8	14.1	66.1	0.89	0.30
1767/68 to 1776/77	20.6	13.8	65.6	0.95	0.31
1777/78 to 1786/87	19.1	14.3	66.6	0.83	0.29
Theoretical needs*	13.7	10.5	75.8	1.00	0.18

*Computed on the basis of Lucie Randoin et. al., *Tables de composition des aliments* (Paris, n.d.), pp. 12-13, for boys between the ages of twelve and fifteen.

Table 5.4—Vitamins and Minerals in the Average Daily Ration (in milligrams)

School	Vitamins							
	A	B_1	B_2	B_6	C	D	E	PP
Auch	0.34	4.15	3.02	0.66	19.0	0.0045	22.8	44.8
Toulouse	0.62	3.97	3.01	1.00	8.5	0.0146	18.5	62.2
Molsheim	0.43	3.73	2.93	1.19	58.3	0.0062	16.5	46.2
Theoretical needs*	0.25	1.60	2.00	1.00	80.0	0.0030	2.0	16.0

School	Minerals				Ca/P Ratio
	Carotene	Iron	Calcium	Phosphorus	
Auch	0.62	34.6	723	3,173	0.23
Toulouse	0.56	38.5	766	3,388	0.23
Molsheim	0.55	33.7	714	2,919	0.24
Theoretical needs*	2.50	20.0	1,400	1,500	0.90

*Required by growing boys, according to Dr. Jean Lederer, *Encyclopédie moderne de l'hygiène alimentaire* (Louvain, Paris, 1971), 1: 57-77; and Lucie Randoin et al., *Tables de composition des aliments* (Paris, n.d.), pp. 12-13.

calvilles and pippins. It is impossible to draw a conclusion for Toulouse, since the account books give no details about the purchase of these items. But fruits and vegetables did make up 6.7 percent of all expenditures for food—the same percentage found at Molsheim—and more than half of that sum was spent on fruit. But the diet at Toulouse probably was very similar to that at Auch, which consisted of an abundance of dried fruits and vegetables (peas, beans, lentils, chestnuts, and walnuts), all low in vitamin C. At Auch, at any rate, the amount of vitamin C barely exceeded the minimum required to avoid borderline deficiencies, especially during the winter months. Still, garlic and onions, which seem to have occupied a rather important place in the diet, may have been able to palliate the most glaring deficiencies.

The minimum requirement of *calcium* during growth (600-700 milligrams) was met in every case, but there is a relative deficiency of calcium compared with *phosphorus,* which was overabundant. This led to a serious imbalance in the proper ratio between these two minerals. The abundant amount of bread and meat, and the small amount of dairy products, was a chief cause. Let us, however, stress that the Food and Agricultural Organization recently has called into question the validity of the calcium/phosphorus balance as a test for illnesses resulting from vitamin deficiency.[16]

Conclusion   .

On the whole, the three school diets that we studied show both a more than adequate caloric intake and a rather satisfactory balance in nutritive content. The diet at Molsheim incontestably was closest to the recommended norms and was the most well balanced, with no major excesses. Moreover, the diet clearly tended to improve from one decade to the next. The increased caloric intake went hand in hand with certain changes in the ratios between the various foods and between the nutritive components of the foods served. And, slight as they may be, these changes indicate a modernization of the diet: a decrease in the amount of bread and fish and an increased consumption of sugar, oil, fruit, and, above all, potatoes. By the end of the eighteenth century the diet at Molsheim incorporated all the trends that gradually would form the diet of the rich, industrialized countries: an increase in unsaturated fats (at Molsheim the consumption of vegetable oil increased by 44.3 percent in ten years) and of saturated animal fat, at the expense of saturated vegetable fat. The arrival of the potato replaced the starch quota that had been threatened by the reduced consumption of bread; and, although the amount of sugar eaten remained low, it rose sharply, increasing 84.5 percent in ten years. Last—and this may be the best indication of an improved understanding of physical needs—for the first time the diet included abundant vitamin C, thanks to the apple-a-day, which more than satisfied the requirements for that vitamin.

To summarize, although bread remained the basic food in each of the three diets, the food served in these schools was that of the privileged classes and, with few exceptions, always remained above the level of borderline deficiency. The large amount of meat (over 300 grams per day in all the schools) prefigured, within a small social milieu, the most recent of the great dietary revolutions, although this revolution would not occur in the population at large for another century: that is, the shift from a preponderance of wheat to a preponderance of animal protein.

NOTES

1. Charles Sorel, *La Vraye Histoire comique de Francion* (1622), reprinted in *Romanciers du XVIIe siècle*, Bibliothèque de La Pléiade (Paris, 1958), p. 171.
2. V.-M. Vienot, comte de Vaublanc, *Souvenirs* (Paris, 1838), 1: 85.
3. Archives départementales [hereafter cited as A.D.], Calvados, C 2473.
4. A.D., Gers, D 117-25 (*recettes et dépenses,* that is, receipts and disbursements), and 152-66 (*factures,* that is, invoices).
5. A.D., Haute-Garonne, 7 D 44; Louis J. Lekai, ed., "The College of Saint Bernard in Toulouse, 1553-1791," *Analecta Cisterciensia* 27 (1971): 157-211.
6. A.D., Bas-Rhin, D 160-69.
7. We are preparing a study of the students admitted to the major boarding schools (Juilly, Pontlevoy, Tournon, Effiat, Molsheim, and so forth).
8. Archives communales [hereafter referred to as A.C.], Strasbourg, AA 2158, pieces 3 and 6; cf. A. C., Haguenau, GG 25-26; and A.D., Bas-Rhin, C 343.
9. But only 44.6 percent at Toulouse, of a total of 4,996 *livres tournois.* The general budget for Molsheim fluctuated between 8,000 and 14,000 *livres tournois.* In neither of these two cases did total wages exceed five percent of all expenditures.
10. Cf. Abbé Auguste-Charles Hanauer, *Etudes économiques sur l'Alsace ancienne et moderne* (Paris, Strasbourg, 1878), 2: 133-37; Y. Le Moigne, "Population et subsistance à Strasbourg au XVIIIe siècle," in *Contributions à l'histoire démographique de la Révolution française* (Paris: Bibliothèque nationale, 1962), pp. 13-44 (Mémoires et documents, XV).
11. But with marked seasonal variations: from 43 centiliters in January to 74 centiliters during the heat of August.
12. At the most 30 grams. Given the difficulty of calculating the weight of a given number of sausages, we consistently used the minima hypothesis: low weight, great waste, and high price. In reality, the ration certainly should be increased.
13. Cf. Jean-Jacques Hémardinquer, "Les Graisses de cuisine," in *Pour une histoire de l'alimentation* (Paris: Armand Colin, 1970), p. 263.
14. The spread of the potato in Alsace, which brought an end to periodic scarcity, is an important event in the second half of the eighteenth century. Cf. Etienne Juillard, *La Vie rurale dans la plaine de Basse-Alsace* (Paris: Les Belles Lettres, 1953), pp. 213-15.
15. Our calculations are based upon Lucie Randoin et al., *Tables de composition des aliments,* 3d ed. (Paris, n. d.).
16. Cf. *Besoins en calcium,* a report by a group of specialists presented to the Food and Agricultural Organization/World Health Organization, 23-30 May 1961 (Rome: United Nations Food and Agricultural Organization, 1962), p. 16.

6
Coffee and Cafés
in Paris, 1644-1693

Jean Leclant

Midway through his "tableau" of the Regency,[1] Jules Michelet suddenly stopped to cull an insight into the history of mankind from one small detail about customs. "The three ages of coffee," he wrote, "were the ages of the modern mind." And he went on to analyze shrewdly the delicate aroma of Arabian coffee, then the more bitter taste of Indian coffee—"coffee from volcanic soil, which provoked the explosion during the Regency and the new spirit"—and finally the round, full-bodied, nourishing as well as stimulating taste of coffee from the Antilles, which "nourished the adult age of the century, the strong age of the *Encyclopédie* [published between 1751 and 1780]." One can be skeptical about the "visionary historian" when he asserts that "deep in the dark brew the prophets assembled in Procope's den saw the future glint of 1789," but one must admit that the use of coffee gave the eighteenth century a very different physiognomy from the seventeenth century, which was a wine drinker. The poet Saint-Amant [1594-1661] used to haunt taverns, seeking inspiration "in the sweet song of orgies, in the glow of red, bloated faces." Molière, La Fontaine, Racine, Chapelle, and Boileau would go to a cabaret to drink the "septembral purée" [wine] and chat; but a century later the philosophes—Fontenelle, Diderot, Marmontel, d'Alembert, Beaumarchais, and Voltaire—haunted the cafés, those "manufactories of wit, both good and bad,"[2] and sought stimulation of their critical powers from the "somber, exceedingly cerebral liquor." And so the French mind changed with the increasing use of a new beverage that marked a step in the conquest of French society by influences from the East.[3] Both the history of ideas and the history of customs can profit from an inquiry into the place of "coffee liquor" and the "coffeehouse" in Paris, as early as the seventeenth century.[4]

Annales, E.S.C. 6 (January-March 1951): 1-12. Translated by Patricia M. Ranum.

The story of Monsieur Coffee has a very modest beginning. After a long series of vicissitudes, it became an adopted French subject and gradually won public favor. The bean was brought into the country in 1644; its success was certain by 1693. Hence, it took coffee fifty years to overcome all the obstacles in its path.

As one might expect, it was through travelers that France first became acquainted with coffee, at the time a very common beverage in the lands of the Turks, from the Bosphorus to the Nile Valley. Marseilles, "the gateway to the East," welcomed coffee in 1644. Upon his return from Constantinople, where he had accompanied [ambassador] la Haye [de Ventelet], sieur la Roque[5] brought back both coffee and the utensils needed to make and drink it. He was especially proud of the "old porcelain cups of great beauty and the small napkins of fine muslin, embroidered in gold, silver, and silk," collector's items rather than everyday ones. His little Turkish-style study "was considered a real curiosity," and the public invited to taste the beverage was made up of traveler friends, who, like la Roque, were familiar with the ways of the Levant. At that point, other wholesale merchants of Marseilles also began to drink coffee to some extent. But for fifteen years the drink rarely was consumed outside a very small social circle.

In 1657 coffee made its appearance in Paris, thanks to Jean de Thévenot.[6] This famous traveler had brought back from Egypt a supply of the precious beans and offered a taste to some friends,[7] who may not all have been as familiar with the Levant as Monsieur de la Croix, the king's interpreter of Turkish, who recorded the event for us.[8] Several aristocrats, on the lookout for new pleasures, even boasted of having Italians to make their coffee. In 1660 a sieur More ["Moor"] was appointed to the kitchen staff by Cardinal Mazarin's maître d'hôtel, while Andrea Salvator came regularly to prepare the new drink at the home of Marshal de Gramont, who was "very curious about these sorts of things." These two skillful Italians excelled "in distilling all sorts of flowers, fruits, grains, and other things, using both heat and cold, and in preparing chocolate, tea, and coffee."[9] The scarce and costly bean sold for eighty francs a pound.

The number of purchasers was still rather small. The general public remained unaware that coffee existed. Hence the surprise when, in 1666, readers of the Muse de Cour [Court Muse] found a poem by Subligny praising the merits of kavé, "which heals you in less time than an Ave Maria, when the rest cannot heal in a year."[10]

Then, a very "Parisian" sort of event provoked the sudden infatuation that "launched" the black brew.

For a number of years, relations between the sultan and the king of France had been broken off as a result of the insults, thefts, molestations, and so forth, that French ambassadors and merchants were subjected to among the Turks. An army corps commanded by the Duke of Beaufort had even recently been sent to help the Venetians, who were besieged in Candia by the grand vizir. Suddenly it was learned that Mohammed IV, experiencing a favorable change of heart, was sending an ambassador to Paris.[11] The latter disembarked at Toulon on 4 August 1669, accompanied by some two dozen notables and servants; and all eyes henceforth were turned toward Suleiman Aga, Mutaferraca.[12] Cities along his route fired cannons in greeting. In Paris, the king himself received the ambassador with unusual ceremony;[13] but instead of being touched by all this attention, the Turk, on the contrary, complained of the king's failure to rise when receiving his letter and withdrew in great irritation. The mission ended in failure politically; but it was far from a failure for literature and manners, for Mustapha Raca inspired Molière's *Bourgeois Gentilhomme** and spread the use of coffee throughout France. If we are to believe one of La Martinière's anecdotes, it was in order to make fun of the Sublime Porte that Molière created the "Turkish" buffoonery in the *Bourgeois Gentilhomme.*[14] By putting a fancy-dress Levant on the stage, Molière was avenging Louis XIV.[15]

Having demonstrated his pride to Louis XIV, Suleiman Muta Faraca, a handsome man in his fifties, began to receive guests, above all ladies. "Handsome young slaves, dressed in opulent Turkish costumes, offered ladies little damask napkins fringed with gold and served coffee in porcelain cups from Japan." People crowded into the exotically decorated lodgings, although they were drawn more by the charm of lively conversation—the Turk was a "witty man"[16] —than by the rather bitter brew being provided. But Mustapha Raca pushed gallantry to the point of offering sugar in the coffee he served. And the craze caught on. After his departure,[17] all those who had been granted the inestimable privilege of being received by him considered it a point of honor to offer guests a taste of the drink that everyone was talking about. And so, throughout noble society, it gradually became the fashion to serve coffee when receiving guests.

Soon the bourgeoisie also wanted to sample the new flavor. The fame of the "arabesque liquor" was exploited by shopkeepers of the capital, who were always ready to satisfy the public's curiosity. Thus, by 1671 there were in Paris "several shops where coffee was sold publicly," as we learn from the treatise "on the use of coffee, tea, and chocolate," published that year at Lyons.[18] It summarized several different opinions about the *bunchum,* or coffee bean, and the drink made from it. Sold in bean form, the new product was used more as a drug than as an agreeable drink. Indeed, its therapeutic qualities were extolled in a prospectus distributed by coffee sellers.[19] And so, coffee would have been merely a prefiguration of medicinal quinine had it not, during these same years, been hawked as the perfect beverage by stallkeepers at fairs.

At this point the Armenians, who by 1666, as Subligny noted, were bringing bales of coffee into Paris, realized that they could profit from the Parisians' infatuation with the concoction by opening shops that would sell nothing but the

---

*In this comedy, Monsieur Jourdain, a vain and uneducated bourgeois who is motivated by a desire to resemble a nobleman, refuses to approve his daughter's marriage with a commoner. The rejected suitor masquerades as the son of the Grand Turk, who has come to Paris specifically to seek the girl's hand. Speaking an incomprehensible gibberish, the young man confers the title of *mamamouchi* upon Jourdain, who swallows the bait and grants his daughter's hand to the so-called Turk. The *mamamouchi* ceremony, which brings the play to a close, is a veritable costumed ballet in which everyone, even Jourdain, wears exaggerated Turkish garb.—Trans.

murky brew.[20] Perhaps they were inspired by the city of Marseilles, the real innovator as far as coffee is concerned, where a "coffee liquor" store had opened in 1671. Thus, in 1672,[21] at the Saint Germain Fair of Paris, a "caffé house" run by a certain Harouthioun or Pascal opened and was a great success.[22] At the end of the fair, Pascal moved his business to the quai de l'Ecole,[23] where he served a cup of coffee for two sous, six deniers. But this venture failed. Passersby along the quay refused to enter the establishment, whose only customers were Levantines and a few Knights of Malta. Pascal therefore had to close up shop and move to London. Did he continue his business there? Probably. In the English capital, coffeehouses, first opened in 1652, had already won such public approval that, in 1675, Charles II tried to do away with "these resorts of disaffected persons, who devised and spread abroad divers false, malicious, and scandalous reports, to the defamation of His Majesty's government and to the disturbance of the peace and quiet of the nation."[24]

In Paris, Pascal had been a sign of things to come. Drawn by the abundant and easily attracted clientele of the Saint Germain Fair, his aide, Procopio, joined his meager savings earned as a waiter in Pascal's café to the earnings of a certain Logerot and, when the fair reopened, rented booth 121, located at the corner of the rue Mercière and the rue de la Quatrième Traverse. The idea of a coffee house in town was tested once again by Maliban, another Armenian, who opened a business on the rue de Bussy, near the Metz tennis courts. After a brief move to the rue Férou, he returned to his first shop and began to sell tobacco and oriental pipes. His business probably failed, for he soon went to Holland. His helper, a certain Grigor or Grégoire, from Ispahan, took over. Grégoire had a very clever idea: he set up shop near the French Comedy, which at the time was located on the rue Mazarine. Actors and literary figures fell into the habit of meeting at Grégoire's shop. Thus, the café, a place for conversing, was established.[25]

In order to drink coffee it no longer was necessary to enter the little shops of Levantine coffee brewers. Vendors strolled through the streets, distributing coffee at one's door. The most famous of them, a short, lame fellow called "Le Candiot" —surely he was from Crete [otherwise known as Candia]—would go through the streets crying out, "Coffee!" His waist was swathed in a very clean white napkin; he carried in one hand an alcohol burner on which sat a coffee pot and in the other a water container with a faucet. In front hung a tin basket with all the necessary utensils.[26] For two sous, sugar included, he would fill a mug.

Le Candiot had rivals. There are records of a certain Joseph, a Levantine, and of an Etienne d'Alep [that is, from Aleppo].[27] All these men from the Levant are the unknown builders of coffee's acceptance in Paris. During the second half of the seventeenth century "Armenian" was synonymous with "coffee seller."[28]

The retreats where coffee was sold were, however, merely shops reeking of tobacco smoke. Then, in the rue des Fossés-Saint-Germain, a very different sort of establishment appeared—a welcoming, clean, even luxurious place—the first true café, founded by Francesco Procopio Coltelli.

Much has been said, and the debate is not over, about his origins, Was he born in Palermo, Sicily; or in Florence, Italy, as Dubuisson, his successor, claimed;[29] or in Paris, where a Procopio Coltelli had settled in the days of Catherine de Medicis? This question is answered by an "extract from the records of the Chambre des Comptes of Paris, for the year 1684, page thirteen," attesting that Francesco Procopio Coltelli was a Sicilian.[30] In addition, his marriage certificate reveals that he was born in 1650 to Onofrio Coltelli and Domenica Semarqua.[31] After what tribulations did this Sicilian (we must give up imagining him an impoverished nobleman)[32] end up at the Saint Germain Fair, where he became Pascal's aide? No one knows. He followed his employer to the quai de l'Ecole and, when that shop was closed, returned, as we have seen, to the Saint Germain Fair. There, with Logerot, he rented a shop, where he earned enough money to marry Marguerite Crouïn by 1675. Between 1676 and 1688 he fathered eight children. His social contacts seem to have been limited to the Italian community.[33] In 1684 this Sicilian, head of a prosperous business, became a naturalized Frenchman. Known as Procope Couteau, he henceforth was part of the history of French customs, if not the history of France itself.

But, by 1676, before his naturalization, Procopio had become one of the distilleurs-limonadiers of Paris. Although his wedding certificate of 1675 lists him as a "shopkeeper," in the baptismal records of his daughters he is called a "distiller" in 1677 and a "master distiller" in 1677 and 1678. Indeed, in 1676 the "master limonadiers, brandy sellers" had been given new bylaws; article III granted them the "right to compound and sell . . . coffee in the bean, as powder, and as a drink."[34] As a distilleur-limonadier, Procope left the Saint Germain Fair to set up a business on the rue de Tournon.[35] In 1686,[36] he moved to the rue des Fossés-Saint-Germain and established the business that in the coming centuries would become famous as the Café Procope.[37] In addition, Procope rented two adjacent houses, giving him a considerable amount of space. "The terrain ran along the city's dry moat between the gates of Saint-Germain and Bussy and served as their counterscarp."[38] Tearing down the inner walls, the daring Sicilian fused the street floors of the two buildings to form his café, furnished it with convenient and attractive little marble tables, hung crystal chandeliers from the ceiling, and decorated the walls with an elegant tapestry and, for a final luxury touch, small framed mirrors and large wall mirrors. The café was becoming a worthy meeting place for respectable people—and for gourmets.

To his talents as café owner, the "master distiller" added those of preparer of alcoholic liquors and a multitude of drugs. He also stocked a gamut of heady wines: muscat, wines from Spain, from Saint-Laurent, and from La Ciotat, as well as a whole spectrum of masterful blends. There was rossoly, or "sun dew," which permitted the gourmet to savor the harmonious blend of fennel, anise, coriander, dill, and caraway, crushed and then left to steep in brandy in the heat of the sun. There was populo, which mingled the flavors of cloves, musk, amber, long pepper, sugar, anise, coriander, and spirit of wine; or citron water and "perfect love liquor"; or sorbec made of citron, musk, amber, and sugar; candied fruits, cherries, raspberries, or nuts; fruit jellies diluted with water; and, last of all, a variety of fruit or flower ices, for, in the late seventeenth century, the Sicilian "artist"[39] launched the combined trade of *café glacier* [cafékeeper and ice cream vendor] to satisfy both the customer who wanted to warm himself and the customer who wanted something cool.

At this point, through a lucky coincidence, a large clientele virtually came knocking at Procope's door. Forced to leave the rue Mazarine in 1687 as a result of hostility from their Jansenist neighbors, the King's Players moved to the tennis court of sieur de l'Etoile on the rue des Fossés-Saint-Germain, just opposite the Café Procope, and built a new theater. On 18 April 1689 the French Comedy opened its new home with an exciting performance of Racine's *Phèdre* and Molière's *Médecin malgré lui*.[40] Procope had his own spot in the theater, for he had rented the *limonade* stand and had installed a "dispenser of sweet liquors." But, most important of all, the Café Procope became the headquarters of everyone having anything to do with the Comedy.

Until then, most of Procope's customers had been bowlers from the Malus bowling green just behind the café, tennis players from l'Etoile's courts, or a few swashbucklers from the neighborhood. He also had gained a clientele from among the many people passing through the Bussy crossroads, at that time the real center of left-bank Paris. After all, from the rues Dauphine, Mazarine, Saint-André-des-Arts, des Boucheries, and de Condé, people were willing to go a bit further to the rue des Fossés-Saint-Germain for an ice cream or a cup of coffee. But, once the French Comedy had been built, a clientele of authors, actors, newsletter writers, and men of letters, as well as fine lords or farmers general poured in, drawn to these parts by the actresses' charms. Waiters in Eastern garb, draped in loose garments and wearing fur hats, brought tiny cups of the steaming beverage to an extremely varied clientele:[41] well-built young horsemen, courtly abbés savoring sweetmeats, quiet couples seeking privacy in the midst of the crowd and noise, and scholars and men of letters who "conferred on erudite questions, without constraint and without ceremony, while having fun, so to speak."[42] They chatted with their coffee cups before them; "conversation obligatorily accompanies coffee or tea, it is even their real reason for existing." Scarcely was it born before the café became a literary café.

From the very beginning the café also was political. The more serious government matters were discussed there. And people in power soon became interested in those potential centers of opposition. On 27 December 1685, Colbert de Seignelay [a secretary of state] wrote to La Reynie [chief of the Paris police]: "The king has been informed that, in several places in Paris where coffee is served, there are assemblies of all sorts of people, and especially foreigners. Upon which His Majesty ordered me to ask whether you do not think it would be appropriate to prevent them from assembling in the future."[43]

But the new establishments were such a dazzling success that the chief of police did not act upon the secretary of state's suggestion. Many other cafés sprang up near Procope's. At the Saint Germain Fair modest booths were transformed into elegant rooms, where "Armenian" waiters poured from silver coffee pots. At the corner of the rue Dauphine and the rue Christine, Laurent started a café that soon would become famous.[44] After years of moving through the Paris streets shouting "Coffee!," Etienne d'Alep settled down on the rue Saint-André-des-Arts. In short, by 1690 the entire heart of elegant Paris—from the Bussy crossroads to the Saint Germain Fair and on to the Seine River—had been won over to the new practice. It was considered good form to go to a café.

During these years, coffee also had gained a foothold in private homes, but not without difficulty. After the craze of the 1670s came a reaction led by the medical school. Alarmed by the stimulating properties of coffee, many physicians virtually outlawed it by forbidding it to their patients. Madame de Sévigné's correspondence offers proof of the medical profession's opposition to the new drink and of the changing attitude of courtly and society figures toward it. On 10 May 1676 she informed her daughter, Countess de Grignan, that coffee had just been "chased shamefully" from Mademoiselle de Méri's house: "After such a fall from favor, can one count on its rise?"[45] In 1679 she again reported to Madame de Grignan that Du Chesne, her friends' physician, had forbidden it: "The strength you think you gain from coffee is only a false well-being."[46] That same year, in an examination for admission to the College of Physicians of Marseilles, sieur Colomb demonstrated that the use of coffee was harmful to the inhabitants of that city.[47]

Yet many people remained fond of coffee. In February 1680 the Marquise de Sévigné was perplexed: "Du Chesne still hates coffee; Brother [Ange, a Capuchin monk reputed to be a healer] has only good to say about it," she wrote to her daughter. "Must one take it as if it were a medicine? Caderousse constantly sings its praises; coffee makes one person fat and someone else thin. That is how foolish people are about it. I do not think that it is possible to talk more favorably about something for which there are so many unfavorable experiences."[48]

The partisans of coffee gradually won; coffee, in its turn, soon was the subject of scholarly treatises, showing how it could be used to "avoid and treat illnesses."[49] But the wheel of fortune turned once again. "Coffee is in total disgrace," wrote Madame de Sévigné to her daughter on 1 November 1688. "The Chevalier [de Sévigné] believes that it heats him up and makes his blood course; and I, at the same time, copycat that you know me to be, I don't drink it any more."[50] A week later, however, the marquise thought that coffee might "return to favor."[51] But the members of the royal court appeared to be permanently censuring it. "Coffee is in disgrace here and consequently I no longer drink it; I did, however, find that it had some good effects upon me; but I no longer think about them."[52] Then Monin, a physician from Grenoble, conceived the notion that coffee could have milk and sugar added to it.[53] This mixture defeated the last remaining opponents, and the marquise, who was following the advice of Aliot, ordinary physician to the king, henceforth praised "coffied milk" or "milky coffee"[54] as the "nicest thing in the world."[55]

As long as the consumption of coffee remained low, the government did not view it as a potential source of revenue. Once coffee began to appear regularly in account books, the government realized it could be the source of substantial income. Indeed, an edict of January 1692 made the sale of coffee a monopoly of the public treasury.[56] The tax farmers were the only people entitled to import and sell coffee, tea, chocolate, cocoa, and vanilla; selling these items retail required written authorization, renewable yearly for a fee of thirty livres. The price of coffee beans was fixed at four francs a pound, and a "dose" of coffee at three sous, six deniers. And Master François Damame, bourgeois of Paris, became holder, for the "next six consecutive years," beginning 1 January 1692, of the privilege of "selling, causing to be sold, and distributing alone, to the exclusion of everyone else, all coffees, both in the bean and in powder, tea, *sorbecs,* and chocolates."[57]

From then on coffee had an official existence within the state.[58] But could it stand up to the enormous price increase that the tax farm would bring? In 1690 it had been worth between twenty-seven and twenty-eight sous a pound;[59] suddenly the price climbed to four francs a pound. There was a pronounced drop in consumption—or official consumption, at least, for an enormous amount of smuggling went on. A letter of 10 March 1692 from Bérulle, intendant at Lyons, to the comptroller general informs him that "the assistants of Damame have seized at a customs post and have brought to their office a bale containing between seven and eight quintals [that is, between 700 and 800 pounds of coffee beans], which the Princess of Würtemberg, who is in a convent here, wants returned to her as her property and which she claims to have ordered for her personal use."[60] Although the intendant pointed out in vain that, "this princess drinks a great deal of it and has no pleasures other than coffee drinking," it probably was a simple matter of smuggling.

Yet, overall consumption must actually have decreased. "Most of those who drank it, now abstain," states the preamble of a decree of the Council of State of 19 August 1692, "which reduces and moderates the price of coffee to a sum of fifty sous a pound, including the seller's costs and other taxes."[61] This decrease did not give renewed vigor to a system that slowed consumption and encouraged smuggling. A decree of the Royal Council[62] revoked Damame's privileges in May 1693.[63] Coffee sales were freed of restrictions; yet it could "enter the kingdom only through the city of Marseilles, after paying upon entry into the port the sum of ten sous per pound, mark weight, above and beyond all previous taxes."

Henceforth, "coffee liquor" and "coffeehouses" could satisfy the growing public favor without restrictions. The *caffé* that had quietly made its appearance at Marseilles fifty years earlier, thanks to exotic personages—travelers, Italians, Turks, Armenians, and Sicilians—and thanks to a variety of lucky circumstances, had become permanently rooted in Paris. Even today, "the only cafés will always be those of Paris."

NOTES

1. Jules Michelet, *Histoire de France* (Paris, 1867), 17: chap. 5, "La Régence."
2. *Encyclopédie ou dictionnaire raisonné des sciences, des arts et des métiers* (Paris, 1751), 2: 529, s.v. "Caffés."

3. P. Martino, *L'Orient dans la littérature française aux XVIIe et XVIIIe siècles* (Paris, 1906), p. 347.

4. For coffee, the researcher has nothing comparable to the volume on chocolate by Albert Bourgaux, *Quatre siècles d'histoire du cacao et du chocolat* (Brussels, 1935). The most basic work on coffee is Alfred Franklin's *Le Café, le thé et le chocolat* (Paris, 1893), part of his series entitled *Le Vie privé d'autrefois*. However, this book has very serious limitations: Franklin's sources of information are only rarely indicated, and he makes numerous assertions with no proof; on several points his solutions are unacceptable today (for example, he states that the Café Procope was not established until 1702). Yet this book makes the use of older volumes unnecessary, for these older texts are bad compilations or collections of insipid anecdotes dealing almost exclusively with eighteenth-century cafés.

I should, however, like to call attention to a number of older volumes. John Ellis, *An Historical Account of Coffee* (London, 1774), tried chiefly to trace the glorious career of a product that had brought wealth to Dominique, whose agent he was. Gentil, *Dissertation sur le café* (Paris, 1787) is written mainly from a medical point of view.

Contrary to expectations, there is almost nothing in Jacques Savary des Bruslons, *Dictionnaire universel de commerce, d'histoire naturelle et des arts et métiers* (Paris, 1719, 1721, etc.). The same is true for Nicolas Delamare, *Traité de la police* (Paris, 1722 and 1738), 2: 797 ff., bk. 5, chap. 47, "Des liqueurs."

For general books on cafés, see E. F. Bazot (presumed author), *Les Cafés de Paris par un flâneur patenté* (Paris, 1819); A. Constantin, *Histoire anecdotique des cafés et cabarets de Paris* (Paris, 1862); Auguste Lepage, *Les Cafés artistiques et littéraires de Paris* (Paris, 1882), all of which set out to guide their readers through eighteenth- and nineteenth-century cafés, paying virtually no attention to the earliest cafés. François Fosca (pseud. for Georges de Traz), *Histoire des cafés de Paris* (Paris, 1934), is a crisp but too rapid synthesis of earlier works.

5. Jean de la Roque, *Voyage dans l'Arabie heureuse... Traité historique de l'origine et du progrès du café...de son introduction en France et de l'établissement de son usage à Paris* (Paris, 1718), p. 363. Jean, a resident of Marseilles, added the treatise on coffee to his father's account of a journey to Arabia. This is the source that historians of coffee have consulted, usually with no critical sense. (Available in the collection of the Arsenal of Paris, call number 8° H 1230.)

6. Jean-Marie Carré, *Voyageurs et écrivains français en Egypte* (Cairo, 1932), 1: 15.

7. Jean Thévenot devoted several pages to the Turkish *cahvé* and *cahvehanes* ("public cabarets for *cahvé*") in the narrative of his travels, *Voyages de M. de Thévenot en Europe, Asie, Afrique* (Paris, 1664).

8. Of special interest is Antoine Galland, early-eighteenth-century French translator of the *Arabian Nights*, who commented upon an Arab manuscript about *cahvé* in the Royal Library, in a seventy-six-page brochure, *De l'origine et des progrès du café* (Caen, Paris, 1699), Arsenal, call number 8° S 113.

9. Audiger, *La Maison réglée...avec la véritable méthode de faire toutes sortes d'essences, d'eaux et de liqueurs* (Paris, 1692), which provides information about the first "private coffee sellers," and the way coffee was made (collection of the Bibliothèque nationale of Paris, call number V 31,048).

10. 2 December 1666, p. 225. In order to be understood by his readers, the witty lawyer felt obliged to explain the origins of the product and to praise its qualities:

C'est une liqueur arabesque,
Ou bien si vous voulez turquesque
Que dans le Levant chacun prend....
Elle a passé dans l'Italie,
En Hollande et chez les Anglois
Où l'on la trouve fort utile,
Et des Arméniens qui sont en cette ville
L'apportent encore aux François....

[This an arabesque liquor, / Or turkesque if you prefer / That in the Levant everyone drinks.... / It has gone to Italy, / To Holland and to the English / Who find it very useful, / And Armenians in this city / Are introducing it to the French....]

11. A. Vandal, "L'Ambassade de Soliman Aga Mutaferraca," *Revue d'Art Dramatique* 11 (1883): 65-80, a study of these diplomatic negotiations and their literary repercussions, although it does not discuss coffee. Vandal seems to have used only a part of the available documents, in a partial way and with marked partiality.

12. *Mutaferraca* was a Turkish title indicating the holder's role in the sultan's household. It was mistaken for part of the ambassador's name, so in Paris he was called "Muta Faraca" or "Mustapha Raca."

13. Olivier Lefèvre d'Ormesson, *Journal d'Olivier Lefèvre d'Ormesson,* ed. Adolphe Chéruel (Paris, 1860-61), 2: 577; *Gazette de France,* 7 and 19 December 1669, pp. 1165 and 1197, an account of the "audience given by His Majesty to the envoy of the Grand Turk."

14. Eugène Despois and Paul Mesnard, *Oeuvres de Molière,* collection des Grands Ecrivains de France (Paris, 1873-1900), 8: 10. Cf. Marcel Paquot, *Les Etrangers dans les divertissements de la Cour* (Brussels, 1931), pp. 161 ff.

15. Vandal, "L'Ambassade de Soliman Aga Mutáferraca," p. 80.

16. Lefèvre d'Ormesson, *Journal,* 2: 577.

17. He took his leave of sieur de Lionne at the end of May 1670 and left Toulon on 22 August (Laurent d'Arvieux, *Mémoires du chevalier d'Arvieux* [Paris, 1735], 4: 251).

18. Spon, *De l'usage du caphé, du thé et du chocolate* (Lyons, 1671), Arsenal, call number 8° S 1887, published anonymously. Franklin, *Le Café, le thé et le chocolat,* p. 30, n. 1, cites it under the name of Girin, the publisher. In 1716 la Roque, *Traité historique,* p. 306, called it a "French translation by Dufour [see below, note 48] of a Latin manuscript that he had got his hands on." Pierre Bayle, *Nouvelles de la République des Lettres,* said the author was Spon. Like the bibliophile Jacob, I tend to favor the hypothesis that Spon, a scholar from Lyons, was the author of this first French treatise on coffee. The work includes a summary of earlier works (Prosper Alpini, etc.) and a study of the *bunchum* or *bon* (coffee bean), and of *caphé,* the drink made from it.

19. Coffee is a seed that grows in the deserts of Arabia, from where it is transported into all the dominions of the Grand Turk; the which being drunk, dries up all cold and damp humors, dries out winds, fortifies the liver, eases dropsy by its purifying nature; likewise infallible against gall and corruption of the blood; freshens the heart and its vital beats, comforts those with stomach pains and those who have lost their appetite; is likewise good for the indispositions of cold, damp, and heavy brains.

The steam that comes from it is good for discharges from the eyes and noises in the ears; infallible also for shortness of breath, for colds in the chest, and pains in the spleen, for worms, for especial relief after having eaten and drunk too much. Nothing better for those who eat a great deal of fruit.

(Spon, *De l'usage du caphé, du thé et du chocolate,* pp. 23-25.)

20. Historians of the café (such as Franklin, *Le Café, le thé et le chocolat,* p. 32) all indicate that as early as 1643 a Levantine opened an unsuccessful café in the covered passageway under the Petit-Châtelet, leading from the rue Saint-Jacques to the Petit-Pont. None of them gives references, and I have been unable to confirm this fact.

21. The date 1672 seems to have been given for the first time by Constant d'Orville, *Mélanges tirés d'une grande bibliothèque,* cited by Auguste Jal, *Dictionnaire critique de biographie et d'histoire* (Paris, 1867), p. 445. Cf. P. Fromageot, "La Foire Saint-Germain-des-Prés," *Bulletin de la Société de l'Histoire du VIe arrondissement de Paris* 4 (1901): 185-248, and 5 (1902): 46-140.

22. F. Macler, "Les Arméniens: Leçon d'ouverture du cours à l'Ecole des Langues Orientales vivantes," *Revue internationale de l'enseignement,* 1912, p. 28, and *La France et l'Arménie à travers l'histoire* (Paris, 1917), pp. 18-19. Macler cites the works of P. Alighan, *Sisakan* (Venice, 1893), pp. 456-57, and *Honchik hayreneats Hayots* (Venice, 1869), 1: 73.

23. Today the quai du Louvre.

24. *Encyclopedia Britannica,* 11th ed., s.v. "coffee."

25. Grégoire passed the business of the rue de Bussy to a Persian named Makara, who in turn sold it to a Fleming known as "Le Gantois" [the man from Ghent].

26. La Roque, *Traité historique,* p. 377.

27. They made enough money to set up business independently, Joseph on the Notre-Dame bridge, Etienne d'Alep on the rue Saint-André-des-Arts, almost opposite the Saint-Michel bridge.

28. Alfred Franklin, *Dictionnaire historique des arts, métiers et professions exercées dans Paris depuis le XIIIe siècle* (Paris-Leipzig, 1906), s.v. "Arméniens." In Dancourt's play "La Foire Saint-Germain" (1696), one of the characters, Loranse, "a coffee seller dressed as an Armenian," confesses that he has been a "naturalized Armenian for three weeks."

29. The distiller Dubuisson, *L'Art du distillateur et marchand de liqueurs considérées comme aliments médicamenteux* (Paris, 1779).

30. Archives Nationales, P 2695, published in A. Bruel, *Bulletin de la Société de l'Histoire du VIe arrondissement de Paris* 1 (1898): 155. The fire in the Chambre des Comptes in 1737 destroyed the original text of the naturalization papers, which surely would have provided more complete information about Procopio's origins.

31. Solemnized in the Church of Saint-Sulpice on 26 February 1675. "The marriage of Procope

Couteau, shopkeeper, age twenty-five, son of the late Onofre Couteau and Dominique Somarque [sic], residing on the rue Tournon." The French form, Couteau, that is, knife—and not the plural, Couteaux—is the exact translation of Coltelli.

32. Moura and Louvet, *Le Café Procope* (Paris, 1929), p. 22, still believed that Procopio was a nobleman, "Procopio dei Coltelli." They based this assumption on the existence of a parlementary family, de Cousteau. In reality, the de Cousteau were merely the café owner's descendents, become rich and respectable, who had been granted letters of nobility (Bruel, *Bulletin*, pp. 156-58). This book is very superficial and full of errors; its authors are unaware that Procope became naturalized, state that the treatise by Dufour is the first book on coffee, and so forth.

33. His first daughter had as a godfather an "Italian nobleman," and his third "a nobleman from Messina." In 1688 Marie-Anne's godfather was Don Cristofolo Papi, duca di Pratoamene. Could it be that the most loyal clients of Procopio Coltelli were compatriots, happy to find, in Paris, cafés like those already well established in Italy? Baptismal records in Jal, *Dictionnaire critique*, p. 446.

34. René de Lespinasse, *Histoire générale de Paris, Les métiers et corporations de la ville de Paris. Ordonnances générales. Métiers de l'alimentation* (Paris, 1886).

35. Felix de Rochegude and Maurice Dumoulin, *Guide pratique à travers le Vieux Paris* (Paris, 1923).

36. Georges de Wissant, *Le Paris d'autrefois, cafés et cabarets* (Paris, 1928), p. 65, gives the year 1684 with no reference to his source. Nor does he mention the interim stay on the rue de Tournon.

37. Perhaps a distant relative had attracted him to that particular spot, for the place he set up shop, a bathing house bearing the sign of "The Holy Shroud of Turin," had been kept by descendants of the Procopio Coltelli who had come to Paris in the suite of Catherine de Médicis.

38. Memoranda for A. Couteau, shopkeeper, grocer-limonadier in Paris, respondent, against Jean Maurice Durand de Chastas, secretary of the king, receiver general of finances for Champagne, appellant (Wissant, *Le Paris d'autrefois,* pp. 66-67).

39. The term used by his successor, Dubuisson, author of the *L'Art du distillateur.*

40. Cf. A. Joannidès, *La Comédie Française de 1680 à 1920* (Paris, 1921). Further information about the French Comedy can be found in Béatrix Dussane, *La Comédie Française* (Paris, 1921), and Emile Genest and E. Duberry, *La Maison de Molière connue et inconnue* (Paris, 1922).

41. The café provided an inexhaustible mine of word *portraits* and *caractères*, that is, verbal sketches of mores. By 1694 the diversity of the clientele prompted an unsuccessful comedy, "Le Café," printed by P. Aubouin. It was performed only once. All these *caractères* are also described by the Chevalier de Mailly, *Les Entretiens des Cafés de Paris et les Différents qui y surviennent, par M. le C. de M^XX^* (Trévoux, 1702). This volume seems to be one of the first devoted to "coffeehouses." The author sketches a series of *portraits* and analyzes a number of *caractères* with some finesse. In addition, the very precious illustrations give us some of the first pictures of café life. The Musée Carnavalet [devoted to the history of the city of Paris] has no document as old as this book, which is part of the collection in the Bibliothèque historique de la ville de Paris, call number 921,425.

42. La Roque, *Traité historique*, p. 380.

43. Archives Nationales, Registers of the Secretary of State for the Royal Household, O¹ 29, folio 568; published in Georges-Bernard Depping, *Correspondance administrative sous le règne de Louis XIV* (Paris, 1850-55), 2: 575.

44. On the Café Laurent, see Franklin, *Le Café, le thé et le chocolat*, pp. 64 and 279.

45. Letter of 10 May 1676, Marie de Rabutin-Chantal, marquise de Sévigné, *Lettres,* ed. Gérard-Gailly, Pléiade (Paris, 1960), 2: 92. On 16 March 1672 the marquise had written to her daughter: "Racine is writing comedies for La Champmeslé [a famous actress]; they are not written for posterity. . . ." (ibid., 1: 498); by oversight Voltaire probably mixed up the letters of 16 March 1672 and 10 May 1676, when, in his preface to *Irène* (1776) he quoted Madame de Sévigné's famous remark, "The craze for loving Racine will pass, like the craze for coffee."

46. Letter of 8 November 1679, ibid., 2: 498.

47. The burnt parts with which it abounds are, indeed, so fine and so very movable that, having spread throughout the mass of blood, they first draw all the serosity into the reservoirs of urine and into the other parts of the body. From there, attacking the brain, after having dissolved all its humidity and its large corpuscles, these burnt parts keep all the pores open and prevent the animal spirits that cause sleep from moving to the center of the brain, since these pores are plugged. Hence these burnt parts cause, by their nature, wakefulness that often is so stubborn that the nervous sap whose strength is very necessary for the distribution of these spirits is

completely lacking, and so the nerves give way, which results in paralysis or impotence. And through the bitterness and dryness of a blood that is already entirely burnt up, all the parts of the body together become so drained of sap that the entire body is in the end reduced to a horrible thinness.

48. Letter of 16 February 1680, Sévigné, *Lettres,* 2: 610.

49. "Filled with sulphur and volatile salt," it was a true panacea, according to Philippe-Silvestre Dufour, *Traités nouveaux et curieux du café, du thé et du chocolate* (Lyons, 1685), part of the collection in the Arsenal of Paris, call number 8° S 8117. The author, a druggist from Lyons, presents a "chemical" study of coffee and its therapeutic uses. At the end of the volume is a "Lettre de M. Bernier sur le café," where François Bernier, the famous traveler [to the empire of the "Great Mogul"] discusses the countries from which the bean comes. Dufour's text was outdone by that of Nicolas de Blégny, "councillor, physician, and ordinary *artiste* of the King and of Monsieur [the king's brother] and appointed, by order of His Majesty, to search out and verify new discoveries in medicine." His volume, *Le Bon Usage du thé, du café et du chocolat pour la préservation et pour la guérison des maladies* (Lyons, 1687), is available in the Arsenal, call number 8° S 9777.

50. Letter of 1 November 1688, Sévigné, *Lettres,* 3: 230.

51. Letter of 8 November 1688, ibid., 3: 239.

52. Letter of 23 November 1688, ibid., 3: 254.

53. Franklin, *Le Café, le thé et le chocolat,* p. 59. *Café au lait* [coffee with a liberal dose of warm milk added] was first used as a remedy to stop coughs and fatten the patient.

54. Letter of 29 January 1690, Sévigné, *Lettres,* 3: 664.

55. Letter of 19 February 1690, ibid., 3: 682.

56. Royal edict regulating the sale and distribution of coffee, tea, chocolate, cocoa, and vanilla, January 1692. If we are to believe the preamble, almost no more wine was being drunk in France: "The drinking of coffee, tea, *sorbec,* and chocolate has become so common that the taxes of the *aides* have considerably decreased." Not wishing to deprive his subjects of these drinks, "which most deem useful for good health," the king was leasing them as a tax farm, "proposing to receive some aid from it in view of the current war."

57. Decree of the Royal Council of State, 19 August 1692.

58. There were precautions to assure the effectiveness of the monopoly. Those with stocks of coffee had only one day to make their declaration: "The aides and employees of the said Damame" were given very extensive investigative and supervisory powers; it was henceforth forbidden to bring coffee into the country "by ports other than those of Marseilles and Rouen... with the exception, however, of coffees taken at sea and those coming from the French islands." To prevent smuggling, it was decided that coffee could not be "mixed or mingled with grain, peas, beans, or other things of that nature... under penalty of corporal punishment and a fifteen-pound fine."

59. Decree of the Royal Council of State, 19 August 1692.

60. Arthur Michel de Boislisle, *Correspondance des contrôleurs généraux des finances avec les intendants des provinces* (Paris, 1874), 1: 280, doc. number 1057.

61. Decree of the Royal Council of State reducing and moderating the price of coffee to the sum of fifty sous per pound, including the seller's price and other duties, 19 August 1692.

62. Decree of the Royal Council of State revoking the privilege for the sale of coffee, tea, *sorbec,* chocolate, cocoa, and vanilla, established by the edict of the month of January 1692, dated 12 May 1693.

63. The tax farm seems to have been done away with as a result of the poor functioning of the system. The preamble of the decree indicates that Damame himself was requesting its revocation. However, there is reason to wonder whether other influences did not come into play, for example, pressure by importers at Marseilles who wanted the product to be widely available. To answer this would require a study of the archival materials at Marseilles.

7
The Art of Using Leftovers: Paris, 1850-1900

Jean-Paul Aron

Like history, economics has its shadowy zones. It is built upon silences, to which it pays little attention, for by definition such silences do not fit into statistics and reassuring correlations. There are a great number of references about food during the nineteenth century. The records of high schools, hospitals, and customs posts provide specific information about the food eaten over long periods of time. Paris during the Restoration outdoes itself as far as details are concerned: we know apparently everything about the items sold—and theoretically eaten—per inhabitant and per food item. True, we have only a vague idea about the people who did the eating. But this does not upset demographers and anthropologists, who are less concerned about details—that is, about differences—than about underlying structures, about abstract and mathematically significant generalizations. The fact that only two thousand people of the ten thousand upon whom their computations are based actually ate what is attributed to the population at large does not affect the essential points: the amount purchased, the price, and the commercial categories represented, such as poultry, meat, or fish.

But economic history cannot accept being cut down to size by such considerations, being drained of a good part of its substance, and answering impertinent questions. There, on its own territory, it would be caught in flagrant breech of trust! After all, the calculations of the amount of food eaten in Paris are based upon such detailed research. We must remember that the food marked is distorted from the beginning by something we do not know: the wholesomeness of the products. Under the heading "food" is grouped everything that is eaten and edible, everything sold and salable. Yet, this is an area where quantitative and qualitative historians should coordinate their efforts. Evaluating the wholesomeness of food would shed some new light upon the conclusions about illness, poverty, and rebellion being drawn by historians working on the nineteenth

Annales, E. S. C. 30 (March-June 1975): 553-562. Translated by Patricia M. Ranum.

century. Here I hope to show that two parallel sorts of food were eaten during the last half of the nineteenth century. First, there were what might be called "second-hand" foods, that is, foods that had been prepared, served once, and then sold, sometimes even resold—foods whose itinerary through the city and the surrounding area often ended in decay. Second, there were foods in a poor state of preservation that were sold as damaged goods and ranged from what the city police department called "overripe"[1] to totally rotten.

I. Leftovers

Leftovers formed an important part of the Parisian diet in the nineteenth century. Every household, even among the bourgeoisie, even among the affluent, knew what eating leftovers meant. Toward the end of the century a man who had been a bon vivant during the Second Empire recalled his former revelries and described leftovers:

It is chiefly within the family itself, where they must bear up to Homeric assaults, that such venerable debris, pepped up by a different gravy, gaily comes back to life thanks to the art of using leftovers.... Of all these culinary metamorphoses, I know none more appealing and more attractive than "croquettes Périgord style" [that is, with truffles], an exquisite memory from the days of my gluttonous youth. These croquettes are truly delicious, the day after such luxurious feasts as those served on meat-eating days. With subtle and patient skill the finely chopped meat of the preceding day blends, mingles, harmonizes, somehow comes together in a single dish. Garlic-scented roast beef and leg of lamb, a subtle hint of roast veal rump, the delectable aroma of chicken, quail, and partridge with their exquisite bouquet—each makes its own contribution and adds its own touch to the admirable whole.... It perfumes the entire house. Then they arrange it on a platter, a masterpiece, a golden pyramid browned in fat, topped with a bonnet of green parsley.... Sometimes these croquettes made from a variety of meats are hidden by an artistically browned batter, similar to the way some cooks prepare salsify or artichoke hearts. But when served in this way it is at least a venial sin if the chopped meats are not ornamented with lovely slices of black truffles, cooked in champagne. This makes a subtle and stylish dish—I don't say an economical one.

It is not hard to believe him, and, after this recollection of such culinary spendors, we can understand Fulbert Dumonteil's peroration: "Ah, I beg you, do not be disdainful of the art of using leftovers, which, ultimately, is the great art of living,"[2] an art that is still alive in this world of plenty, with its refrigerators. But in the nineteenth century the food left on the tables of embassies and leading restaurants encountered strange vicissitudes before it ended at the city dump.

The Parisian trade in leftovers had three networks of distribution.

A. PRIVATE SALE

Sometimes prepared in renowned kitchens and fine hotels, but more often by restaurants and caterers, leftovers were the object of secret transactions. Sometimes they were handled by a specialist with a network all his own. An example is the egg whites that the bakery chef in large establishments—who made parfaits, Bavarian creams, ice creams, and chocolates—sold to macaroon makers, since his own work generally involved the use of only the yolks.[3] Sometimes the chef or owner disposed of all items left over from the previous day. There were two sorts of clients: either the specialized businesses I shall discuss shortly or else other restaurant owners who deposited these treasures in their pantries for more or less lengthy stays. Tasty the first day, acceptable the second, languishing the third, and after that increasingly nasty!

Another way of sampling all these voluptuous things, for a low cost, is the seventeen-sous restaurant. A choice of two main dishes, a dessert, a half-bottle of wine, and as much bread as you can eat. And what a menu! For fish there is salmon with green herb sauce, Normandy sole, pike. Then filet of beef with Périgueux sauce [flavored with truffles and madeira], veal cutlet Milanese. And wild game too: jugged hare, roebuck [that is, venison] steak with poivrade [pepper] sauce, salmis of woodcock. Mayonnaise appears frequently on this fantastic menu, and lobster bisque is no rarity; sometimes one finds extraordinary dishes that only fat purses usually permit. Trustworthy sources claim to have found swallow's nests and onager steaks. Moreover, on the counter are displayed enormous piles of fruit worthy of Chevet, pears as big as a baby's head, peaches and grapes that doubtlessly came from Montreuil [famous for some of the best peaches in France] or the land of Caanan; and, wonder of wonders, just the thing to convince the admiring throng on the sidewalk outside, a stag, a real stag, hanging by its hind feet and dragging on the floor its bloody muzzle and authentic ten-point antlers, while partridges, their beaks in the air, hang in bunches just beside the poster upon which gleam tempting prices—1 franc 25, 1 franc 15, or 85 centimes—just above a menu fit for a king upon which no skeptic would dare cast doubt, since with his own eyes he can see at the door still raw, still feathered and furred, the beasts that he will be eating cooked inside. And they say food is expensive in Paris!

Alas! Alas! the stag is only there as a decoration, the partridges have been rented, and the fruit too. If they were stuffed or made of papier maché, as in the theater, it would amount to the same thing. But—you say—the sole and the salmis and the roebuck steaks exist. They do. In the morning, at dawn, a great basket was brought to the restaurant, a basket covered with a dark cloth that, in the jargon of pantries and kitchens, is called the black flag. In it were all the relics of fine banquets and suppers of the previous night, all the morsels that fine gentlemen and ladies with no appetite toyed with, in mansions or in night restaurants. Cooks and chefs sell for almost nothing the left-over salmon, the virtually intact filets of Normandy sole, the poultry carcasses, and the roebuck steaks. . . . This is why you have a menu rivaling that of Rothschild when he hosts important figures, rivaling the menus that Lulu and Cuddles force their lovers to order for them during nocturnal love feasts. A little disinfectant over it all, a little decoration, and for seventeen sous you can eat the feast of Luculus—oh naive schoolboy, oh dreamy and tempestuous office boy—hypnotized by the ten-point stag hanging in the window, the stag who soon will go back home to its owner, the man who runs the big food store, when a week of aging has ripened it for actual sale. But do not weep! For this stag will return to you in pieces, under the black flag![4]

Perhaps the pieces will be served rotten, like the serving of cooked ray seized by food inspectors at a restaurant on the avenue des Ternes on 10 February

1862.[5] The reports of the Paris police never specify whether these leftovers came from elsewhere or had been prepared by the restaurant itself. But the way Parisian restaurants were operated makes me lean toward the first conjecture. Bistros rarely accumulated leftovers, for the turnover was very rapid, even if the food served consisted of leftovers purchased cheaply. Besides, even rotten, it was good enough for their impoverished clientele, who, in the case of the avenue des Ternes, were surely workers employed near the toll gate of the Roule. This lends weight to the evidence supplied by the many self-satisfied administrative reports of food inspectors. One of these reports, dated 10 February 1862, a mere two weeks after these inspections began, reads: "Although I have already stated this in my daily reports, I feel obliged to repeat it here: the working-class people who are regular customers of these cheap restaurants are showing very evident and clearly demonstrated approval of the creation of this new service."[6]

B. PUBLIC SALE

Near the poultry building in the centrally located Halles, or market—both before and after the construction of Baltard's cast-iron covered market complex in the 1850s—was a well-known section loved by customers and watched over by the police. Here every morning little zinc-lined carts would have their precious merchandise unloaded. This marked the end of a long journey through Paris, a tedious door-to-door trek from the major hotels to the famous restaurants, from government ministries to embassies, from fine dwellings to noble palaces. Their itineraries were not left to chance, for each cart went to specific addresses, often at a fixed time. The tradesman who accompanied them was known as the "jeweler," a title bestowed through either gratitude or derision. In a cellar reserved for him, the "jeweler" would sort the foods. And, by nine o'clock, dishes had been set out and decorated, to be sold for prices ranging from three to five sous circa 1860[7] and four to twelve sous at the very end of the century.[8] Pieces of meat, filet of game, fish heads and tails, cold cuts, desserts, cakes with only a few slices missing, and virtually intact bonbons were put on sale. And vegetables too. The cheapest platters had more vegetables than meat, which usually was stewed. More appealing were the six- to eight-sous mixed platters. But for ten to twelve sous one was better treated and could have attractively displayed poultry legs, a lobster claw, a filet of sole, a bit of pastry, and some pistachio custard. Or else a half a pig's food, with truffles alongside a slice of galantine, a breaded cutlet, and a fish head, crowned by a chocolate eclair. Or even—for there was an admirable variety of jewels available—sauerkraut keeping company with crayfish in Bordeaux wine, sautéed rabbit, calf's head, roebuck filet, and apple charlotte.[9] Imagine how exhausted the "jeweler" would be after arranging these plates and distributing the leftovers equally, in terms of price and ingredients, with a mind to the combination of colors, odors, and dimensions. But he had to satisfy his faithful customers, who ranged all the way from people working for starvation wages to women trembling with fever to minor clerks and on to housewives from lower-class neighborhoods.

These neighborhoods of the city, it is true, had similar local resources. In the markets spread throughout the city were stalls specializing partially or entirely in this strange trade. Frédéric Le Play pointed out the role that leftovers played in the working-class diet. Take, for example, the family living near the Place Maubert*—a ragpicker, his wife, and his daughter—with a total annual income of 631 francs 1 centime (roughly 4,500 francs, or $950, today), 457 of which went for food. Once a week during the four winter months his wife bought ready-cooked meat in the market of the quarter of Saint-Honoré, and throughout the year she purchased fat made of a blend of butter, drippings, pork fat, and poultry fat, all leftovers from middle-class kitchens. In order to purify this mixture and keep it for two weeks, her husband melted it down and added a little white salt.[10]

The reports of the Paris police refer without comment to daily seizures of merchandise in the markets along the outskirts of the city (in the region now incorporated into Paris proper and corresponding totally or partly to today's 12th, 13th, 14th, 15th, 16th, 17th, 18th, 19th, and 20th arrondissements). For items that were intact—a pike, ten whitings—but rotten or well on the way to being so, the hypothesis that these were discards can be rejected. But when it is a question of morsels—especially game—and luxury items to boot, we can well assume that these were leftovers. In the 17th arrondissement, at the market on the rue des Ternes, on 8 February 1862, the inspectors ordered the disposal of a duck and three pieces of roebuck; on 12 February, in the same arrondissement, but this time in stall twenty-five of the market at Clichy, three putrified pieces of roebuck were ordered destroyed.[11]

C. CLANDESTINE SALES

Whatever their state of conservation, these leftovers, or "jewels," were—if I dare use the term—first-hand leftovers from well-stocked tables. They passed from plate to plate, to use the language of the consumer, or, in economic parlance, from the producer (cooks, chefs, owners) to the second-hand dealers. The latter ran clearly marked shops along a street. But other people were interested in these leftovers: wholesalers selling second-hand (or second-table) food, who remained camouflaged on the outskirts of the market, the departure point of an amazing journey. The jewels remaining on the second-hand dealer's hands and already well on the way to being rotten were carted away for a few sous by unlicensed hucksters who put them back into circulation: bones with bits of meat that had now been gnawed off, contaminated fish bones, cake crumbs. This refuse went by the sobriquet of "harlequin," probably owing to its motley appearance. It remained on the spot as long as it lasted—usually a few days

---

*Before wide avenues were cut through the populous quarter surrounding the Place Maubert, during the Second Empire, the neighborhood housed one of the largest open markets of the city. Located in the southeastern quadrant of the city, the *place* lay at one end of a diagonal line through the old medieval heart of Paris, while the market in the Saint-Honoré quarter was at the other end. To make her purchases, the woman in question had to cross most of the city, presumably on foot.—Trans.

—tolerated, if not monitored, by the food inspectors, who, like all Parisians, knew about these sordid transactions. "Fish heads or cutlets, remains of legs of lamb, fragments of pastries, all mixed together pell-mell, soaked with twenty different gravies, already four or five days old and awaiting customers at a certain corner of the central market of the Halles. But there this refuse is at least under the eyes of the authorities, who order it removed from the counter before it is totally rotten."[12] But no one worried excessively on this score. This garbage did not go to waste. It found surreptitious buyers: disreputable peasants nicknamed "coal miners," who peddled it in the suburbs.

So now we have reached the third-hand stage of the trade in leftovers. The castoff waste thus illegally carried off was sold as chance and the all-pervasive poverty dictated. Exaggerating the value of his wares, the "coal miner" would offer some game. His merchandise was carefully wrapped, "in order not to attract the attention of the police," he would say. "Having vainly peddled for a week the game that was already spoiled when he bought it, he would get rid of it in the greasy spoons of the suburbs."[13] Deep down, he felt he had nothing to be ashamed of. Many of his colleagues obtained their wares from even less appetizing sources. During the Second Empire people were arrested who for years had been collecting the rotten fish that the sanitary services of the Halles had been throwing into the dump of La Villette.[14]

II. Fraud

Now I come to the supervision of grocery stores, caterers, and secondary markets and the confiscation of spoiled products—which at first glance seem very closely related to the practices I have just described. Actually, they are not the same at all. Although leftovers used in this loathsome traffic are indistinguishable from the rotten foodstuffs that caused the police to step in and halt such sales, the two are distinct from one another on three levels: hygiene, for leftovers could be healthful, while the fraudulent sale of foodstuffs involved solely rotten items; the economy, for fraudulent items moved through the regular market and were tallied by the customs agents when entering Paris as well as by the accountants at the Halles; and "mentalities," or ways of thinking, since leftovers are related to a specific frame of mind made up of a need to economize and a hankering for luxury. "Of late, two of these sidewalk gourmets nearly came to blows over a cutlet with Soubise sauce that, according to the shopkeeper, had been on the plate of the president of the republic himself."[15] And, after all, the fact that spoiled articles put on sale formed a part of the chain comprising the first-hand market made them subject to stricter surveillance than leftovers whose luxurious origins seemed to guarantee their respectability.

In January 1862 the police department of Paris inaugurated a system of food inspection independent from that which had long been in force in the central Halles and in the neighborhood markets. It was intended to check on the healthfulness of the products and the objects with which they came into contact (scales, copper utensils, pottery, and so forth) in the various food stores of Paris and, more specifically, in the twenty auxiliary markets of the former suburbs. After a slow start, the service was broken in rather rapidly, as seen by its reports, which soon became more concise and illuminating. Yet the modest means at the inspectors' disposal made verification difficult, despite the superficial and shaky optimism of the administration. And we remain uncertain about the nature of the items confiscated: were they leftovers or uncooked foods? Thus, the incomplete evidence at our disposal limits the extent of any research. We can only trace an outline of the sale of commodities that were rotten *before sale* compared with those that were sold for direct consumption, two, three, or even four times.

Shortly after its creation, the new agency drew up a list of the food stores in Paris (table 7.1), either because it thought this the logical way to begin or, perhaps, because it wished to show its efficiency. The list included over fourteen thousand businesses, not counting the stalls in the twenty auxiliary markets. The job of inspecting all these businesses was put in the hands of twenty inspectors, and no more, so it is not surprising that confiscations depended upon chance. Summarizing in March 1863 the work accomplished in February of that year, the director of the inspection services wrote: "The number of markets held and each requiring the presence of an inspector, combined with the already small number of employees making up our service, makes it impossible to visit each establishment more than once every two months."[16] Their pitiful harvest therefore comes as no surprise:

Friday, 20 February 1862, the inspection of victuals was made in the seven auxiliary markets of the 13th, 14th, 15th, 17th, 18th, and 20th arrondissements, and in the 1st, 3rd, 4th, 5th, and 6th arrondissements.

Confiscated and destroyed: 3rd arrondissement, no. 8, rue du Pont-aux-Choux, two rotten whitings; 5th arrondissement, no. 301, rue Saint-Jacques, four kilograms of pumpkin; no. 190, rue d'Enfer, one kilogram of pumpkin.

A few objections were made when our employees called at those businesses called *tables d'hôte,* but presentation of their orders removed all difficulties.[17]

A few months after its inauguration, this inspection service began to compile a monthly summary of its activities. In table 7.2 I have combined into one general table the types of businesses involved and the number of confiscations. A few pertinent facts can be discerned:

1. Of the 5,525 confiscations carried out in 1863, 4,386, or almost 80 percent of the total, occurred in three of the fourteen categories of shops: fruit stores, retail groceries, and markets. This can be explained by the perishability of the fruits, especially in summer; by the tendency of grocery stores to sell fraudulent merchandise during the nineteenth century (and indeed, in July four grocers were taken to court for such serious offenses as adulterating salt); and by the nature of the auxiliary markets, whose customers were the poor creatures of the close suburbs and the scarcely less well off inhabitants of the periphery of the city.

2. Other categories—pastry shops and fish stores—appear infrequently. This

Table 7.1—Number of Food Stores, Per Arrondissement and Per Category, 1862

Arrondissements	Caterers, Restaurant Owners	Pork Butchers	Food Store Keepers	Dairy Store Keepers	Grocers	Fruit Sellers	Pastry Shop Keepers	Poulterers	Total
1	565	35	164	118	131	112	31		1,156
2	277	35	25	95	115	105	23		675
3	365	79	7	120	178	178	41	22	875
4	224	70	39	132	169	134	49	28	845
5	210	38	5	129	165	157	27	14	745
6	291	30	13	99	179	78	45		725
7	109	30	6	87	158	110	26		534
8	116	14	9	75	100	78	29	8	443
9	165	44	59	157	158	152	32	22	767
10	267	40	9	107	161	127	33		763
11	274	37	35	147	205	137	25	19	866
12	259	34	32	96	215	52	19		687
13	189	24	17	54	151	73	8	5	521
14	285	31	6	86	184	109	12	1	714
15	238	25		34	144	101	9	4	555
16	145	16	2	34	88	56	16		357
17	190	33	31	92	147	101	25	8	627
18	455	50	18	130	283	155	19		1,110
19	285	39	5	111	172	85	15	3	715
20	189	38	3	71	147	84	21	11	564
Total	5,098	702	485	1,964	3,234	2,109	505	151	

Table 7.2—Confiscations according to the Various Categories of Food Stores, 1863

Month	Bakeries	Pork Butchers	Food Stores	Commission Merchants	Dairy Stores	Wholesale Grocers	Retail Grocers	Fruit Sellers	Stallkeepers in Markets	Itinerant Hucksters	Pastry Shops	Fishmongers	Caterers	Poulterers,	Game Suppliers	Cookshop Keepers	Total
Jan.	11	16	5	5	10	11	107	120	89	2	1	2	14	3		11	374
Feb.	11	33	13	11	4	1	63	88	69	4	11	1	10	3		11	289
Mar.	11	22	7	7	15	1	82	100	91	11	11	1	14	11		11	340
April	11	13	12	19	4	11	85	112	61	11	1	11	24	5		11	336
May	11	13	16	12	5	3	101	105	140	5	11	11	15	3		11	418
June	11	40	16	11	19	11	157	139	115	11	11	1	17		1		505
July	11	35	14	7	8	2	146	194	160	1	3	11	21	11			596
Aug.	11	66	22	27	11	1	122	138	312	4	3	1	39	11			738
Sept.	11	61	17	9	10	6	106	107	231	4	1	11	17				578
Oct.	11	46	20	12	10	2	121	198	158	1	1	2	21		4	5	601
Nov.	11	34	10	5	5	1	74	122	128	1	11	6	17		12	1	420
Dec.	11	29		8	9	3	83	87	75	8	11	1	16		7		330
Total	11	408	166	111	110	20	1,247	1,510	1,629	30	10	14	225	45		5,525

Source: Archives of the Prefecture of Police, File D ^{a} 179, notebooks 5, 6, and 7.

Note: Tallied together in June and from September through December in the records of the food inspectors, poulterers and cookshop keepers were considered separate categories from January through May. During those months the cookship keepers [who sold poultry as one of their roast meats] were cited more frequently for infractions than the poulterers; but in July-August the poulterers seem to have regained their leadership in the poultry trade.

is all the more unusual since fish (herrings, sardines, whitings) were among the leading victuals continually being discarded in the markets.

3. Only a very modest proportion were caterers. In view of the great number of restaurants in Paris and the countless complaints of the day about the rotten food they served, it is tempting to interpret this as a confirmation of the inefficiency of the surveillance.

4. The disparity in the number of confiscations cannot be explained by seasonal factors. Naturally, the percentage is lowest in February, a cold month, and highest in August, a hot month and the month with the highest number of infractions. But what about October, a temperate month, sometimes even cool, which is a close competitor of August for the accolade of most-putrid-month? The reply to this question can be found by comparing the list of visits made by the police and the list of disciplinary actions. In February, 120 inspections were made in the twenty arrondissements of the city. In only three of them (the 7th, the 16th, and the 20th) were three of the four quarters making up that arrondissement inspected. In August, 149 inspection rounds were made. In six arrondissements (the 1st, 7th, 8th, 12th, 15th, 16th) only three quarters were involved. Another eloquent detail: the visits were distributed unevenly. Twelve were made in the 1st arrondissement, with its many food businesses adjacent to the Halles; a total of 48 were made in six other arrondissements combined, 84 were spread over another twelve arrondissements, and 5 were made in the 4th arrondissement alone, one of the smallest in Paris. This distribution was at least relatively general and produced a rather high number of confiscations. In October there were 169 visits. Only three quarters were visited in the 4th arrondissement; only two quarters of the 1st arrondissement were visited, although 15 inspections were made. Apparently, despite the obstacles faced by the inspectors—the number of businesses, the distances separating them, and the limited personnel—the efforts nonetheless brought results, because the visits were spread about judiciously according to the specific problems of each arrondissement and of the various quarters making up each arrondissement.

The conclusions to be drawn from these data must remain tentative. The few products confiscated and destroyed would seem of little importance when compared with all the items eaten in Paris each year. But in reality they arouse suspicions about:

1. The existence of the parallel market that I discussed so briefly in the first part of this chapter and that certainly merits a patient and detailed study to reveal its exact extent;

2. Above all, the existence of what could be called *hazardous foods,* which interest both specialists in public health and historians of the Parisian poor, and hence of the economy. Among the roughly 1,200,000 Parisians during the Second Empire who theoretically ate their share of the food allocated them abstractly by official statistics, I have shown elsewhere[18] that between 300,000 and 400,000 of them ate well or decently and that the rest ate very poorly. Naturally it was the latter who ate the "ripe," decaying, or even rotten foods. Banned, along with a number of other subjects, from the usual scholarly studies, an analysis of the

inedible is a way—and one of the better ways—to study a civilization. Such an approach is essential for an understanding of nineteenth-century France.

NOTES

1. Archives of the Prefecture of Police of Paris [hereafter cited as A. P. P.], file $D\frac{a}{179}$, notebook 1.

2. Jean-Camille Fulbert-Dumonteil, *La France gourmande* (Paris: Librairie universelle, 1906), pp. 57-59.

3. Eugène Chavette, *Restaurateurs et restaurés* (Paris: Le Chevalier, 1967), pp. 38-39.

4. Emile Goudeau, *Paris qui consomme* (Paris, 1893), pp. 134-39.

5. A. P. P., file $D\frac{a}{179}$, notebook 1.

6. Ibid.

7. Emile Zola, *Le Ventre de Paris* (Paris: Garnier, Flammarion), p. 308.

8. Alfred Suzanne, *Art culinaire* (Paris, 1892), 10: 46.

9. Ibid.

10. Frédéric Le Play, *Les Ouvrier européens*, pt. 4, *Les Populations désorganisées* (Tours, 1878), 6: 264-66.

11. A. P. P., file $D\frac{a}{179}$, notebook 1.

12. Chavette *Restaurateurs et restaurés*, p. 110.

13. Ibid., p. 112.

14. Ibid., p. 113.

15. Suzanne, *Art culinaire*, 10: 47.

16. A. P. P., file $D\frac{a}{179}$, notebook 1.

17. Ibid.

18. Jean-Paul Aron, "Essai sur la sensibilité alimentaire à Paris au XIXe siècle," in *Cahiers des Annales* 25 (Paris: Armand Colin, 1967); and *Le Mangeur du XIXe siècle* (Paris: Laffont, 1973).

8
Water Supplies
in Nineteenth-Century
Nivernais

Guy Thuillier

Water pollution is not a recent phenomenon. Until the early twentieth century, and even later, virtually everyone used unhealthful water, and the medical and social consequences of water scarcity in both city and country were significant. It is, of course, difficult to write a history of water,[1] and few historians are tempted to write one, precisely because water is part of the "invisible aspects of daily life"[2] that leave so few traces. Moreover, such a history involves material living conditions, demography, and even mentalities. The "water revolution" was too diffuse to permit an easy grasp of its full dimensions.[3] Yet it should be possible, for a limited region, to make a rough sketch of water conditions during the *ancien régime* that preceded this revolution.

First of all, water was relatively scarce in Nivernais.* Indeed, although the water table in the Loire and Allier valleys is abundant and springs are numerous in the granite terrain of the Morvan, almost half the townships of Nivernais had only more or less rudimentary cisterns,[4] and a few had copious springs. Water in shallow wells[5] often became low in summer, and at times peasants had to go a half kilometer to fetch water. The daily burden of getting water was one of the age-old chores of rural life,[6] even in hamlets and market towns.[7] In the cities, both public and private wells were too few and they often ran dry in summer,[8] requiring extreme conservation of water.[9] In addition, the maintenance of wells and fountains was poor. In Saint-Benin-d'Azy,

Annales, E.S.C. 23 (January-February 1968): 49-68. Translated by Patricia M. Ranum.

*Nivernais (capital: Nevers) was one of the provinces of the Kingdom of France; after the Revolution of 1789 the region became known as the department of Nièvre. Even today both terms are used interchangeably.— Trans.

It is noteworthy that from time immemorial no public repairs have been made at the expense of the township, despite the sizable sums levied for that purpose. Of the twelve fountains used daily in a total of eleven villages, only one, Mongoublin, is in proper working condition and well kept up at the expense of citizen Saint-Phalle. Among the eleven others, some are dug out like square wells, some have basins, all are without well curbs and have no pulley of any sort. Sewers and gullies run into these wells, contaminating the water and filling it with sludge; . . . complaints are made that on occasion such things as garden produce and swaddling clothes have been washed in them.[10]

A half-century later, the subprefect of Clamecy noted that "in the various regions of the department of Nièvre, most public or private fountains and ponds are totally dry during the hottest days of summer. This unfortunate state of affairs results from lack of upkeep and cleansing; so the sludge accumulates to a considerable degree and noticeably decreases the amount of water they can hold. In a few of them up to two meters of sludge have built up; sometimes this sludge is, in addition, covered by a layer of muddy water that is unhealthy and undrinkable."[11] There was little to protect these fountains from animals or from also being used as watering troughs and laundry tubs.[12] Above all, the local people often used water contaminated by the many manure piles found in villages. "If only," declared a subprefect in 1832, "they would give up the pernicious habit of steeping their hemp in the same ponds or streams where they do their laundry and fetch their drinking water! If only they would become convinced that it is there that, in most instances, they catch the germs of illnesses whose cause seems unexplicable to them!"[13]

Second, drinking water was polluted in a thousand different ways. In cities and market towns, wells were contaminated by refuse, by seepage, and by excrement emptied into the garden. People slaughtering livestock at home, tripe merchants, tanneries, and factories threw their waste water into the street,[14] and most houses had no privies. At Nevers, the Nièvre River and certain streets had become a veritable sewer;[15] at Clamecy the water of the Yonne River was "saturated with lime sulfate"[16] and clouded by all kinds of organic matter from the logs that were floated down the river. During the early years of the century, only rich bourgeois had charcoal filters.[17] This widespread water pollution must be considered the source of the multitude of infectious illnesses and intermittent fevers that were endemic in Nivernais.[18] As early as the Napoleonic Empire, physicians specializing in epidemics all pointed out that their patients had nothing but the muddy water of ponds or marshes to drink. "Only unfortunate paupers, and especially those paupers whose dwellings are along the edges of a marsh, fall victim to these fevers," noted a physician at Fours.[19] Woodcutters, charcoal makers, raftsmen, harvesters, and blacksmiths were sapped by the fevers and dysentery provoked by this unhealthy water,[20] and by the intestinal parasites (roundworms and pinworms) that infected the streams and shallow wells.[21]

Third, since water frequently was scarce, it was used very sparingly, and personal hygiene was almost nonexistent in city and country alike. The man from the Morvan, a schoolteacher noted soberly in 1886, "washes his face a bit when he shaves, but the rest of his body has not felt a drop of water since the day he was born. Baths...are unknown in the Morvan. The only baths are those taken in the river, whose cold water is not always healthful. His feet and hands are filthy."[22] These traditions persisted until 1910 or 1920 in much of Nivernais.[23] Where there was little water, laundry was often a cursory process, and the women in poor families settled for soaking their linens in fountains or streams.[24] In town, doing the laundry was an expensive operation, for there were no public washhouses.[25] Traditions and superstitions complicated this task,[26] which usually was done two or three times a year. In addition, for lack of water, houses—even overcrowded ones—were not cleaned, further increasing the unhealthiness and fostering epidemics. The inquiry triggered by the cholera epidemic of 1849 is eloquent on this subject.[27] Religious communities, hospices, and secondary schools traditionally lacked water.[28] In 1852 the psychiatric asylum of La Charité could not carry on hydrotherapy because "water is lacking at the asylum, for its baths, its showers; in short, the water that is an indispensable item for treating the insane should be amply available."[29] It is difficult for us to account for this total absence of hygiene throughout the nineteenth century. Of course, the poverty of the inhabitants was one of the fundamental causes,[30] but even the well-off classes showed a general scorn for these conditions of material life.[31] This can partly explain the high mortality rate in city and country alike, and not enough stress can be placed upon the demographic consequences of this scarcity of water, which aggravated the already shaky physical health of the population.

This *ancien régime* of water lasted virtually unchanged until the beginning of the twentieth century. It is difficult to study the factors involved in the changes that eventually took place, for in this area changes in attitude and daily customs leave very little concrete evidence. Therefore, it is not easy to recreate the attitudes of the various social groups about a problem of this sort.[32]

First of all, physicians exerted some degree of pressure upon the authorities whenever epidemics occurred, and especially during the cholera epidemics of 1834, 1849, and 1884. As early as 1850 the departmental committee on public health denounced the unwholesome water, the prevalence of manure piles and private animal slaughtering, and the pollution of fountains and wells.[33] But its protests were not always heeded, for it was fighting both age-old practices and personal interest. In addition, medical theory was still uncertain on this point; intermittent fevers usually were attributed to the harmful fumes from stagnant water or to the direction of the wind,[34] and contagion from contaminated water was not yet acknowledged as the water-borne source of typhoid fever.[35] This position did not gain acceptance until the end of the century (1887), and then in Paris but not the provinces. The uncertainty shown by the medical profession, combined with the absence of any reliable way of making a chemical analysis of water prior to the 1880s, partially explains this general indifference.

Yet, on the other hand, as part of their customary tasks, administrators were obliged to check on the healthfulness of water, and the subprefects carried on very active campaigns to make sure that market towns and rural areas had suitable water supplies. In 1831 Delamarre, subprefect at Clamecy, deplored the absence of a government policy for water. "Many townships lack healthy and perfectly safe water; some even are totally deprived of it. The creation of artesian wells...would produce the most fortunate results in the townships." He even talked with the Flachat Company about drilling artesian wells, especially at the Maison Dieu [a hospital], which "already, following my suggestion, has allocated a sum of 10,000 francs."[36] Delamarre promoted the creation of a well that "should be equipped with pullies and iron chains," and the rebuilding of the fountains.[37] He wanted to have cemeteries moved out of town, marshes drained, and manure piles removed from doorways. In 1856 Marlière, another subprefect at Clamecy, tried to install pumps at the fountains, have the fountains scraped out, and construct public laundry tubs, latrines, and showers and baths at Clamecy. He proposed bringing spring water to that city. "It would suffice that all house owners be willing to subscribe for several years, for a company to take charge of this project immediately without its costing the township a thing."[38] Marlière had a hydraulic ram installed at Rix to bring water from the Beuvron, and at Anthien he had water conveyed via cast-iron pipes from a spring 500 meters away.[39] Thus, we see the important role played by these subprefects, who were trying to shake mayors out of their apathy and force them to make investments for the good of all (which aroused considerable resistance, for the local notables often refused to vote the necessary increases in the tax rate). Still, between 1840 and 1870 small townships made considerable efforts to construct fountains and covered laundry tubs[40] and to repair public wells. Indeed, such investments—very small ones, ranging from 200 to 2,000 francs—represented considerable progress,[41] although it is difficult for us to trace the true extent of that progress. But finances remained limited, and in the absence of subsidies, the only recourse was borrowing or subscriptions, which were distasteful to landowners. And so it took twenty or thirty years—and a change of mayor—to drill a well or build a fountain, for no systematic policy existed before 1890.[42]

Last, changing ideas played a part, at least in cities, where residents in bourgeois houses wanted an unlimited water supply, as in Paris. In 1823 Achille Dufaud wrote to his father from England: "We lack one major thing [back home]: water in the house. Here water provides an ease, a facility for servants, and marvelous cleanliness; with a compression pump and lead pipes, you could get the same effect, but the expense is necessary in order to live in comfort."[43] The bourgeoisie filtered their water and installed pumps in their homes.[44] Intercity rivalries played a part, for Nevers wanted water, like Moulins and like Paris. But in reality this frame of mind changed very slowly, for provincial life was in a rut and the city fathers overestimated the costs involved. Yet, investing in water companies became a profitable speculation, once the technical details of production and distribution had been worked out.[45] However, the mass of the population remained indifferent until the 1890s, through poverty, ignorance, or lack of concern.[46]

Pressure exerted by physicians, intervention by the government, and a change in mentality—it is difficult to determine the exact role of each of these different factors.[47] It seems that there was little interest in water "production" until the end of the century, as events at Nevers clearly show.

In 1827 Monsieur de Bouillé, mayor of Nevers, undertook to provide a water distribution system for the city. He planned to supply six hundred cubic meters of water from the Loire River, allowing ten liters per inhabitant and thirty liters per horse.[48] In actual fact, "for many years the colonels of the various regiments stationed one after the other at Nevers continually requested transfer, basing their demand upon the extreme difficulty they encountered in finding water for the soldiers and their horses."[49] Political concerns were reinforced by the desire to keep these regiments garrisoned at Nevers. The plan called for a twelve-horsepower steam engine that would pump the six hundred cubic meters to a reservoir holding six hundred and fifty cubic meters of water. This reservoir was to stand thirty-two meters above the Loire, so the water would be supplied to Nevers by gravity.[50] Installation was completed in 1830 at a cost of more than 250,000 francs.[51]

But the distribution system did not work perfectly. The steam pump located in the port of Médine functioned very erratically, and there were complaints about the smoke it emitted,[52] its inadequate power, and the cost of upkeep. Above all, distribution was only partial, for only hospices, the army barracks, and a few institutions were connected to it, while entire quarters of the city received no water. In 1842 it was decided that the network must be expanded and that twenty roadside fountains would be built. But a large part of the city, including the slaughterhouse, remained outside the network.[53] The number of private homes willing to be connected to the system was reduced as a result of the high cost: thirty francs a year for two hectoliters per day, with consumption computed on the basis of the probable amount used.[54] Hence, the fees paid by subscribers did not exceed 4,000 francs for 1857. And so for thirty years the inhabitants of Nevers had to be satisfied with water of a deplorable quality, muddy in winter, too hot in summer.[55] During periods of drought, the water reached the reservoir clouded by sand and mud.[56] Purification procedures were still rudimentary, and the water was pumped from a spot just three hundred meters downstream from the laundry raft and at the very spot where the Nièvre River, a veritable cloaca that served as a sewer for the entire lower city, flowed into the Loire.

Nonetheless the amount of water used by public services was increasing markedly. In 1851, 106,000 cubic meters were used, and in 1855, 151,000; yet the consumption per inhabitant was a mere twenty-eight liters per day,[57] although even in those days a minimum of fifty liters per inhabitant was deemed normal. True, the city had installed only twenty-three street fountains, and only ninety-seven buildings, both public and private, were connected to the system. "Production will soon be insufficient," wrote the mayor in 1857, "either because the steam engine is not powerful enough or because the water tower lacks sufficient capacity. It is also felt that the water should be filtered.... Interruptions in service are rather frequent, and their length is sometimes very distressing."[58] As early as 1849 there had been a plan to get water from the fountains of Veninges and Les Bouillons,[59] for spring water was considered superior to river water.[60] But no one knew how to calculate the exact amount produced by these springs, and Grillot de Passy, the engineer for the department of bridges and roads, was totally wrong about the amount produced by the springs of Veninges and Jeunot, which had to be brought to Nevers by aqueducts 3.8 and 7.9 kilometers long.[61] Once the work had begun, at a cost of 300,000 francs, and an onerous agreement had been signed with a concessionary company,[62] it became apparent that the springs could not supply even half the water needed. The city had to fall back on water from the Loire and pay an additional 150,000 francs to install a new steam engine capable of pumping eight hundred cubic meters a day. And so, until 1920 the inhabitants of the city had to be content with a mixture of water from the Loire River and spring water that was scarcely safer than before. For more than fifty years the water system of Nevers remained very archaic.

First of all, the city had many financial disputes with the concessionary company, headed by Girerd, lawyer and future deputy. Most of these disagreements involved interpretations of the clauses in the agreement.[63] The city was supposed to pay an annuity of 17,500 francs for fifty years in order to obtain an additional eight hundred cubic meters of water, and nine centimes for each additional cubic meter. Costs soon increased alarmingly. A commission was established in 1875 "to seek the causes for the constantly increasing water consumption." Of the total production of 670,000 cubic meters for 1872-73, 180,000 were "for no known uses."[64] The commission blamed permanent leaks, errors in calculating the amount of water pumped, and above all excessive use by consumers, whose unmetered allocation was two hundred cubic meters per day. Consumers used water heedlessly, and one industrialist billed for twenty-five hectoliters actually used eighty or even one hundred. Rates had been based upon faulty reasoning, for the consumer did not pay according to his true consumption but according to a flat rate. A hectoliter of water cost five francs for those customers who paid a fee of less than fifty francs, ten francs for those whose flat rate was between 500 and 1000 francs, and fifteen francs after that. Boarding schools, religious communities, and workshops had an estimated per capita consumption of ten liters a day, so a hectoliter of water cost ten francs—and ten liters was a very small allowance.[65] Under these circumstances, abuses were sure to occur. Two new commissions, one created in 1880 and another in 1885, proposed requiring meters for all major consumers and establishing a rate based upon the cubic meter,[66] but they encountered strong resistance. The Union of Commercial and Industrial Syndicates lodged a protest with the prefect about the water company's exorbitant demand, and the plan was never implemented.[67] Not until 1910 were consumers obliged to install water meters and to pay for water by the cubic meter.[68]

Second, increasing water needs brought many difficulties, and the water company, keeping to the letter of the agreement, obstinately refused to expand the distribution network. But although the amount of water used had climbed from 150,000 cubic meters in 1855 to 670,000 cubic meters in 1875, by 1906 it was still only 711,000 cubic meters. Until 1910 the Malthusian approach of the water company, which was making large profits,[69] aroused many protests. Numerous new quarters of the city received no water, and no water could be installed in the upper stories of houses. Since the sanitation department was short of water the streets were not washed down. In addition, the water pipes had to be turned off at night, which was potentially dangerous in the event of fire.[70] The sewers were in a wretched state for lack of water. Finally, in 1885, the departmental board of public health stated its opinion that "the slaughterhouse, sewers, public urinals, and a certain number of streets do not receive enough water. We cannot understand how Nevers, which is located along the banks of such a beautiful and limpid river, could be short of water."[71] Indeed, in 1886 a plan was drawn up for a new steam engine and an additional reservoir at Les Montapins, so that water could be installed in upper stories;[72] but for reasons that are not clear, this work, which would cost 168,000 francs, was never carried out, even though the city council had allocated the money. The inhabitants of the city therefore had to wait until the water concession expired in 1909. In short, for fifty years water consumption was prevented from increasing, despite an increase in the population, because the water company and the municipal government shirked their responsibilities. Deplorable sanitation was the result.

Third, until 1910 the quality of the water remained very unsatisfactory. Most important, the water from the fountains of Veninges and Jeunot lacked the desired purity. They were contaminated by manure from stables near the outlet of the springs and became very questionable during rainy spells. No protective measures were taken prior to 1908.[73] In addition, the new water intake, installed in 1860, was downstream from two gelatin factories, the laundry rafts, the sewers of Nevers, and the mouth of the Nièvre River, which was a gigantic sewer for several kilometers. "The liquid mass that forms the Nièvre is not really water but a dilution of all the most abject, the most nasty, the most rotten things possible, and consequently of the things most likely to provoke serious illnesses or at least multiply the germs of such illnesses." In short, continued Dr. Ranque in 1884, "if any municipal assembly had been so cruelly facetious as to offer a prize for the best solution to the proposal 'Try and find out what conditions and what means can provide the inhabitants of Nevers with the dirtiest, most impure, and truly the most disgusting water,' the creator of the current system would surely have won the prize, for it is impossible to find a more satisfactory solution to this paradoxical problem."[74] The gravity of the epidemics of typhoid fever made his statements perfectly justified, but despite the criticism of the board of health,[75] no modifications were made in the filtration system until 1924. True, the procedures for analyzing the bacteriological and chemical components of water were still rudimentary,[76] but the concessionary company seemed omnipotent. Hence, in 1910, scarcely 3,000 of Nevers's 27,000 inhabitants had water, and that water came from the Loire; it was of more than dubious quality and was not tested for bacteriological content.[77] The other inhabitants used three hundred and fifty wells, which all too frequently were contaminated by organic matter and were located near leaky septic tanks.[78] In 1912 the national board of health demanded an "improvement in the water supply" of Nevers, in order to reduce the death rate from typhoid.[79]

In 1909 the city assumed direct control of the water system, but the plan drawn up at that time was not fully completed until 1923. Eight filtering tanks of reinforced concrete were installed at the place called the "Solitary Poplar," upstream from the Nièvre River, but downstream from "a second Nièvre, a bypass canal whose water was more or less polluted,"[80] and also downstream from a gelatin and glue factory. But bacteriological texts existed by then, the legal snarls had been ironed out, and by 1927 consumption had increased to 1,400,000 cubic meters.[81] Twenty more years had to pass, however, before private wells were eliminated in certain parts of the city.[82]

The same slowness can be seen in the towns of Nivernais, doubtlessly due to the cost of the work but also to a certain widespread indifference that led to continual delay in carrying out plans. At Clamecy, where "the water question first came up fifty years ago," and where "typhoid fever is endemic and causes between five and ten deaths a year,"[83] it was decided in 1896 to bring water from the spring at La Fontainerie, some thirteen kilometers away, at a cost of 189,000 francs.[84] By 1888 La Charité had installed filtration tanks in the Loire River,[85] as Decize did in 1891 and Cosne in 1905. These tanks used the so-called "Marnier and Abraham process" of sterilization by ozone, which alone offered real security.[86] At Château-Chinon springs were tapped in 1856 to provide between sixty and one hundred cubic meters of water; in 1895 that amount was deemed insufficient, for the hospital had no water. "In certain quarters of the city water was only available at certain hours during the summer months. It was impossible to do the laundry at home. The streets were never washed down." It was decided to pump water from the Yonne River and at the same time to provide lights for the city with an electric power plant.[87] At Varzy, with its normal school, sanitation was deplorable. Not until 1898/99, and then only with difficulty, was water brought to the school in response to its threatened removal.[88] Other townships gradually developed public water supplies:[89] Saint-Révérien (1888), Sémelay (1898), Pouges-les-Eaux (1902); but despite the ravages of typhoid fever caused by contaminated wells, Fourchambault had no filtration tanks until 1925[90] and Saint-Pierre-le-Moutier had none until 1927.

True, water was expensive in small cities. At La Charité water "at the unmetered tap" cost between fifteen and thirty-five francs a year per household in 1908 and 0.18 centimes per cubic meter if metered. At Clamecy it cost thirty centimes, with a minimum charge of fifteen francs per year. Since this was a financial burden for modest households, the number of subscribers was small (150 at Decize, 140 at Clamecy, 100 at Cosne).[91] Paying for water had not yet become a part of life in 1914, and resistance to the spread of water-for-a-fee continued for many years in the market towns and countryside.[92]

But the water question determined the entire policy of making cities more healthy, a policy that for the first time had specific rules fixed by the law of 15 February 1902, which obliged cities to have sanitation laws. This law was complemented by various circulars about water pollution.[93] There were practically no adequate sewers, no sewage purification systems, no watertight septic tanks.[94] At Clamecy "there are many latrine holes in private homes, and their contents usually leech through the soil. Watertight tanks are rare. Part [of the night soil] is collected by the nightmen, who in most cases secretly throw it into the river." In Nevers proper, septic tanks were not illegal until 1918—illegal in principle, that is. "Their insufficiently purified run-off contaminates the sewers and spreads foul odors into the street through sewer grates."[95] In short, despite government control,[96] and despite the subsidies granted after 1902, efforts remained limited in the face of such great social or psychological resistance. In 1905 the labor inspector noted soberly that "owners and workers generally are equally indifferent to the care the body should receive. Few industries, even the dirtiest and most unhealthful, are equipped with clean, practical washbasins. Workers are almost never provided with soap and towels. No establishment in the department of Nièvre has as yet installed a bathroom, although several factories in a neighboring department have had excellent baths, showers, and washbasins for some years. We do not despair at being able to bring owners and workers to a better understanding of their dignity and their personal interest."[97] The influence of the school system—and of the army—upon actual practice remained minimal.[98] Depending upon the locality, it would take one or two generations before any changes would be noticeable, and until the 1930s the comfort of daily life seems to have lagged behind the rising income.[99]

It is somewhat difficult to grasp this *ancien régime* of water, for living conditions have changed so much in the past forty years.[100] Pure water long was a privilege of the few, and until the end of the nineteenth century physiological distress in large part resulted from an unsatisfactory water supply and the total absence of hygiene, which fostered epidemics. Before anyone can formulate a precise description of this *ancien régime* of water and explain the reasons for the time lag and the general apathy about this innovation that was changing daily living conditions, the archives of townships and of boards of health must be examined, the records of technical services must be studied, oral evidence must be taken down, a great many monographs must be written, and the points of view of physicians, sociologists, historians, engineers,[101] and even city planners must be collated. The task undoubtedly is a thankless one, but it would contribute to a better understanding of this important revolution.

NOTES

1. The work of the National Commission on Water has called attention to the importance of problems involving water, and especially water pollution. See the *Receuil des travaux de la Commission de l'eau*, July 1959-June 1963, 323 pages; and *Ve Plan* (1965), 2: 415-30, appendices. No history of water has been written for France, although technical, legal, and medical literature on the subject is quite abundant. Cf. Alphonse Debauve, *Distributions d'eau, Egouts*, 2 vols. (Paris, 1897); B. Buffet and R. Evrard, *L'Eau à travers les âges* (Liège, 1951); and P. Gille, "L'Eau," in *Histoire des techniques* (1964), vol. 2. On legal questions, cf. Edouard Copper-Royer, *Des sociétés de distribution d'eau* (Paris, 1896).

2. Paul Leuilliot, "Défense et illustration de l'Histoire locale," preface to my *Aspects de l'économie nivernaise au XIXe siècle* (Paris, 1966); English translation in Robert Forster and Orest Ranum, eds., *Rural Society in France, Selections from the Annales, E.S.C.* (Baltimore, 1977), pp. 6-30.

3. The psychological aspects of this revolution have not been studied, doubtlessly because it is too recent. Even literary evidence is scarce, with the exception of Jules Renard's works.

4. In 1930, 131 out of 163 townships had springs, wells, and cisterns. On the geological structure of the region, see *Annuaire statistique et descriptif des distributions d'eau,* 3rd ed. (1931), 1: 651. Roger Dion, *Le Val de Loire* (Tours, 1934), was not interested in the question of the "consumption" of the water of the Loire, which posed multiple problems, even at Nantes; cf. the typewritten "Historique du service des eaux de Nantes," (1945).

5. We have no information about well construction. In the nineteenth century there was a tendency to replace "the wooden frame holding the wheel with iron supports that were more durable and solid," and to replace ropes with iron chains. The curbs were raised and the wells were covered.

6. In winter the problem of ice came up. Thus, during the winter of 1788, "the major rivers froze to a depth of five and even six feet...; man and beast could not... find enough water to quench their thirst," Guillaume Paillard, parish priest at Ourouer, quoted by Carré, *Mémoires de la Société académique du Nivernais* (1919), p. 72.

7. They went to fetch water with barrels or carts. The water of the Loire was often preferred over well water, and people went quite far to get it. Thus, in 1859, the mayor of Pouilly stated that "even in summer a good number of his constituency goes to fetch water at the Loire each day...; that those who live rather far away have it placed in earthenware urns and keep it in a cool place." Note that in order to carry the pails or buckets, they used barrel hoops, "which they hold with both hands or lean against the handles, or else they use *courges,* that is, sticks with straps, which they lay over their shoulders." Jean Drouillet, *Folklore nivernais* (1961), 2: 60-61. The pails were made of wood, leather, tin, or pewter, and less frequently copper. In the eighteenth century the firemen of Nevers used willow pails "lined with leather and tarred inside."

8. Nevers had thirteen public wells, Clamecy had five; cf. Louis Gueneau, *L'Organisation du travail à Nevers au XVIIe et au XVIIIe siècles* (Paris, 1919), pp. 8-9; and V. Gueneau, "Recherches sur les rues de Nevers," *Mémoires de la Société académique du Nivernais* (1927-29). Not until the Restoration were a number of pumps provided; by year X [1802] Clamecy was requesting a pump on the public well (Archives départementales of Nièvre, series O, Clamecy. [Archives départementales will be cited hereafter as A.D., Nièvre]).

9. Inventories after death refer to "water pots," pottery wall-fountains with their basins, jars or pots in earthenware or terra cotta—known by the names *coquasse* or *coquassons* in the Morvan—and *casses,* which were copper recipients for dipping water from pails; cf. Drouillet, *Folklore nivernais.*

10. Town council, 28 December 1800. We would need many more samples from the records of town councils in order to trace the situation for fountains and public wells; cf., as examples, Alfred Massé, *Le Canton de Pouges* (Nevers, 1912), and *Le Canton de Nevers* (Nevers, 1913), passim.

11. A. Marlière, *Département de la Nièvre, Statistique de l'arrondissement de Clamecy* (Clamecy, 1859), p. 121. Elsewhere there were covered fountains, as in Corvol-l'Orgueilleux, which "presented the inconvenience of being low, lacking ventilation, and retaining the water, which became stagnant and caused the paving stones to heave," Delamarre, *Statistique de l'arrondissement de Clamecy* (1832), p. 53.

12. Women dipped dirty pails into the fountain or built dams nearby in order to dam up the water and do their laundry, causing the dirty water to run back into the fountain; cf. Dr. Fichot's report of 15 May 1888, *Conseil d'hygiène* (1889).

13. Delamarre, *Statistique de Clamecy,* p. 33. About the many manure piles in each and every village, see the inquiry into unhealthy living quarters conducted in 1883, A.D., Nièvre, series M.

14. On the unhealthfulness of Nevers during the eighteenth century, see Gueneau, *L'Organization du travail,* pp. 8-9, and during the nineteenth century the *Rapports du Comité départemental d'hygiène.* The annual reports and related papers submitted by this departmentwide board, created in 1850, are in A.D., Nièvre, series M.

The reports about epidemics of typhoid fever by Dr. Fichot, physician in charge of epidemics, enable us to glimpse the deplorable situation in certain towns at the end of the century. At Moulins-Engilbert, in 1889, the Coulon spring was "covered by a small courtyard that contains a manure pile, a stable, a pigsty, and privies," and the river also was contaminated by latrines. "As soon as the first hot weather arrives and water becomes scarce, fecal matter forms a black pulp that gives off a noxious odor and surely mingles with the water in a number of wells" (*Conseil* [1889], pp. 15-22). At Fourchambault, the well in a workers' barracks housing 250 people was contaminated by seepage from the nearby privies, piles of garbage, and manure from the numerous rabbit hutches (*Conseil* [1894], p. 75). At Saint-Saulge, the Fontaine d'Argent, which supplied the town's water, was polluted by privies (*Conseil* [1893], p. 28). In villages the situation was even worse.

15. See below, note 74.

16. "In such a sizable proportion that they interfere with the digestive process," Marlière, *Statistique de Clamecy,* p. 138.

17. Very little is known about filters, which seem to have been rather widely used by the bourgeoisie. In 1808 it was noted that Dufaud the elder, director of the postal system, "has available a stock of fountains with charcoal filters made by Messieurs Cuchet and Ducommun. These wall-fountains have the double property of abundantly clarifying cloudy and silty water and of purifying fetid and rotten water" (*Annuaire de la Nièvre pour 1808*). But the muddy water of the Loire often was difficult to filter; in 1859 Jules Hochet asserted that he had never "been able to obtain, even with the best filters, the clear water necessary for his table" (*Notice sur une déviation des eaux de la Loire pour l'alimentation de la ville de Paris... présentée par MM. E. Girard et Robin-Duvernet, concessionaires des eaux de Nevers* [1859], p. 18 [to be found at the Bibliothèque nationale in Paris, call number V 14916]).

18. Cf. my "Problèmes médico-sociaux," *Aspects de l'économie nivernaise.*

19. Archives nationales, Paris [hereafter cited as A.N.], F⁸ 64; and A.D., Nièvre, series M, epidemics, 1800-1830.

20. Cf. Thomas, *Annuaire statistique, administratif et commerical du département...* (1829), pp. 36 ff.; and the inquiry of 1848 on agricultural and industrial labor, in my *Aspects de l'économie nivernaise,* pp. 515-23.

21. Cf. Dr. Fichot, *Les Causeries du Dʳ Fichot...* (Nevers, 1882?), p. 70; and Dr. Mallet, "Aperçu de l'état sanitaire d'il y a soixante ans," *Journal du Centre,* 27 January 1964.

22. Simon, *Statistique de Frétoy* (1889), p. 180.

23. According to Romain Baron, describing the village of Marcy, circa 1910. Note that Ernest de Toytot, *L'Ouvrier d'Imphy* (1886), pointed out that "taking cold baths in the Loire is common." A swimming school was created at Nevers in 1846, *Union libérale,* 17 June 1846.

24. They still used ashes—and soapwort; cf. Ernest Le Play, "Monographie du fondeur de Vandenesse," *Ouvriers européens* (1865). Soap was relatively expensive. The washing was done in tubs; laundry boilers only appeared at a late date, toward the end of the Second Empire: "Housewives! Clean laundry—done at home, in two hours, at half the cost, by using the circulating sudser.... Easy to use, fits on any range—four sizes, 12, 20, 36, and 65 francs" (*Impartial du Centre,* 10 May 1869).

25. At Clamecy, circa 1858, women went to the common laundry tubs, which "almost always charged a rather high fee and where, since items were air-dried, the procedure was so slow that it did not meet the urgent needs of the poor to get their items quickly, since they usually had a small quantity" (Marlière, *Statistique de Clamecy,* pp. 120-21).

26. It was forbidden to do the laundry between the "two Christmases," that is, from Christmas to the feast of the Purification [2 February], during Holy Week, during the entire month of May, and so forth. No laundry was done and no sheets were changed, for if one were to become sick, one would die in those very sheets; cf. Drouillet, *Folklore nivernais,* 2: 67-69, and S. Commeau, "Folklore de la région de Fours," *Mémoires de la Société académique du Nivernais* (1928), pp. 65-66. When the linens of a dead person were laundered, notes Commeau, "all the inhabitants of the village had to add a piece of personal linen, so that the dead person's soul would be peaceful in heaven."

27. *Rapport fait au Comité Central d'Hygiène et de salubrité publique... sur l'épidemie de choléra asiatique qui a régné dans ce département pendant l'année 1849 par MM. Senelle, Robert Saint-Cyr et Leblanc-Bellevaux* (1851), 131 pp, available at the library of Nevers, call number NM 1046/3.

28. No study has been made of the hygiene in these institutions.

29. *Conseil général* (1852), p. 97 [reports of the General Council of the department of Nièvre]. In 1866 an inspector general was still inveighing against the inadequate water supply (*Conseil général* [1866], p. 130). Incidentally, at Nevers there was an office for "electrohydrotherapy" in 1859.

30. Everyone was aware of this. Thus, Heulhard d'Arcy, the physician in charge of epidemics at Clamecy, wrote about a hamlet near Corbigny with absolutely no water, whose inhabitants "are of a dirtiness that has become proverbial in the region." "Making the countryside more healthful is the goal the authorities should set for themselves; when roads are created to make it accessible, an easier life will be born and, with it, the hygienic precautions necessary for the preservation of health. In vain do physicians prescribe sobriety, cleanliness, and so forth... to people who are unanimously illiterate; they will be talking to the deaf until the inhabitants of this countryside leave behind that almost barbarous state in which they now squat" (10 February 1834, A.D., Nièvre, series M). In a like vein, Dr. Fichot wrote in 1882, "In our countryside the question of money will prove a long-term obstacle. Poverty is still very great there. In general it is a silent poverty. The poor man eats his black bread and often drinks impure water without complaining.... When poverty is less great, in the countryside, epidemics will be less dangerous and less frequent" (*Les Causeries du Dʳ Fichot,* p. 125). Questions of cleanliness and income cannot be separated.

31. For example, we have only to recall the absence of dental hygiene. When plans were being

made to install water at Nevers, the *Chronique* of 9 June 1827 insinuated that "our ladies could hope to keep their tooth enamel longer." Cf also Auguste Doudard, *De l'eau, du vin et du pain, au point de vue de la santé publique par M. Bourdard, pharmacien et médecin, inspecteur des pharmacies . . .* (Nevers, 1862), p. 12, on women's failure to shampoo their hair. (The trade of hair shampooer did not exist until the 1880s.)

32. Here is a simple example. To make their bread dough, bakers used well water, which often was contaminated. During baking, the center of the loaf never rises above the boiling point. In Paris, bakers had to be forbidden to use well water; it is almost impossible to determine the date when such a change occurred in the provinces, although the *Instruction contre la fièvre typhoïde* (1890) reiterated for bakers the prohibition about using well water (*Rapports du Conseil d'hygiène* [1890], p. 155).

33. Annual reports of the *Comité d'hygiène* (see note 14), and A.D., Nièvre, series M.

34. Vincellet, *Réflexions sur les fièvres intermittentes* (1826).

35. Once again, in 1893, Dr. Fichot, physician in charge of epidemics, maintained that typhoid fever was spread not only through drinking water but also on the air, "although for the moment this view is not accepted." Cf. *Conseils d'hygiène et de salubrité, Procès-verbal des délibérations* (1893-94 and 1895), p. 56.

36. The Flachat Company charged 800 francs for transporting the teams of workers, 35 francs for each eleven-hour working day to a depth of 300 feet, 32 francs for each ten-hour night, and so forth, plus a bonus of thirty percent of the total expenditures if a flow of 100 cubic meters was obtained (Delamarre, *Statistique de Clamecy,* p. 31). Concerning this corporation created by Stéphane and Jules Flachat, engineers and disciples of Saint-Simon, see *Entreprise de sondages de MM. Flachat frères and Cie . . . pour les recherches d'eaux souterraines et de mines* (1829); and *Bulletin de la Société nationale d'Encouragement* (February 1829), pp. 58-72. We must remember that among the major projects advocated by the *Globe* (8 March 1832) were "the establishment of a system of water distribution and a sewer system, as required for public health in all the major cities of France."

37. At Metz-le-Comte the inhabitants "are obliged to go half a league to draw water to drink; a well would be useful and easy to drill in the middle of the square." Delamarre also wanted to drain a swamp whose exhalations in summer were bound to be unhealthy and certainly caused the epidemic illness that abounded in that hamlet each year, and so forth. He studied the situation in village after village.

38. Especially along the river ports and in certain quarters; he judged "this measure all the more useful since most houses located in the suburbs and lower streets lack privies." The situation has not changed all that much today.

39. This was an old plan, already proposed by Delamarre in 1832, that involved bringing water from the fountain of Creux via a five-kilometer-long aquaduct. The cost would be 75,000 francs. Nothing was done for fifty years. See below, p. 116.

40. Covered laundry tubs were quite helpful, especially for "women whose main income comes from going as dayworkers to do laundry and who consequently wash almost every day and work from dawn to dusk in all sorts of weather. Sometimes in winter their work days were agonizing" (Daniel Halévy, *Visites au paysans du Centre* [Paris, 1921], p. 34).

41. On this undertaking, see A.D., Nièvre, series O, and the monographs by Massé, *Le Canton de Pouges* and *Le Canton de Nevers*. These very dispersed but substantial investments influenced economic activity, especially during the Second Empire, when they became more numerous. At times, projects were undertaken in order to provide work for the poor, as at Magny in 1831 (Massé, *Le Canton de Nevers,* p. 371).

42. For example, many villages still had cemeteries that provoked seepage into water fountains and wells. At Saint-Parize-le-Châtel the cemetery was located on unstable, permeable soil and "directly overlooked the laundry tubs and a fountain" several meters below (*Conseil* [1890], p. 114). At Tamnay, "the way the cemetery was placed acted as a veritable filter, for the liquids produced by the decomposing bodies . . . ran through a part of the town and in summer slowly drained, open to the air and the sun, into the river at the place used for watering animals and doing the laundry" (*Conseil* [1891], p. 73). Since 1878 the board of health had made no headway with the town council!

43. Letter by Dufaud, 19 June 1823, in the archives of Monsieur Dezautières.

44. After 1840 plumber-coppersmiths began to appear on the scene and undertook to install sanitary facilities. Thus, Thoulet installed "lead water pipes and everything associated with them, a pump, and odorless waterclosets, all guaranteed for a year" (*Almanach de la Nièvre pour 1846*), p. 230). Indeed, we have little information about the pumps being used (compression pumps, with lubricating cups), about their cost (at Poiseux it ran to 358 francs a year) and manufacture, and how their use spread.

45. At Nevers, the pipes originally were made of lead and later of cast iron with lead joints, then of

iron cast by the Chameroy system, and after 1914 of steel. Cf. *Procès-verbal de reprise du service des eaux...* (1909), A.D., Nièvre, series O. The factories of Torteron made the water pipes for the city of Paris during the Napoleonic Empire.

46. There was such indifference that, as the board of health observed on several occasions, the wells of recently constructed schools (after 1880) often had only bad water, and the pupils frequently came down with typhoid fever. At La Brosse, near Donzy, the school pump was located "at the place where all the rain water running down from the village converges and becomes stagnant after having filled the laundry ponds and seeped through manure piles, absorbing along the way harmful germs from the excrement of the ill" (*Conseil* [1893], p. 69). At Saint-Benin-des-Bois the township's well water was contaminated by seepage from the nearby latrines of the new school (*Conseil* [1894], p. 166). And on and on. Only after 1893 was it obligatory to consult the departmental boards of health about the construction of new schools. Also, in elementary schools, "the children drink a great deal of water during the hot spells of summer; the water they drink frequently is too cold; on other occasions it has remained standing in the classroom in a covered black pail" (*Conseil* [1884], p. 85). Hygiene in schools remained primitive for a long time.

47. No history of water distribution in cities has as yet been written for the nineteenth century; but the problem was a major one. Virtually all we possess are theses by pharmacy students or technical brochures; for Lille, see Pierre Pierrard, *La Vie ouvrière à Lille sous le Second Empire* (Paris, 1965), pp. 38, 54.

48. Cf. De Bouillé, *Observations au Conseil municipal de Nevers sur la possibilité d'établir des fontaines publiques en cette ville* (Nevers, 7 February 1828). Bouillé estimated the installation costs at 140,000 francs. "At first glance this project may seem gigantic, I agree, and the expenditures involved may be frightening," but the advantages were considerable, "from the viewpoint of healthfulness, especially during summer heat, of convenience, of the cleanliness of the streets, which can only be achieved with water, and of the help provided by fountains in the event of fire." In reality, Bouillé wanted to win popularity before the elections; cf. *Revue des candidats au collège électoral de Nevers* (n.d.), and *Chronique*, no. 24, 9 June 1827.

49. Bouillé calculated that this garrison "provides a sure outlet for farm products from the vicinity of Nevers, spends a sum of 300,000 francs a year in the city, and produces revenues of about 24,000 francs at the customs gates," which more than justified the expense of installing the steam pump.

50. Since the initial bid was for an eight-horsepower steam engine, the costs rose by an additional 100,000 francs, which provoked a series of disputes between the city and La Pique, Hornsteiner, Wagnien, and Company, the successful bidder for the project. After 1830 the new mayor refused to pay the additional costs authorized by Bouillé, who had supported the recently deposed king. Wagnien and Company asked authorization from the Council of State to sue Bouillé in order to make sure that the work would be paid for, but this request was rejected on 3 May 1832. The city had to pay 84,422 francs to Wagnien, but the city accountant opposed payment and even demanded the opinion of the *procureur général* at the Cour des Comptes. (The files for these quarrels are in A.D., Nièvre, series O, Nevers, 5, and A.N., F³ II, Nièvre, 12.)

51. In a letter of 15 January 1829, E. Martin had thought it absurd to pump the total 600 cubic meters up to the reservoir of the water tower, thereby needlessly increasing the water pressure and the amount of pipe to be laid. In June 1826 Dufaud had inspected in London a 120-horsepower steam engine, "placed next to the business of Messers Crawshay and pumping water from the Thames and sending it to the various parts of London supplied by the company. This machine pumps and forces through its pipes 12,000 liters of water per minute.... What is remarkable about it is that the main piston is reversed, that is, the principal effort is underneath instead of above."

52. Georges Dufaud proposed to Monsieur de Bouillé, who was complaining about "the harm that the smoke of the steam pump would do to houses along the quay" of the Loire, that he would establish at his own expense "a system of boilers that would emit no smoke," on condition that he be supplied with fuel "on the same footing as the system now in effect." The plan was never carried out (*Journal,* 7 March 1830).

53. In 1857 the network comprised 4,085 meters of pipe (970 meters of cast-iron pipe with a diameter of 13.5 centimeters, 2,330 meters of pipe with a diameter of 7.5 centimeters, 260 meters of four-centimeter pipe, and 535 meters of three-centimeter lead pipe). There were only twenty-four street-fountains. Cf. *Extrait du rapport de M. Adolphe Boucaumont, ingénieur en chef des chemins du Centre et de M. de Passy, ingénieur du service hydraulique sur le projet d'alimentation de la ville de Nevers par les sources de Veninges et de Jeunot* (1857), pp. 15-20.

54. The subscription was supposed to be for a minimum of two hectoliters per day. Cf. *Conditions projetées des abonnements temporaires et des concessions à perpétuité d'eau de Loire provenant du Château d'eau...* (1828); and "Etablissement de fontaines publiques dans la ville de Nevers," *Almanach*

de la Nièvre (1829), p. 124, and (1830), pp. 228-32.

55. In 1850 the departmental board of health denounced the muddy, turbid water, which contained a multitude of foreign bodies (*Rapport général fait par la Comité Central d'Hygiène et de salubrité publique, 1848-50* [1851], p. 16.

56. The water intake was "adjacent to a sand bar, which separated it so completely from the river that a channel had to be dug at great expense for almost 150 meters in order to send the water over the purification tank" (A. Coupechoux, "L'Eau d'alimentation à Nevers," thesis, University of Montpellier, 1904, p. 17). In addition, the openings of this tank "became plugged every time the Loire flooded, and the tank soon became filled with mud and silt, which finally blocked all connections with the sump; hence the need to scrape it out frequently and the resulting interruption in service." Also, the odor of the water "became disagreeable and its taste repulsive whenever the tank was full of sediment."

57. Between 60 and 65 liters per day at Grenoble, 50 at Montpellier, Clermont, and Auxerre. True, these figures are meaningless, since only a small part of the population was connected to the network.

58. Letter of 3 June 1857, A.D., Nièvre, series O. Actually, since 1851 the city had leased its steam pump to the central railroad company, which agreed to sell all the water needed (up to 500 cubic meters) at a rate of nine centimes per cubic meter; hence, the city had paid 9,540 francs in 1851 and 13,590 francs in 1855.

59. See *Extrait du rapport de M. Adolphe Boucaumont.*

60. It so happens that Girard and Robin-Duvernet, the very same company that had sought and obtained the concession for the fountains of Veninges and Jeunot, proposed to the government that it divert 100,000 cubic meters of water from the Loire to supply Paris. It boasted of the superiority of the water of that river and provided a quantity of testimonials and certificates. This project, worked out by Grillot de Passy, who was in charge of the hydraulic services of the department of Nièvre, was submitted to the emperor and the board for bridges and rivers. See *Notice sur une déviation des eaux;* and *Constitutionnel,* 10 October 1859.

61. The debate over spring water versus river water was of long standing. In his *Albert Savarus,* Honoré de Balzac made fun of such projects: "Rebuilding the Roman aquaduct in order to drink the water the Romans drank in a city along the Doubs River is one of those foolish ideas that only catch on in the provinces, where the most exemplary seriousness reigns. If this fantasy were to become rooted in the hearts of the inhabitants of Besançon, it would require huge expenditures, and these expenditures would make money for the influential man. Albert Savarus de Savaron decided that the Doubs was only good for flowing under suspension bridges and that the only drinkable water came from the Arcier River."

62. See A.D., Nièvre, series O, Nevers, 5; and Coupechoux, "L'Eau d'alimentation à Nevers." For the protests at Nevers about spring water, see Boudard, *De l'eau, du vin et du pain.*

63. See *Ville de Nevers. Fontaines publiques. Traité du 8 janvier 1869* (Nevers, 1887).

64. See *Ville de Nevers. Service des Eaux. Rapport de la Commission* (Nevers, 1875), 50 pp., Bibliothèque nationale, call number Lk 18 2116. In 1872-73 the springs produced 494,000 cubic meters and the Loire supplied 175,000 cubic meters. For fountains and sewers the city used 1,175 cubic meters per day during the summer and 839 in winter, or a total of 375,000 cubic meters. The amount used by customers was estimated at 200 cubic meters each, or 73,000 cubic meters in all, eleven percent of all water used. Public institutions, which received water free of charge, used 165 cubic meters per day, or 60,000 cubic meters per year.

65. According to the rates set on 31 May 1857—in effect until 1909—daily consumption was estimated at two hectoliters per household, plus 0.04 hectoliters per luxury or traveling vehicle, and 0.60 hectoliters for gardens under 400 square meters in size. Bathhouses and breweries paid for 25 hectoliters, pottery works and hotels were charged for 10 hectoliters, inns and laundries for 6 hectoliters, and bakeries and cafés for 4 hectoliters. These amounts seem to have been purely theoretical ones (A.D., Nièvre, series O).

66. See the report of the water commission, 11 June 1885, A.D., Nièvre, series O; and J. Ramond, *Rapport de la Commission des Eaux lu au Conseil municipal le 2 août 1886* (Nevers, 1886), 12 pp. The debates of 10 and 11 June 1885 establishing the rates came under attack from members of the opposition party on the city council and the matter became a purely political issue.

67. Letter of 18 March 1886, asking the prefect to withhold approval of the decision: "The water company wants to force water meters upon consumers, and even make them pay for their installation; moreover, the amount charged for these meters is far in excess of their worth" (A.D., Nièvre, series O). Besides, it was no easy matter to install meters, owing to the very low pressure in many parts of the city.

68. *Ville de Nevers. Distribution publique d'eau potable. Règlement et tarif* (1909). Water sold for thirty centimes per cubic meter at the metered tap. But this regulation of 1 December 1909 maintained the unmetered concedssions already existing. According to article 3, meters were to be of a type approved by the city of Paris, for Nevers chose the "meters with an oscillating disk." We know that the choice of meters was the subject of lively polemics. See, for example, E. Mathieu, *La Question municipale des compteurs d'eau à Reims* (Reims, 1911).

69. In 1906 the dividend was forty francs for each five-hundred-franc share. I have been unable to find the records of this company, whose history merits study.

70. See A.D., Nièvre, series O, Nevers, 5.

71. Report by Dr. Fichot, *Rapport du Comité d'hygiène* (1884), p. 65. The board called for the installation of a second steam engine beyond the connecting canal (ibid. [1892], p. 22).

72. Cf. Ramond, *Rapport de la Commission des Eaux,* and the reports that the departmental engineer submitted to the prefect on 9 November 1886, A.D., Nièvre, series O, Nevers.

73. See Coupechoux, "L'Eau d'alimentation à Nevers."

74. *Mémoire sur l'insalubrité des eaux alimentaires de la ville de Nevers par le D' Ranque* (1884). On pages 11-16 of this memorandum, Ranque drew an impressionistic picture of the filth of the Nièvre River, into which the latrines of the lower city directly poured their contents. The board of health had on several occasions asked that these latrines be suppressed. The old port of Médine, wrote Ranque, "now is nothing more than a stinking mudhole, a foul marsh whose mud emerges virtually throughout the year and reveals here and there glimpses of the most filthy debris: kitchen garbage, animal cadavers, putrid things of all sorts, to say nothing of the privies overhanging it." The situation in these unhealthy parts of the city seems to have remained virtually unchanged until the 1930s.

75. Typhoid fever was endemic in Nevers. The reports by physicians in charge of epidemics submitted to the board of health are eloquent on this subject: for example, *Rapport* (1893), pp. 42, 54, 56. There was also the problem of disposing of the city's night soil (10,000 tons in 1886), which was poured into leaky ditches that "produced in the soil seepage liable to mingle with the underground water table that feeds adjacent wells, and perhaps even the well of the water company" (*Rapport du Conseil* [1886], pp. 45-46). And there was the problem of the sewers of Nevers and the very significant report on Fichot's inquiry (*Rapports du Conseil* [1862], pp. 21-26, and (1884), pp. 65 ff).

76. See *Rapport du Conseil* (1884), p. 99, and Coupechoux, "L'Eau d'alimentation à Nevers." We must not forget that the water-borne origin of typhoid fever was not announced by Brouardel until 1887.

77. There were 4 fountains, 74 street-fountains, 18 storm drains, 40 fire hydrants, 2 public wells, and 350 private wells. In reality, there were only 1,300 private customers out of a total of 3,620 houses in the city. The average total consumption was 1,949 cubic meters per day in 1906. See Dr. Edouard Imbeaux, *Annuaire statistique et descriptif de la distribution d'eau de France,* 2nd ed. (1909), pp. 483-85.

78. Until 1911 water came from three very polluted springs within the city. Privies usually were not watertight.

79. "The water supply," ran the report, "is insufficient both in quantity and quality—for the spring water is bad. A plan is being prepared. The sewers are inadequate; the network is very incomplete. Untreated waste water is poured into the Nièvre and the Loire" (28 November 1912, A.N., F⁸ 220).

80. Dr. O. Simonot, "Rapport sur divers projets de captage d'eau d'alimentation de la ville de Nevers," 15 May 1909, 17-page manuscript in the library of Nevers, call number 2 N 858; and Dienert, *Rapport présenté à la municipalité sur la captation des eaux de la Loire . . .* (1911).

81. See *Annuaire statistique et descriptif des distributions d'eau,* 3rd ed. (1921), 1: 650-51; and A.D., Nièvre, series O.

82. There is no recent study of the latest developments in the water system of the city, administered by the S.A.D.E. [Société anonyme de la distribution d'eau]. After having stagnated for twenty years, production rose from 1,800,000 cubic meters in 1959 to 2,000,000 in 1961 and 2,500,000 in 1964. This sharp increase reflects new water sources put into use in 1960 and improvements to the pumping system made in 1964.

83. Jacquot's report to the advisory board of health, 7 January 1895, A. N., F⁸ 199. At the time the city had 14 public wells and 100 private ones, and the population even went to the Yonne or the Nivernais canal to fetch water, although privies and the city's garbage were emptied into that water.

84. In 1881 the general water company had proposed pumping the water from the Yonne and the Beuvron at a cost of 150,000 francs, but the plan had seemed too costly. The work done in 1896 cost more than that.

85. The sample taken from the Loire was "of dubious quality. The results of the biological analysis . . . show that microbes are passing through the sand, despite the thick layer of filtering

material" (A.N., F^8 199, 1888). But the advisory board did not oppose the plan. In 1907 1,000 cubic meters were used in summer and 600 in winter.

86. See E. Sancenot, *Notice sur la distribution d'eau de Cosne* (Cosne, 1906). Sterilization by ozone was an innovation. The Marnier process had been used experimentally at Lille by industries but had not yet been employed by any city. According to the analyses made by Dr. Roux of the Pasteur Institute, the Loire water taken from the filtration tank had over 4,000 bacteria per cubic centimeter and contained a high concentration of *bacterium coli*. After ozonification it had less than one bacterium per cubic centimeter and no *bacterium coli* at all. This analysis, one of the first serious ones every made, shows the pollution of the Loire River and above all the inadequacy of the filtration tanks that were in use everywhere—at Decize, at Nevers, and at La Charité, for example.

87. The system made available 186 liters per day for each inhabitant and permitted the city to install electrical lighting (86 street lamps and 72 subscribers in 1900). The plan aroused new resistance owing to the preference for spring water (*Journal de la Nièvre*, 8 August 1896, and A.N., F^8 199). Cf. Pochet, "Notice sur l'adduction des eaux de l'Yonne pour l'alimentation de Château-Chinon et l'éclairage électrique de la ville," *Annales des ponts et chaussées* (1900), pp. 213-31.

88. Since 1881 the inspectors of the regional office of education had been concerned about the sanitary situation in the city, owing to Professor Bataillon's revelation that the water in the spring of Sainte-Eugénie was polluted. See Jacquot's report of 14 June 1897, A. N., F^8 199. The General Council of the department of Nièvre did not agree until 1900 to do the needed work (see *Procès-verbaux du Conseil général,* April 1896 and August 1896). In December 1909 another epidemic of typhoid fever broke out at Varzy: "Since 20 September the city had had no drinking water, as a result of the breakdown of a boiler. The population was reduced to using either the old wells that had been closed following a typhoid epidemic or a spring whose water was connected to a reservoir used as a laundry tub and watering trough" (*Conseil général* [1910], p. 143). Yet the water at the normal school was "filtered regularly."

89. The advisory board of health, to which all water plans were submitted, opposed the plan for Corbigny in 1886. "The water of the Yonne at the place where the water will be collected . . . contains a considerable quantity of organic matter. The use of this water must be categorically outlawed." But two-thirds of the public wells ran dry during several months of the year, and water was constantly lacking (A.N., F^8 119). A detailed study should be made of all the records submitted to this board. In passing, I should like to point out the difficulty that the board encountered in obtaining correct analyses of water samples.

90. Cf. Hostier, *Fourchambault, 1854-1954,* (n.p., 1955), pp. 57-59. In 1907 they considered bringing water from the spring of Beaumont-la-Ferrière, since Pouges brought its water from Saint-Aubin-les-Forges.

91. On the conditions for use, see Imbeaux, *Annuaire statistique,* pp. 481-86. An attempt should be made to trace the increased water consumption of these towns. At Cosne it increased by fifty percent between 1907 (400 cubic meters per day) and 1912. Individual consumption seems to have remained rather limited, as at Fourchambault, where circa 1930 public services used 32,000 cubic meters of the 45,000 produced.

92. The problems involved in expanding pumping stations and extending the network, as well as sanitations problems, still exist in Nivernais, even in towns. Many villages still have no piped water; see, for example, *Rapports du Conseil général, Procès-verbaux des délibérations* (January 1965), pp. 19-26.

93. Circular of 20 August 1906, about the pollution of the underground water tables by sewer water; and the minister of agriculture's circular of June 1906 forbidding people to throw or allow waste water to run into streams. In addition, article 9 of the law of 15 February 1902 stated that if for three consecutive years the number of deaths in a township exceeded the average death rate for France, "the prefect was to make an inquiry and order the necessary sanitation projects."

94. The reports of the supervising board of health are eloquent (A.N., F^8 220). Night soil was emptied into gardens in all townships of Nièvre, even at such spas as Pougues and Saint-Honoré, which had no water systems.

95. Septic tanks were considered a threat to public health. "These sanitary installations . . . have brought only disappointment," said Calmette, "and cost a lot of money for those owners of buildings who are caught up by the fallacious promises set forth in the brochures of their inventors." Cf. Dr. O. Simonot, "Fosses septiques et hygiène publique," *Mémoires de la Société académique du Nivernais* (1911); Dr. Simonot was director of public health for Nevers.

96. See, for example, the reports by the departmental vetinerary to the General Council of Nièvre in which, year after year, he deplored the unsanitary conditions at the slaughterhouses. In 1911 he stated that the slaughterhouse of Nevers "lacks water, and [that] the sewer is a focus of infection." At

Cosne, "a ditch carries to the Loire the waste water sullied by organic debris; the ditch is plugged and the liquids form a foul pond" (*Conseil général* [1911], pp. 298-99).

97. *Conseil général* (1905), p. 195.

98. The woman inspector for nursery schools noted in 1908 that "the cleanliness of the children is often only apparent cleanliness—clean face, clean hands, and clean outer clothing" (*Conseil général* [*1908*], pp. 142-43). Until 1930 the "cleanliness checkups" in schools had to take into account the frequently poor living conditions.

99. At Nevers the number of lodgings with washroom or bathroom was infinitesimal in 1940, and many had no running water. Whole sections of the city were considered unhealthful. According to the census of 1946, 13,975 buildings out of 68,882 had water (in Nevers, 4,088 out of 5,371; at Clamecy, 755 out of 1,258; at Cosne, 1,195 out of 2,192). In towns with over 10,000 inhabitants, 75 percent of the dwellings had running water in the apartment, or at least in the building, and 12.3 percent had wells. In urban townships of less than 10,000 inhabitants, 53 percent of all dwellings had water, but 15 percent had well water and 30 percent used public fountains. In rural townships, running water was available in only 11 percent of cases, and wells in 49 percent. The number of bathrooms was infinitesimal: 609 out of 11,527 dwellings in towns with over 10,000 inhabitants, 965 out of 71,000 lodgings in other townships; 2,800 out of 82,000 dwellings in the department had a sewer main, and so forth (see *Résultats statistiques du recensement général de la population*, vol. 4, *Nièvre* (1951), tables VI, 2, 3, and 4).

100. Today we take hygiène measures and plumbing in houses for granted ("water on every floor, toilet, bathroom," run the ads), and we are rapidly forgetting the old living conditions of not so long ago. Charles Péguy attacked this illusion in *L'Argent* (Paris, 1913), p. 10: "The world has changed less since Jesus Christ than it has changed in the past twenty years.... A farm in the Beauce, even after the war, was infinitely closer to the Gallic farm during Roman occupation, or rather virtually the same as that Gallic farm, in customs, status, solemnity, gravity, structure and institutions, dignity,... than it is to the farm we see there today."

101. It is impossible to overemphasize the importance of the materiel used (meters, conduits, pumps) and the methods of chemical analysis and purification employed, none of which have been the subjects of historical research. Even today the public water supply in towns is not very closely monitored for bacterial content. In one market town, the water is only checked every two months.

9
The Semiotics
of Food in the Bible

Jean Soler

How can we explain the dietary prohibitions of the Hebrews? To this day these rules—with variations, but always guided by the Mosaic laws—are followed by many orthodox Jews. Once a number of false leads, such as the explanation that they were hygienic measures, have been dismissed, the structural approach appears to be enlightening.

Lévi-Strauss has shown the importance of cooking, which is peculiar to man in the same manner as language. Better yet, cooking is a language through which a society expresses itself. For man knows that the food he ingests in order to live will become assimilated into his being, will become himself. There must be, therefore, a relationship between the idea he has formed of specific items of food and the image he has of himself and his place in the universe. There is a link between a people's dietary habits and its perception of the world.

Moreover, language and dietary habits also show an analogy of form. For just as the phonetic system of a language retains only a few of the sounds a human being is capable of producing, so a community adopts a dietary regime by making a choice among all the possible foods. By no means does any given individual eat everything; the mere fact that a thing is edible does not mean that it will be eaten. By bringing to light the logic that informs these choices and the interrelation among its constituent parts—in this case the various foods—we can outline the specific characteristics of a society, just as we can define those of a language.

The study of my topic is made easier by the existence of a *corpus* whose boundaries cannot be considered arbitrary; the dietary laws of the Hebrews have been laid down in a book, the Book, and more precisely in the first five books of the Bible, which are known as the Torah to the Jews and the Pentateuch to the Christians. This set of writings is composed of texts from various eras over a wide span of time. But to the extent that they have been sewn together, have coexisted

Annales, E.S.C. 28 (July-August 1973): 943-55. Translated by Elborg Forster.

and still do coexist in the consciousness of a people, it is advisable to study them together. I shall therefore leave aside the historical dimension in order to search for the rules that give cohesion to the different laws constituting the Law.

It is true, of course, that these five books tell a story, running from the creation of the world to the death of Moses, the man to whom these laws, and even this set of writings, are attributed. Attention will therefore have to be given to the order of the narrative; but whether and when the events mentioned in it actually occurred, whether or not the persons mentioned actually existed, and if so, when, has no bearing whatsoever on my analysis, any more than does the existence or nonexistence of God.

Man's food is mentioned in the very first chapter of the first book. It has its place in the plan of the Creation: "Behold, I have given you every plant yielding seed which is upon the face of all the earth, and every tree with seed in its fruit; you shall have them for your food" (Gen. 1: 29),[1] says Elohim. Paradise is vegetarian.

In order to understand why meat eating is implicitly but unequivocally excluded, it must be shown how both God and man are defined in the myth by their relationship to each other. Man has been made "in the image" of God (Gen. 1: 26-27), but he is not, nor can he be, God. This concept is illustrated by the dietary tabu concerning the fruit of two trees. After Adam and Eve have broken this prohibition by eating the fruit of one of these trees, Elohim says: "Behold, the man has become like one of us, knowing good and evil; and now, lest he put forth his hand and take also of the tree of life, and eat, and live forever" (Gen. 3: 22). This clearly marked distance between man and God, this fundamental difference, is implicitly understood in a threefold manner.

First, the immortality of the soul is unthinkable. All life belongs to God, and to him alone. God is Life, and man temporarily holds only a small part of it. We know that the notion of the immortality of the soul did not appear in Judaism until the second century B.C. and that it was not an indigenous notion.

Secondly, killing is the major prohibition of the Bible. Only the God who gives life can take it away. If man freely uses it for his own ends, he encroaches upon God's domain and oversteps his limits. From this it follows that meat eating is impossible. For in order to eat an animal, one must first kill it. But animals, like man, belong to the category of beings that have within them "a living soul." To consume a living being, moreover, would be tantamount to absorbing the principle that would make man God's equal.

The fundamental difference between man and God is thus expressed by the difference in their foods. God's are the living beings, which in the form of sacrifices (either human victims, of which Abraham's sacrifice represents a relic, or sacrificial animals) serve as his "nourishment" according to the Bible; man's are the edible plants (for plants are not included among the "living things"). Given these fundamental assumptions, the origins of meat eating constitute a problem. Did men, then, at one point find a way to kill animals and eat them without prompting a cataclysm?

This cataclysm did indeed take place, and the Bible does speak of it. It was the Flood, which marks a breaking point in human history. God decided at first to do away with his Creation, and then he spared one family, Noah's, and one pair of each species of animal. A new era thus began after the Flood, a new Creation, which coincided with the appearance of a new dietary regime. "Every moving thing that lives shall be food for you; as I gave you the green plants, I give you everything" (Gen. 9: 3).

Thus, it is not man who has taken it upon himself to eat meat; it is God who has given him the right to do so. And the cataclysm does not come after, but before the change, an inversion that is frequently found in myths. Nevertheless, it must be understood that meat eating is not presented as a reward granted to Noah. If God has wanted "to destroy all flesh in which is the breath of life from under heaven" (Gen. 6: 17), it is because man has "corrupted" the entire earth: "and the earth was filled with violence" (Gen. 6: 17), in other words, with murder. And while it is true that he spares Noah because Noah is "just" and even "perfect" (Gen. 6: 9), the human race that will come from him will not escape the evil that had characterized the human race from which he issued. The Lord says, after the Flood: "I will never again curse the ground because of man, for the imagination of man's heart is evil from his youth; neither will I ever again destroy every living creature as I have done" (Gen. 8: 21). In short, God takes note of the evil that is in man. A few verses later, he gives Noah permission to eat animals. Meat eating is given a negative connotation.

Yet even so, it is possible only at the price of a new distinction; for God adds the injunction: "Only you shall not eat flesh with its life, that is, its blood" (Gen. 9: 4). Blood becomes the signifier of the vital principle, so that it becomes possible to maintain the distance between man and God by expressing it in a different way with respect to food. Instead of the initial opposition between the eating of meat and the eating of plants, a distinction is henceforth made between flesh and blood. Once the blood (which is God's) is set apart, meat becomes desacralized—and permissible. The structure remains the same, only the signifying elements have changed.

At this stage the distinction between clean and unclean animals is not yet present, even though three verses in the account of the Flood refer to it. Nothing is said that would permit Noah to recognize these two categories of animals, and this distinction is out of place here, since the power to eat animals he is given includes all of them: "Every moving thing that lives shall be food for you."

It is not until Moses appears that a third dietary regime comes into being, one that is based on the prohibition of certain animals. Here we find a second breaking point in human history. For the covenant God had concluded with Noah included all men to be born from the sole survivor of the Flood (the absence of differentiation among men corresponded to the absence of differentiation among the animals they could consume), and the sign of that covenant was a cosmic and hence universal sign, the rainbow (Gen. 9: 12-17). The covenant concluded with Moses, however, concerns only one people, the Hebrews; to the new distinction between men corresponds the distinction of the animals they may eat: "I am the Lord your God, who have separated you from the peoples. You shall therefore make a distinction between the clean beasts and the unclean; and between the unclean bird and the clean; you shall not make yourselves abominable by beast or by bird or by anything with which the ground teems, which I have set apart for you to hold unclean" (Lev. 20: 24-25). The signs of this new covenant can only be individual, since they will have to become the distinctive traits of the Hebrew people. In this manner the Mosaic dietary code fulfills the same function as circumcision or the institution of the Sabbath. These three signs all involve a cut (a cut on the male sex organ: a partial castration analogous to an offering, which in return will bring God's blessing upon the organ that ensures the transmission of life and thereby the survival of the Hebrew people; a cut in the regular course of the days: one day of every seven is set apart, so that the sacrificed day will desacralize the others and bring God's blessing on their work; a cut in the *continuum* of the created animals—added to the already accomplished cut, applying to every animal, between flesh and blood, and later to be strengthened by an additional cut within each species decreed to be clean between the first-born, which are God's, and the others, which are thereby made more licit). The cut is at the origin of differentiation, and differentiation is the prerequisite of signification.

Dietary prohibitions are indeed a means of cutting a people off from others, as the Hebrews learned at their own expense. When Joseph's brothers journeyed to Egypt in order to buy wheat, he had a meal containing meat served to them: "They served him by himself, and them by themselves, for the Egyptians might not eat bread with the Hebrews, for that is an abomination to the Egyptians" (Gen. 43: 32). It is likely that the nomadic Hebrews already had dietary prohibitions but, according to Biblical history, they began to include their dietary habits among the defining characteristics of their people only after the exodus, as if they were taking their model from the Egyptian civilization.

Dietary habits, in order to play their role, must be different; but different from what? From those, unquestionably, of the peoples with whom the Hebrews were in contact. Proof of this is the famous injunction: "You shall not boil a kid in its mother's milk," for here a custom practiced among the people of that region was forbidden. Yet the dietary regime of the Hebrews was not contrary to the regimes of other peoples in every point; had this been the case they would have had very few things to eat! Why, then, did they strictly condemn some food items and not others? The answer must not be sought in the nature of the food item, any more than the sense of a word can be sought in the word itself. (It is contained in the dictionary, which defines that word by other words, which refer to yet other words, with all of these operations taking place within the dictionary). A social sign—in this case a dietary prohibition—cannot be understood in isolation. It must be placed into the context of the signs in the same area of life, together with which it constitutes a system; and this system in turn must be seen in relation to the systems in other areas, for the interaction of all these systems constitutes the sociocultural system of a people. The constant features of this system should yield the fundamental structures of the Hebrew civilization or—and this may be the same thing—the underlying thought patterns of the Hebrew people.

One first constant feature naturally comes to mind in the notion of "cleanness," which is used to characterize the permissible foods. In order to shed light on this notion, it must first of all be seen as a conscious harking back to the Origins. To the extent that the exodus from Egypt and the revelation of Sinai represent a new departure in the history of the World, it can be assumed that Moses—or the authors of the system that bears his name—felt very strongly that this third Creation, lest it too fall into degradation, would have to be patterned after the myth of Genesis (whether that account was elaborated or only appropriated by Moses). Man's food would therefore be purest of all if it were patterned as closely as possible upon the Creator's intentions. Now the myth tells us that the food originally given to man was purely vegetarian. Has there been, historically, an attempt to impose a vegetarian regime on the Hebrews? There is no evidence to support this hypothesis, but the Bible does contain traces of such an attempt or, at any rate, of such an ideal. One prime trace is the fact that manna, the only daily nourishment of the Hebrews during the exodus, is shown as a vegetal substance: "It was like coriander seed, white, and the taste of it was like wafer made with honey" (Exod. 16: 31). Moreover, the Hebrews had large flocks, which they did not touch. Twice, however, the men rebelled against Moses because they wanted to eat meat. The first time, this happened in the wilderness of Sin: "Would that we had died by the hand of the Lord in the land of Egypt, when we sat by the flesh-pots" (Exod. 16: 3). God thereupon granted them the miracle of the quails. The second rebellion is reported in Numbers (11: 4): "O that we had meat to eat," wail the Hebrews. God agrees to repeat the miracle of the quails, but does so only unwillingly and even in great wrath: "You shall not eat one day, or two days, or five days, or ten days, or twenty days, but a whole month, until it comes out at your nostrils and becomes loathsome to you" (Num. 11: 19-20). And a great number of the Hebrews who fall upon the quails and gorge themselves die on the spot. Here, as in the myth of the Flood, meat is given a negative connotation. It is a concession God makes to man's imperfection.

Meat eating, then, will be tolerated by Moses, but with two restrictions. The tabu against blood will be reinforced, and certain animals will be forbidden. The setting apart of the blood henceforth becomes the occasion of a ritual. Before the meat can be eaten, the animal must be presented to the priest, who will perform the "peace offering," in which he pours the blood upon the altar. This is not only a matter of separating God's share from man's share; it also means that the murder of the animal that is to be eaten is redeemed by an offering. Under the elementary logic of retribution, any murder requires in compensation the murder of the murderer; only thus can the balance be restored. Since animals, like men, are "living souls," the man who kills an animal should himself be killed. Under this basic assumption, meat eating is altogether impossible. The solution lies in performing a ritual in which the blood of the sacrificial animal takes the place of the man who makes the offering.[2] "For the life of the flesh is in the blood, and I have given it for you upon the altar to make atonement for your souls; for it is the blood that makes atonement, by reason of the life" (Lev. 17: 11). But if a man kills an animal himself in order to eat it, "bloodguilt shall be imputed to that man; he has shed blood; and that man shall be cut off from among his people" (Lev. 17: 4); that is, he shall be killed. The importance of the blood tabu thus becomes very clear. It is not simply one prohibition among others; it is the *conditio sine qua non* that makes meat eating possible.

It should be noted that this ritual is attenuated in Deuteronomy. With the institution of a single sanctuary in Jerusalem, it became difficult for the Hebrews who lived outside the city to go to Jerusalem every time they wanted to eat meat. In this case, they were permitted to perform the offering of animals themselves. The procedure was to be the same as for hunting, where ritual offerings obviously could not be performed: "You may slaughter and eat flesh within any of your towns . . . as of the gazelle and as of the hart. Only you shall not eat the blood; you shall pour it out upon the earth like water" (Deut. 12: 15-16). This is a tangible example of how the variations of a system must adapt to the given infrastructure of geography.[3]

As for the prohibition of certain animals, we must now analyze two chapters (Lev. 11 and Deut. 14) devoted to the distinction between clean and unclean species. Neither of these texts, which are essentially identical, provides any explanation. The Bible only indicates the particular traits the clean animals must possess—though not always; for when dealing with the birds, it simply enumerates the unclean species.

The text first speaks of the animals living on land. They are "clean" if they have a "hoofed foot," a "cloven hoof," and if they "chew the cud." The first of these criteria is clearly meant to single out the herbivorous animals. The Hebrews had established a relationship between the foot of an animal and its feeding habits. They reasoned like Cuvier, who said, "All hoofed animals must be herbivorous, since they lack the means of seizing a prey."[4]

But why are herbivorous animals clean and carnivorous animals unclean? Once again, the key to the answer must be sought in Genesis, if indeed the Mosaic laws intended to conform as much as possible to the original intentions of the Creator. And in fact, Paradise was vegetarian for the animals as well. The verse dealing with human food, "I have given you every plant yielding seed which is upon the face of all the earth, and every tree with seed in its fruit; you shall have them for your food," is followed by a verse about the animals (and here, incidentally, we note a secondary differentiation, serving to mark the distance between humankind and the various species of animals): "And to every beast of the earth, and to every bird of the air, and to everything that has the breath of life, I have given every green plant for food" (Gen. 1: 29-30). Thus, carnivorous animals are not included in the plan of the Creation. Man's problem with meat eating is compounded when it involves eating an animal that has itself consumed meat and killed other animals in order to do so. Carnivorous animals are unclean. If man were to eat them, he would be doubly unclean. The "hoofed foot" is thus the distinctive trait that contrasts with the claws of carnivorous animals—dog, cat, felines, etc.—for these claws permit them to seize their prey. Once this point is made, the prohibition against eating most of the birds that are cited as unclean becomes comprehensible: they are carnivorous, especially such birds of prey as "the eagle," which is cited at the head of the list.

But to return to the beasts of the earth. Why is the criterion "hoofed foot" complemented by two other criteria? The reason is that it is not sufficient to classify the true herbivores, since it omits pigs. Pigs and boars have hoofed feet, and while it is true that they are herbivores, they are also carnivorous.[5] In order to isolate the true herbivores it is therefore necessary to add a second criterion, "chewing the cud." One can be sure that ruminants eat grass; in fact, they eat it twice. In theory, this characteristic should be sufficient to distinguish true herbivores. But in practice, it is difficult to ascertain, especially in wild animals, which can properly be studied only after they are dead. Proof of this is the fact that the hare is considered to be a ruminant by the Bible (Lev. 11: 6 and Deut. 14: 7), which is false; but the error arose from mistaking the mastication of the rodents for rumination. This physiological characteristic therefore had to be reinforced by an anatomical criterion, the hoof, which in turn was strengthened by using as a model the hoof of the ruminants known to everyone: cows and sheep. (In the myth of Creation, livestock constitutes a separate category, distinct from the category of wild animals. There is no trace of the domestication of animals; livestock was created tame). This is why clean wild animals must conform to the domestic animals that may be consumed; as it happens, cows and sheep tread the ground on two toes, each encased in a layer of horn. This explains the third criterion listed in the Bible: the "cloven hoof."

One important point must be made here: The presence of the criterion "cloven hoof" eliminates a certain number of animals, even though they are purely herbivorous (the horse, the ass, and especially the three animals expressly cited in the Bible as "unclean": the camel, the hare, and the rock badger). A purely herbivorous animal is therefore not automatically clean. This is a necessary, though not a sufficient condition. In addition, it must also have a foot analogous to the foot that sets the norm: that of domestic animals. Any foot shape deviating from this model is conceived as a blemish, and the animal is unclean.

This notion of the "blemish" and the value attributed to it is elucidated in several passages of the Bible. Leviticus prohibits the sacrificing of animals, even of a clean species, if the individual animal exhibits any anomaly in relation to the normal type of the species: "And when any one offers a sacrifice of peace offerings to the Lord, to fulfill a vow or as a freewill offering, from the herd or from the flock, to be accepted it must be perfect; there shall be no blemish in it. Animals blind or disabled or mutilated or having a discharge or an itch or scabs, you shall not offer to the Lord or make of them an offering by fire upon the altar to the the Lord" (Lev. 22: 21). This prohibition is repeated in Deuteronomy (17: 1): "You shall not sacrifice to the Lord your God an ox or a sheep in which is a blemish, any defect whatever; for that is an abomination to the Lord your God." The equation is stated explicitly: the blemish is an evil. A fundamental trait of the Hebrews' mental structures is uncovered here. There are societies in which impaired creatures are considered divine.

What is true for the animal is also true for man. The priest must be a wholesome man and must not have any physical defects. The Lord says to Aaron (Lev. 21: 17-18): "None of your descendants throughout their generations who has a blemish may approach to offer the bread of his God. For no one who has a blemish shall draw near, a man blind or lame, or one who has a mutilated face or a limb too long, or one who has an injured foot or an injured hand, or a hunchback, or a dwarf, or a man with a defect in his sight or an itching disease or scabs or crushed testicles; no man of the descendants of Aaron the priest who has a blemish shall come near to offer the Lord's offerings by fire." The men who participate in cultic acts must be true men: "He whose testicles are crushed or whose male member is cut off shall not enter the assembly of the Lord" (Deut. 23: 1). To be whole is one of the components of "cleanness"; eunuchs and castrated animals are unclean.

To the blemish must be added alteration, which is a temporary blemish. Periodic losses of substance are unclean, whether they be a man's emission of semen or a woman's menstruation (Lev. 15). The most unclean thing of all will therefore be death, which is the definitive loss of the breath of life and the irreversible alteration of the organism. And indeed, death is the major uncleanness for the Hebrews. It is so strong that a high priest (Lev. 21: 11) or a Nazirite (Num. 6: 6-7) may not go near a dead body, even if it is that of his father or his mother, notwithstanding the fact that the Ten Commandments order him to "honor" them.

The logical scheme that ties cleanness to the absence of blemish or alteration applies to things as well as to men or animals. It allows us to understand the status of ferments and fermented substances. I shall begin with the prohibition of leavened bread during the Passover. The explanation given in the Bible does not hold; it says that it is a matter of commemorating the exodus from Egypt when the Hebrews, in their haste, did not have time to let the dough rise (Exod. 12: 34). If this were the reason, they would have been obliged to eat poorly leavened or half-baked bread; but why bread without leavening? In reality, even if the Passover is a celebration whose meaning may have changed in the course of the ages—and this is the case with other institutions, notably the Sabbath—it functions as a commemoration of the Origins, a celebration not only of the exodus from Egypt and the birth of a nation but also of the beginning of the religious year at the first full moon after the vernal equinox. The Passover feast is a sacrifice of renewal, in which the participants consume the food of the Origins.[6] This ritual meal must include "bitter herbs," "roasted meat," and "unleavened bread" (Exod. 12: 8). The bitter herbs must be understood, it would seem, as the opposite of vegetables, which are produced by agriculture. Roast meat is the opposite of boiled meat, which is explicitly proscribed in the text (Exod. 12: 9): the boiling of meat, which implies the use of receptacles obtained by an industry, albeit a rudimentary form of it, is a late stage in the preparation of food. As for the unleavened bread, it is the bread of the Patriarchs. Abraham served cakes made of fine meal to the three messengers of God on their way to Sodom (Gen. 18: 6). These cakes were undoubtedly identical to those that Lot prepared shortly thereafter for the same messengers: "and he made them a feast, and baked unleavened bread, and they ate" (Gen. 19: 3). But unleavened bread is clean not only because it is the bread of the Origins. It is clean also and above all because the flour of which it is made is not changed by the ferment of the leavening: it is true to its natural state. This interpretation allows us to understand why fermented foods cannot be used as offerings by fire: "No cereal offering which you shall bring to the Lord shall be made with leaven; for you shall burn no leaven nor any honey as an offering by fire to the Lord" (Lev. 2: 11). A fermented substance is an altered substance, one that has become other. Fermentation is the equivalent of a blemish. Proof *a contrario* is the fact that just as fermentation is forbidden, so salt is mandatory in all offerings (Lev. 2: 13). Thus, there is a clear-cut opposition between fermentation, which alters a substance's being, and salt, which preserves it in its natural state. Leavened bread, honey,[7] and wine all have the status of secondary food items; only the primary foods that have come from the hands of the Creator in their present form can be used in the sacred cuisine of the an offering. It is true, of course, that wine is used in cultic libations. But the priest does not consume it; indeed he must abstain from all fermented liquids before officiating in order to "distinguish between the holy and the common, and between the clean and the unclean" (Lev. 10: 10). Fermented liquids alter man's judgment because they are themselves altered substances. The libation of wine must be seen as the parallel of the libation of blood, which it accompanies in burnt offerings. Wine is poured upon the altar exactly like blood, for it is its equivalent in the plant; wine is the "blood of the grapes" (Gen. 49: 11, etc.).

To return to my argument, then, the clean animals of the earth must conform to the plan of the Creation, that is, be vegetarian; they must also conform to their ideal models, that is, be without blemish. In order to explain the distinction between clean and unclean fish, we must once again refer to the first chapter of Genesis. In the beginning God created the three elements, the firmament, the water, and the earth; then he created three kinds of animals out of each of these elements: "Let the waters bring forth swarms of living creatures, and let birds fly above the earth across the firmament of the heavens" (Gen. 1: 20); "Let the earth bring forth living creatures according to their kinds, cattle and creeping things and beasts of the earth according to their kinds" (Gen. 1: 24). Each animal is thus tied to one element, and one only.[8] It has issued from that element and must live there. Chapter 11 of Leviticus and chapter 14 of Deuteronomy reiterate this classification into three groups: creatures of the earth, the water, and the air. Concerning the animals of the water, the two texts only say: "Everything in the waters that has fins and scales...you may eat." All other creatures are unclean. It must be understood that the fin is the proper organ of locomotion for animals living in the water. It is the equivalent of the leg in the animal living on land and of the wing in the animal that lives in the air. Recall also that locomotion distinguishes animals from plants, which in the Bible are not included in the category of "living" things. In this manner, the animals of the earth must walk, fish must swim, and birds must fly. Those creatures of the sea that lack fins and do not move about (mollusks) are unclean. So are those that have legs and can walk (shellfish), for they live in the water yet have the organs of a beast of the earth and are thus at home in two elements.

In the same manner, scales are contrasted with the skin of the beasts of the land and with the feathers of the birds. As far as the latter are concerned, the Biblical expression "birds of the air" must be taken quite literally; it is not a poetic image but a definition. In the formulation "the likeness of any winged bird that flies in the air" (Deut. 4: 17), the three distinctive traits of the clean bird are brought together: "winged," "which flies," and "in the air." If a bird has wings but does not fly, (the ostrich, for instance, that is cited in the text), it is unclean. If it has wings and can fly but spends most of its time in the water instead of living in the air, it is unclean (and the Bible mentions the swan, the pelican, the heron, and all the stilted birds). Insects pose a problem. "All winged animals that go upon all fours are an abomination to you," says Leviticus (11: 20). This is not a discussion of four-legged insects, for the simple reason that all insects have six. The key expression is "go upon" [walk]. The insects that are meant here are those that "go upon all fours," like the normal beasts of the earth, the quadrupeds. Their uncleanness comes from the fact that they walk rather than fly, even though they are "winged." The exception mentioned in Leviticus (11: 21) only confirms the rule: no uncleanness is imputed to insects that have "legs above their feet, with which to leap on the earth." Leaping is a mode of locomotion midway between walking and flying. Leviticus feels that it is closer to flying and therefore absolves these winged grasshoppers. Deuteronomy, however, is not convinced and prohibits all winged insects (14: 19).

Leviticus also mentions, toward the end, some unclean species that cannot be fitted into the classification of three groups, and it is for this reason, no doubt, that Deuteronomy does not deal with them. The first of these are the reptiles. They belong to the earth, or so it seems, but have no legs to walk on. "Upon your belly you shall go," God had said to the serpent (Gen. 3: 14). This is a curse. Everything that creeps and goes on its belly is condemned. These animals live more under the earth than on it. They were not really "brought forth" by the earth, according to the expression of Genesis 1: 24. They are not altogether created. And like the serpent, the centipede is condemned (Lev. 11: 30) in the expression "whatever has many feet" (Lev. 11: 42). Having too many feet or none at all falls within the same category; the clean beast of the earth has four feet, and not just any kind of feet either, as we have seen.

All these unclean animals are marked with a blemish; they show an anomaly in their relation to the element that has "brought them forth" or to the organs characteristic of life, and especially locomotion, in that element. If they do not fit into any class, or if they fit into two classes at once, they are unclean. They are unclean because they are unthinkable. At this point, instead of stating once again that they do not fit into the plan of the Creation, I should like to advance the hypothesis that the dietary regime of the Hebrews, as well as their myth of the Creation, is based upon a taxonomy in which man, God, the animals, and the plants are strictly defined through their relationships with one another in a series of opposites. The Hebrews conceived of the order of the world as the order underlying the creation of the world. Uncleanness, then, is simply disorder, wherever it may occur.

Concerning the raising of livestock and agriculture, Leviticus 19: 19 mentions the following prohibition: "You shall not let your cattle breed with a different kind." A variant is found in Deuteronomy 22: 10: "You shall not plow with an ox and an ass together." The reason is that the animals have been created (or classified) "each according to its kind," an expression that is a very leitmotif of the Bible. Just as a clean animal must not belong to two different species (be a hybrid), so man is not allowed to unite two animals of different species. He must not mix that which God (or man) has separated, whether the union take place in a sexual act or only under the yoke. Consider what is said about cultivated plants: "You shall not sow your field with two kinds of seeds" (Lev. 19: 19), an injunction that appears in Deuteronomy as: "You shall not sow your vineyard with two kinds of seed." The same prohibition applies to things: "nor shall there come upon you a garment of cloth made of two kinds of stuff" (Lev. 19: 19). In Deuteronomy 22: 11, this becomes: "You shall not wear a mingled stuff, wool and linen together." Here the part plant, part animal origin of the material further reinforces the distinction. In human terms, the same schema is found in the prohibition of mixed marriages—between Hebrews and foreigners—(Deut. 7: 3), and also in the fact that a man of mixed blood (offspring of a mixed marriage) or, according to a different interpretation, a bastard (offspring of adultery) may not enter the assembly of the Lord (Deut. 23: 3). This would seem to make it very understandable that the Hebrews did not accept the divine nature of Jesus. A God-man, or a God become man, was bound to offend their logic more than anything else.[9] Christ is the absolute hybrid.

A man is a man, or he is God. He cannot be both at the same time. In the same manner, a human being is either a man or a woman, not both: homosexuality is outlawed (Lev. 18: 22). The prohibition is extended even to clothes: "A woman shall not wear anything that pertains to a man, nor shall a man put on a woman's garment" (Deut. 22: 5). Bestiality is also condemned (Lev. 18: 20) and, above all, incest (Lev. 18: 6 ff.): "She is your mother, you shall not uncover her nakedness." This tautological formulation shows the principle involved here: once a woman is defined as "mother" in relation to a boy, she cannot also be something else to him. The incest prohibition is a logical one. It thus becomes evident that the sexual and the dietary prohibitions of the Bible are coordinated. This no doubt explains the Bible's most mysterious prohibition: "You shall not boil a kid in its mother's milk" (Exod. 23: 19 and 34: 26; Deut. 14: 21). These words must be taken quite literally. They concern a mother and her young. They can be translated as: you shall not put a mother and her son into the same pot, any more than into the same bed.[10] Here as elsewhere, it is a matter of upholding the separation between two classes or two types of relationships. To abolish distinc-tion by means of a sexual or culinary act is to subvert the order of the world. Everyone belongs to one species only, one people, one sex, one category. And in the same manner, everyone has only one God: "See now that I, even I, am he, and there is no God beside me" (Deut. 32: 39). The keystone of this order is the principle of identity, instituted as the law of every being.

The Mosaic logic is remarkable for its rigor, indeed its rigidity. It is a "stiff-necked" logic, to use the expression applied by Yahveh to his people. It is self-evident that the very inflexibility of this order was a powerful factor for unification and conservation in a people that wanted to "dwell alone."[11] On the other hand, however, the Mosaic religion, inseparable as it is from the sociocultural system of the Hebrews, could only lose in power of diffusion what it gained in power of concentration. Christianity could only be born by breaking with the structures that separated the Hebrews from the other peoples. It is not surprising that one of the decisive ruptures concerned the dietary prescriptions. Matthew quotes Jesus as saying: "Not what goes into the mouth defiles a man, but what comes out of the mouth, this defiles a man" (15: 11). Similar words are reported by Mark, who comments: "Thus he declared all foods clean" (7: 19). The meaning of this rejection becomes strikingly clear in the episode of Peter's vision at Jaffa (Acts 10): a great sheet descends from heaven with all kinds of clean and unclean animals in it, and God's voice speaks: "Rise, Peter; kill and eat." Peter resists the order twice, asserting that he is a good Jew and has never eaten anything unclean. But God repeats his order a third time. Peter's perplexity is dispelled by the arrival of three men sent by the Roman centurion Cornelius, who is garrisoned in Caesarea. Cornelius wants to hear Peter expound the new doctrine he is propagating. And Peter, who had hitherto been persuaded that Jesus' reform was meant only for the Jews, now understands that it is valid for the Gentiles as well. He goes to Casesarea, shares the meal of a non-Jew, speaks to Cornelius, and baptizes him. Cornelius becomes the first non-Jew to be converted to Christianity. The vision in which the distinction between clean and unclean foods was abolished had thus implied the abolition of the distinction between Jews and non-Jews.

From this starting point, Christianity could begin its expansion, grafting itself onto the Greco-Roman civilization, which, unlike the Hebrew civilization, was ready to welcome all blends, and most notably a God-man. A new system was to come into being, based on new structures. This is why the materials it took from the older system assumed a different value. Blood, for instance, is consumed by the priest in the sacrifice of the Mass in the form of its signifier: "the blood of the grape." This is because the fusion between man and God is henceforth possible, thanks to the intermediate term, which is Christ. Blood, which had acted as an isolator between two poles, now becomes a conductor. In this manner, everything that Christianity has borrowed from Judaism, every citation of the Biblical text in the text of Western civilization (in French literature, for example), must in some way be "tinkered with," to use Lévi-Strauss's comparison.[12]

By contrast, whatever variations the Mosaic system may have undergone in the course of history, they do not seem to have shaken its fundamental structures. This logic, which sets up its terms in contrasting pairs and lives by the rule of refusing all that is hybrid, mixed, or arrived at by synthesis and compromise, can be seen in action to this day in Israel, and not only in its cuisine.

NOTES

1. *The Oxford Annotated Bible with the Apocrypha,* rev. standard ed., ed. Herbert G. May and Bruce M. Metzger (New York and Oxford, 1965).
2. That the life of an animal can atone for/save the life of the men who have sacrificed it can be seen in the episode of Exod. 12, where, during the night preceding the exodus from Egypt, the Hebrews sacrifice a lamb (the Passover lamb) and paint the doors of their houses with its blood. During that night, God strikes all the first-born of Egypt, except those who live in the houses marked with the blood. In Abraham's sacrifice also, the life of an animal and the life of a child can be made to stand for each other.
3. In keeping with the principle of the arbitrary nature of the sign, life can have other signifiers than blood. In certain societies, for instance, it is the head, the heart, or the womb. In Leviticus itself, the fat that covers the entrails is forbidden to man and set apart for God (3: 16-17). The metaphoric use of the word also seems to indicate that fat is conceived as the vital substance of the solid parts of the body: "and I will give you the best of the land of Egypt, and you shall eat the fat of the land" (Gen. 45: 18, etc.). The sciatic nerve, which also may not be eaten, is perhaps interpreted as the element *par excellence* of locomotion, a privilege that belongs to living beings only. As Jacob wrestled with the angel, he was paralyzed when this nerve was touched (Gen. 32: 26-33). Fat and the sciatic nerve may well be secondary variants of blood in a different context.
4. Cited in the *Dictionnaire Robert,* s.v. *"sabot."* See also F. Jacob, *La Logique du vivant* (Paris, 1970), p. 119.
5. The boar with its tusks, which are hyperdeveloped canine teeth, was naturally included among the wild beasts of which it is said: "And I shall loose the wild beasts among you, which shall rob you of your children, and destroy your cattle" (Lev. 26: 22).
6. Cf. Mircea Eliade, *Aspects du mythe* (Paris, 1963), p. 59: "To take nourishment is not simply a physiological act, but also a 'religious' act: one eats the creations of the Supernatural Beings, and one eats them as the mythical ancestors ate them for the first time at the beginning of the world."
7. See C. Lévi-Strauss, *Du miel aux cendres* (Paris, 1964), p. 253: Honey is an already "prepared" item; "it can be consumed fresh or fermented"; and it "pours forth ambiguity from each one of its facets."
8. In *Purity and Danger* (London, 1966), a work that came to my attention after I had finished writing the present study, Mary Douglas adopts a similar approach, and the similarity of our conclusions on this particular point is striking indeed.
9. Cf. the Gospel according to John (10: 31-33): "The Jews took up stones again to stone him. Jesus answered them, 'I have shown you many good works from the Father; for which of these do you stone me?.' The Jews answered him: 'It is not for a good work that we stone you but for blasphemy; because you, being a man, make yourself God.'"
10. Cf. the prohibition against taking the mother, the young ones, or the eggs from a bird's nest. Here the eggs are sufficient to represent the young ones, just as the milk represents the kid's mother (Deut. 22: 6-7). See also the prohibition against sacrificing on the same day a cow or a ewe and her young (Lev. 22: 28). Both of these acts might lead to culinary incest.
11. "Lo, a people dwelling alone and not reckoning itself among the nations!" (Num. 23: 9).
12. C. Lévi-Strauss, *La Pensée sauvage* (Paris, 1962), pp. 26 ff. English translation, *The Savage Mind* (Chicago, 1966).

10
The Culinary System in the *Encyclopédie*

Jean-Claude Bonnet

The strawberry is a small red or white fruit; it looks like the tip of a nurse's breast. —Encyclopédie, *s.v. "Fraise"*

The potato is rightly held responsible for flatulence; but what is flatulence to the vigorous organs of peasants and workers?—Encyclopédie, *s.v. "Pomme de terre"*

Apicius: But since reason sometimes makes new acquisitions, why will not the senses do the same? It would be much more important for them to do so. —Fontenelle, Dialogue des morts: Apicius-Gallilé

Among the many statements about cooking dispersed in eighteenth-century texts of all kinds, those of the *Encyclopédie* occupy a special place. They are not used as marginal asides or novelistic incidents, like the menu in the *Voiture embourbée* or Voltaire's pastries, nor are they part of a subject's archives for reporting his bodily experiences, like the culinary passages of autobiography. Issued from a collective venture designed to arrive at a summing-up, they deal with cooking in all of its aspects. Although distributed over time between 1745 and 1772, the culinary statements of the *Encyclopédie* do not lend themselves to serial analyses like those that can be carried out year by year for the successive notices appearing in the *Cuisine bourgeoise,* but must be seen as parts of a whole distributed within the spatial confines of a body of knowledge. As an open and multifaceted verbalization of man's experience with food, they assume the appearance of a complex, multitiered system. One is tempted to use this encyclopedic body of writings on the problem of food directly and to interpret it as the sign of a new collective interest, proof of a historical trans-formation of the forms of desire and the importance of the body, as well as the assertion of a new kind of orality in keeping with the dynamic of the eighteenth century. But in this manner one would be liable to end up with faulty syntheses,

Annales, E.S.C. 32 (September-October 1977): 891-914. Translated by Elborg Forster.

and in any case with a retrospective reading, while actually the main task is to describe how the statements about cooking are distributed and to find out whether they constitute a coherent subject matter.

I have not inventoried the statements about cooking by means of a linear reading in alphabetical order, for the *Dictionnaire Encyclopédique* calls for a mode of reading that is clearly defined by Diderot in the *Prospectus* and in the article "Encyclopédie." The work of the editors, men of genius who perceived relationships between things, consisted of giving many cross references (to "things" and to "words") in order to "perfect the nomenclature." In Diderot's project as it was finally carried out, the cross references must thus serve as "itineraries through the visible world and the intelligible world." Even if, in actual practice, Diderot saw "the nomenclature becoming obscure" in the "byways of an inextricable labyrinth," the system of cross references serves to organize a set of statements explicitly classified and laid out in the index. The cross references that refer to more than just words establish relationships between topics in a common area of knowledge and between the coordinates of a common practice. In this manner the reader is given a multidimensional space whose volume is the product of the two forms of open-endedness we find in the articles: On the one hand, the rubrics containing the various categories and the different approaches taken illuminate any given subject from many sides; on the other hand, cross references to other articles establish a connection between the objects involved in a common practice. One can therefore speak of a culinary system in the *Encyclopédie,* especially since in the preliminary discourse D'Alembert does not use the Biblical image of the tree of knowledge, as Bacon had done, but instead avails himself of such geographical metaphors as the map of the world and the labyrinth and compares knowledge to a voyage leading through terra incognita and well-mapped continents.[1] The very process of reading the *Encyclopédie* with a view to grouping specific statements together under various headings is a seemingly endless voyage; yet there comes a point when certain patterns will emerge out of their sheer accumulation.

My first approach to the *Encyclopédie* has thus been dictated by the *Dictionnaire* itself. I have followed the itinerary mapped out by the cross references without meaning to exhaust the subject. For that reason, the sample used here has no statistical value. It does not sum up a series arrived at in a systematical manner, for I ceased my reading once I observed a certain saturation of the cross references and once a certain describable order came into view. The rubrics enabled me to outline the different areas and a number of specific ways of approaching the subject. The rubrics "Histoire," "Diète," "Cuisine," "Mythologie," and "Littérature" organize a space in which food practices are defined in the context of a religious and moral tradition, including its cultural variants. The rubrics "Histoire Naturelle," "Physiologie," "Médecine," and "Economie Animale" open onto a different category of investigation. Here the experience of eating is approached through the troubled, yet fascinated, description of unusual, deviant behavior. The rubrics "Arts" and "Economie Domestique," as well as the plates and their commentaries, do not ask questions but simply describe as they pursue a straightforward technical approach. I shall attempt to define the connections between these different areas, but I do not feel called upon to reconstruct an entire culinary attitude out of a number of dispersed statements that may only coexist with each other in a heterogeneous manner.

The rubrics "Histoire," "Diète," "Mythologie," and "Littérature" clearly form a set written almost entirely by the Chevalier de Jaucourt, the man who was, according to Jacques Proust, "the veritable maître Jacques of the Encyclopédie."[2] While Diderot took charge of certain technical aspects and occasional recipes, Jaucourt shouldered a more thankless task, one that was fraught with formidable difficulties. The article "Cuisine" and those to which it refers the reader deal with the subject in the widest sense and constitute the basic text that is reused throughout the articles on cooking. Here Jaucourt rapidly outlines the history of cooking and formulates an evaluation of cooking in general.

Because he constantly refers to a mythical nature, Jaucourt does not write a very dialectical history of human eating habits. To him, the history of cooking, like the history of language or of the social structure, is one of progressive complication. The food of the first people to inhabit the earth (dairy products, the fruits of the earth, honey, vegetables, and bread baked in the ashes) was unrefined, but gave strength and health. This was the time when food practices were in a state of balance. Jaucourt explains that this miraculous state of balance was broken by a psychological chain reaction: satiety, spawned by routine, made man eager to try new experiences. Certain historical innovations, such as the commerce between the Persians and the Greeks in Asia, are invoked, but only as to their surface effect: We are told that this commerce disrupted peoples' habits by diversifying them and thus brought about the deterioration of their health. So man "came to make an art out of the most natural activity." The great moments of that treacherous art occurred in Rome under the Empire and in France beginning with the reign of Catherine de Médicis and during the reign of Henry II. The periodization of the history of cooking is based on predominantly moral criteria, without consideration for the social structure itself; new developments in the culinary art are not punctuated by profound historical upheavals, but tied to epiphenomena, such as the coming to power of corrupt or decadent princes. In becoming increasingly refined, the culinary art develops an unwholesome magic: "These people (the Roman chefs) sharpened their masters' appetite by the number, the potency and the diversity of the *ragoûts* they served, and they had carried this diversity so far as to change the appearance of every item they prepared: if their master desired a kind of fish that was not available, they were able to make other fish taste and look like those that the climate or the season witheld from their gourmandise." Jaucourt draws a sharp distinction between Trimalchio's *"farces"* [forcemeats] and fancy preparations and the cooking of "sober or poor" people, which he calls "the most normal art of preparing food for the purpose of satisfying the needs of life."

The history of cooking is thus punctuated by the moral antithesis between a simple, natural way of cooking and the unrestrained proliferation of a spurious art. Yet Jaucourt goes beyond the imagery of the sybarite and the philosopher, which he had borrowed from Tacitus and Seneca, and also beyond the polemic about luxury and frugality, for he feels that new developments in the culinary art hold out exciting prospects for mankind. In certain cases, the destructive chemistry of cooking can become a useful technique and a regenerative pharmaceutical achievement: "Yet it must be admitted that we owe to the art of cooking many very useful preparations, which deserve to be studied by the physicists. Some of these preparations have a bearing on the conservation of foodstuffs, while others make them easier to digest." In this manner, Jaucourt's analysis itself becomes ambivalent and qualified, for the artifices of the art are offset by its useful aspects. Apicius, for example, the very symbol of an unnatural art of cooking, is noteworthy for discovering, in the reign of Trajan, a special technique for preserving oysters. Seen in this perspective, the history of cooking amounts to a history of progress in which the senses and learning are reconciled, because in its course man finds both new pleasures and new practical knowledge.

Concurrently with his rapid historical survey of cooking, Jaucourt makes every effort to evaluate the art of cooking in general. And while he uses a wide variety of criteria for this purpose, it is possible to isolate three areas of concern in which Jaucourt attempts to establish a specific culinary norm. They are: a religious-moral tradition, a body of medical-dietetic knowledge, and a schema of classification. The aspect of cooking that involves seasoning and preparation, that is, the cultural treatment of a raw foodstuff, is defined in the eighteenth century by the generic term *"ragoût,"* which Jaucourt makes explicit in the following terms: "Sauce or seasoning used to titillate or stimulate the appetite when it has lost its edge." The *ragoût,* described as a perversion of nature, a condiment that rekindles the sense of taste by destroying it and by forcing the appetite, is the symbol of *gourmandise,* "the sophisticated and immoderate love of good food." Thomassin, in his *Traité des jeûnes* [Treatise on fasting] (1700), makes this explicit: "Wine was taken away in order to cut off all pleasure in drinking; and by forbidding meat, all the *ragoûts* of the palate were condemned." Similarly, Lorry, in his *Traité des aliments* [Treatise on foodstuffs] (1757), makes a distinction between three kinds of seasonings: those that facilitate digestion, those that correct the poor quality of foodstuffs, and the *ragoûts,* which are used to "improve the taste" and thereby partake of whim and lust of the palate. In the context of a moral and religious discourse, the *ragoût* thus represents a transgression of the norm and a forbidden pleasure: "This art of flattering the sense of taste, this luxury—I almost said lust—of good food" (s.v. "Cuisine"); "this variety of lust" (s.v. "Assaisonnement" [Seasoning]). Here the norm is taken from a Biblical tradition that, harking back to a vegetarian garden of Eden and to an artless diet, sees composite dishes and all culinary activity as signs of a forbidden sensuality.

From the medical-dietetic point of view as well, the *ragoûts* and all fancy preparations are condemned as pernicious to health, and the simple dish is held up as the norm: "The combining and seasoning of different items to be consumed, as in the preparation of *ragoûts,* is usually most pernicious to health, since *ragoûts* not only encourage excessive eating, but also cause the corruption of the humors. The simplest foodstuffs are the best for every kind of temperament" (s.v. "Non-Naturelles" [Non-Naturals]).

Nonetheless, Jaucourt qualifies his position and does not preach a return to the origins of cooking or the total absence of preparation, for he also sees cuisine as the mark of culture: "The art of the chefs consists almost exclusively of the seasoning of dishes; it is common to all civilized nations.... Most seasonings are harmful to health.... And yet it must be granted that by and large only savages can be satisfied with the pure products of nature, eaten without seasoning and as nature provides them. But there is a middle way between such coarseness and the over-refinement practised by our chefs" (s.v. "Assaisonnement"). On the other hand, because of the diversity of temperaments, that which is "poison to one person can be a remedy to another." Here the medical discourse, which does not object to pleasure, produces a certain vacillation. The third concern that leads Jaucourt to pursue his evaluation of cooking in general is the urge to classify, a characteristic concern of seventeenth-century learning.

Jaucourt wants to analyze cooking in general in a way that would enable him to isolate simple categories. He hopes to find "the flavors that must predominate in each *ragoût,*" since they have been progressively falsified in the course of the history of cooking. But in trying to reduce them to a simple list, he meets with insurmountable difficulties, for while there are words with which to define very broad culinary categories and to demarcate major groups of foods (*ragoût,* roast), such words do not exist for seasonings and flavors, whose infinite shadings it is impossible to classify in a concise lexicon. Realizing that the art of flattering the sense of taste is made up of an infinite variety of combinations (s.v. "Glace" [*Ice*]) and that there are composite flavors that "create an infinite number of nuances of taste," Jaucourt gives up all hope of being able to define the essence of cooking in a system of symbols and to establish a complete inventory. Here seventeenth-century learning, in its preoccupation with visible matters that can be classified and described, turns its back on tastes and flavors that defy analysis.[3] While the culinary system [of the *Encyclopédie*] does offer a classification of dishes and recipes, it does not present an inventory of the various flavors, for this aspect of cooking is simply not amenable to any nomenclature. And since the norm is undefinable, the body is open to the vagaries of desire and sensation, whose variations are infinite, but mute.

All of Jaucourt's articles do not come to grief over general problems of classification. Many give precise information on specific culinary practices, on cultural peculiarities, and on historical transformations. Can we speak of a fundamental discontinuity in food practices and in the manner of verbalizing them? The disquisitions of Diderot, who proposes that the butchers' guild be restructured and that "slaughter" be moved out of town, or the physiocratic treatises on the grain trade are no more than scattered statements and do not point to the existence of a general trend. It was only by the end of the century with Restif de la Bretonne or Louis-Sébastien Mercier, and especially during the Revolution, that food practices were systematically thought about in new terms necessitated by urbanization and collective organization, such as distribution, the market, and public health. Yet the *Encyclopédie* was the first to formulate a new set of problems related to food; without proclaiming any radical change, it did show its readers certain brittle points.

The article "Carême" [Fasting] under the rubric "Histoire ecclésiastique" [Church history] is based on the *Traité des jeûnes* [Treatise on fasting] by Father Thomassin, according to whom "the discipline of the Church has imperceptibly become more relaxed with respect to fasting during Lent."[4] The mandatory codes laid down by the Church Fathers (Saint Basil, Saint Gregory of Nyssa, Saint Thomas) have become dead letter, for the concept of fasting has gradually been stripped of its application to food. The latter is replaced by "new exercises" designed to compensate for "inevitable change." The Church's lax attitude toward fasting during Lent was contemporary with the phenomenon of "dechristianization" that is attested by quantitative studies. On the level of discourse, the *Encyclopédie* in its articles "Jeûne" and "Abstinence" testifies to a profound change of attitude. Fasting, a curtailment of man's food habits codified in religious texts, is interpreted from all angles: it is reduced to a moral principle when it is likened to abstinence, a venerable Pythagorean virtue; its symbolic value is interpreted in the same vein in which the relationship between the Eucharist and cannibalism is explained; it is explained as the outgrowth of a superstition "that naturally arose from mourning"; and it is assigned a simple dietetic function. Because "faith is concerned with greater things," fasting is no longer a matter of proscribing the delights of the palate as a cardinal sin, but of avoiding the diseases of gluttony. Fasting thus becomes an aspect of temperance as defined by humoral medicine: "This is why it appears that the fasting practiced by Christians at the beginning of spring should be viewed as a command to self-denial pleasing to God only to the extent that it is a lesson in temperance, a medicinal precept, and a salutary abstinence that tends to give protection against the diseases of the season, which are mainly caused by the superabundance of humors" (s.v. "Jeûne" under the rubric "Médecine"). In all these articles, the interplay of rubrics ("Histoire ecclésiastique," "Médecine," "Mythologie") is arranged in such a way that fasting is no longer defined only in relation to the religious text; instead, it is integrated into a multitiered and pluralistic discourse and thus ceases to be a compelling obligation of faith.

Hunger, likewise, is no longer defined by means of the religious tradition, but in the words of the medical, economic, or political discourse.[5] Dissociated from all notions of sin or punishment, it is no longer a dreadful calamity, but actually becomes a positive experience: "What a unique sensation! What a marvellous sensory experience is hunger! It is not precisely a kind of pain, but a feeling that starts out as a slight tickle" (s.v. "Faim" [Hunger]). Under the rubric "Mythologie," Jaucourt describes a representation of hunger in Greece: "At Chalcidicum in the temple of Minerva the Spartans had a painting of hunger whose very sight inspired terror. It was represented in this temple in the figure of a haggard, pale, dejected and frightfully emaciated woman with hollow temples, dried-out and drawn skin over her forehead, lifeless and sunken eyes; her cheeks were ashen,

her lips were livid, and her fleshless arms and hands were tied behind her back."
Such a representation of the divinity of hunger for the purpose of warding off
death has only esthetic or moral value for the *Encyclopédie* (its proper place is
the "palace of despots" or the "drawing room of an Apicius"), for the eighteenth
century knew all about the historical causes of food shortages: "When the people
starve to death, it is never the fault of Providence, it is always the fault of the
government." This rather abstract physiocratic statement makes it quite clear
that in the eighteenth century hunger and food practices in general were absorbed
into a system of new words. Without unduly simplifying these phenomena, one
can make a connection between these statements of the *Encyclopédie* on hunger
and fasting and such facts as the disappearance of famine or such texts as
Marivaux's description of Harlequin's obsessive appetite (*boulimie*) in which the
oral dimension is insistently brought to the fore.

The *Encyclopédie* clearly shows, and explains, certain changes in food
practices. The article "Hospitalité" precisely defines a historical development.
"We no longer know that noble bond of hospitality, and it must be admitted that
time has wrought great changes among peoples, and above all among us, and
that we are much less bound by the sacred and honorable laws of that duty than
were the ancients." Trade, which elsewhere is presented as a beneficial bond
between peoples, since it fosters exchange and new forms of sociability, is here
explicitly taken to task: "Hospitality has thus naturally been lost in all of Europe,
because all of Europe has taken to travel and trade. . . . The spirit of trade, by
uniting all peoples, has broken the bonds of charity between individuals; it has
wrought much good and much evil; it has produced countless conveniences,
wider knowledge, easy access to luxury, and selfishness. This selfishness has
taken the place of the secret impulses of nature which used to bind men together
by tender and touching bonds." Nowadays travelers are politely received in
proportion to the expenditures they can make. The historical explanation is
overlaid with a theory of nature and its "secret impulses." By emphasizing that
the new commercial era transforms the ties within society, hospitality is construed
exclusively as the effect of a mythical nature, a literary concept unrelated to any
social structure. Hospitality, a value essential to the action of the Odyssey or
Télémaque and a notion dear to Rousseau's heart, runs counter to modernity,
whose fundamental contribution is the restaurant, an institution that was to
become firmly entrenched after the Revolution, when the chefs of the erstwhile
nobles founded famous establishments. In this respect the Revolution did produce
a major shift in the codes of social intercourse and in the exchange of food. Do
the general or incidental remarks of the *Encyclopédie* add up to a semiology of
culinary practices in the Paris of the mid-eighteenth century, the culinary situation
of the 1740s that was characterized as follows by Brillat-Savarin: "From this
period onward, meals were generally served with more order, cleanliness, and
elegance" (*Physiologie du goût,* Meditation 27)? Does the *Encyclopédie* articulate
the criteria and the forms of a set of social conventions specifically applying to
the table?

It is impossible to reconstruct a clear picture of eighteenth-century eating habits from the *Encyclopédie,* for information on the place and time of meals and on the order of courses is inconsistent or very loosely formulated. The article "Salle à manger" [Dining room] merely defines the location of this room in the house in terms of the new architecture, without giving any details as to its use. Eighteenth-century houses usually did not have a room set aside exclusively for eating.[6] Concerning tableware, likewise, the *Encyclopédie* provides, in its plates, details about silversmithing and the art of making porcelain, without defining the ritual of courses. Nor are the meals described more clearly. Dinner is a meal "taking place about the middle of the day, or a little later or a little earlier, depending on the time, the place, and the persons." Supper is defined in its social dimension, but under the rubric "Histoire romaine." Jaucourt explains how in Roman times the supper, which had originally been a veritable family meal, became corrupted in Lucullus's time because of the proliferation of courses. Referring to the article "Histoire des usages de France" [History of French customs], Jaucourt notes that dinner was served at 6 P.M. in the fifteenth century; for the eighteenth century he gives the following indication: "In our century, supper is served at ten o'clock at court and in the great Parisian houses." The article "Etiquette" proclaims that strict adherence to customs is nothing but the effect of despotism, which is uncongenial to the fickleness of the French people. And indeed, it appears that the customs of eighteenth-century Paris were much less uniform than those of the nineteenth century. Meals were not subject to precise rules and had not yet become the sovereign and exclusive form of sociability. Grimod de la Reynière points out that at Madame Geoffrin's and at Julie de Lespinasse's "dinner was not served." Meals were improvised and had the character of a game, if we can believe the memoirs of the time. President Hénault [of the Parlement of Paris], for instance, cites the two *"ateliers"* where Madame Lambert entertained a literary society at dinner and a "more lively" company at night. This was the time of the *salons,* when supper with intimate friends was above all an occasion for the exchange of ideas and the cultivation of friendly relations; it was not yet the time of the dining room presided over by the lady of the house who enforced, along with the code of the meal, a rigid etiquette of conviviality.

The *Encyclopédie* does not stress the social dimension of the meal but is more interested, in the context of its general investigation, in food practices throughout the world and the ages. It is more curious about the dissemination of cultures and about customs brought to light by travelers and archeology than concerned with defining a social norm. (By the end of the century, Abbé Barthélémy devoted one chapter of his *Voyage du jeune Anacharsis en Grèce* to the description of an Athenian meal, and during the Napoleonic Empire the great chef Carême organized Latin meals.) It was not until the Empire that the forms of sociability and dining together were defined in a detailed code of behavior.

Nor does the *Encyclopédie* evaluate food practices through individual foodstuffs. In general, it has very little to say about the price, the use, and the social standing of a given food item and makes no distinction between the truffle and the chestnut. In a few exceptional cases, it indicates the social groups that use a product whose distribution is regulated by quality: One kind of cheese, the "coarse" grade, is given over to the "country people"; but "all the cheeses that have any reputation and are sold in the cities are of a different kind; they are mellow, creamy, delicate, and not liable to turn sour; they have a most agreeable smell and taste." Some items are also defined as the exclusive food of certain social groups. In the article "Vermicelli," Jaucourt notes that "all the dishes of that kind are suitable for a peasant," and the potato, according to him, is the food of "peasants and workers": "People who are a little better off improve it with butter, eat it with meat or make it into a kind of fritter. But however it is prepared, this root is tasteless and starchy. One would not include it among the pleasing foods, but it does constitute abundant and rather healthful nourishment for men who do not want more than sustenance. The potato is rightly held responsible for flatulence; but what is flatulence to the vigorous organs of peasants and workers?" This cynical disquisition rests on medical and dietetic considerations. The ethnosemiotics of the eighteenth century was an outgrowth of humoral medicine, which had a mechanical way of defining the appropriate diet for every occupation. (Tissot, for example, wrote a work on the diet of the man of letters.) Parmentier's works on the potato and domestic economy were published only in the 1770s. They were given very favorable treatment in Grimm's *Correspondance.* Parmentier who was called, somewhat mockingly, "the Homer, Virgil, and Cicero of the poatato" by Grimod de la Reynière (*Almanach des Gourmands,* 1810, p. 104) and hailed as a "friend of mankind" by Louis-Sébastien Mercier (*Tableau de Paris,* bk. 4, ch. 325) was destined to become a great figure in the ideology of the potato and is known in this role even today. In the mid-eighteenth century, a period before the advent of the "French fry," the potato had not yet acquired the "Frenchness" it has today, and the *Encyclopédie* —unlike Mercier—treated it rather casually.[7] The writers and the readers of the *Encyclopédie* did not see the potato as the supremely important food item that had helped eliminate food shortages and was celebrated in humanitarian verses, but felt that it was definitely not quite edible.

Except in the specific cases of cheese, vermicelli, and potatoes, then, the *Encyclopédie* describes food items without clearly showing the dietary context into which they belong. It is not really interested in who eats what. This problem, which aroused the passionate interest of Rousseau, is simply set aside. Too much precision here would amount to ideological rigidity and disturb the consensus within the readership.

Claude Lévi-Strauss, who in *L'Origine des manières de table* postulates the opposition between roast and boiled food, cites the article "Bouilli" [Boiled meat] in the *Encyclopédie,* insisting on its polemical character and deducing from it that "the democratic inspiration of the writers of the Encyclopédie is reflected in their apology of boiled meat." It is true that Mercier in his *Tableau de Paris* described boiled dishes as poor eating and as the basic food of the "petty bourgeois": "At dinner it is soup and boiled meat; at night a beef salad or a *boeuf à la mode*" [stew with vegetables] (ch. 67). Brillat-Savarin was to decree the culinary wretchedness of boiled meat, which he described as "meat without its juice." But in the *Encyclopédie* the categories of roast and boiled do not seem to carry any social connotations. To be sure, the *bouilli* [boiled meat] is presented as "one of man's most succulent and nourishing foods," as a basic foodstuff "like bread"; but it is not placed in opposition to the roast as a totem food nor seen as democratic in relation to the feudal roast. Indeed, it appears that a structural definition of the pertinent contrasting pairs in the *Encyclopédie* as a whole would indicate that the cleavage is, rather, between roast/boiled meat on the one hand and the *ragoût* on the other. Here again, we find the major dichotomy foodstuff/condiment from which cooking derives its specific character. The most important criterion of the *Encyclopédie* is of a medical and moral order. A simple diet is valued positively in inverse proportion to its potential elaborateness. From this point of view the *ragoût,* which represents the danger of culinary activity, is the opposite of roast and boiled meat, the epitome of simple and healthful food. Rousseau or Marmontel in their autobiographies thus naturally include a trout *au bleu* or a roast leg of lamb in the category of frugal cooking, because the criterion is the method and the elaborateness of the preparation. The *Encyclopédie* does not formulate any hierarchy by indicating the social connotations of the various foodstuffs and states, without comment, that beef can be served "boiled, in the form of a roast, as a *ragoût,* or smoked." Nor do the recipes very often include the habitual marks of the treatises on cooking, which call a preparation "à la bourgeoise" or "à la mode."

The articles of the *Encyclopédie* on cooking are clearly set off from the literature on cooking that came into its own by the second half of the eighteenth century. In the article "Cuisine," Jaucourt analyzes the profusion of culinary treatises from a moral perspective, considering it the sign of a corruption of the sense of taste that has led to unrestrained self-indulgence:

Thus, cooking, which had been a simple art in the first ages of the world subsequently became more elaborate and more refined century by century, sometimes in one place, sometimes in another. It has now become a field of study and a most demanding science and is constantly being expounded under such titles as *Le Cuisinier Français, Cuisinier royal, Don de Comus, Ecole des officiers de bouche,* and many others, all of which are forever advocating new methods, thereby furnishing sufficient proof that it is impossible to reduce to a fixed order all the tricks for disguising natural foodstuffs that have been pursued, invented, and imagined by man's self-indulgence and unrestrained taste.

Jaucourt failed to perceive the novelty and to define the function of these series, of which certain volumes were distributed in the *Bibliothèque bleue.** The foreword of 1769 to the *Cuisinière bourgeoise,* for example, is very explicit: "In this issue, as well as in the others, it has been my aim to reduce the expense of cooking, to simplify the method, and to bring down to the level of bourgeois kitchens, as it were, dishes that seemed to be appropriate only to opulent kitchens." All these books give precise recipes adapted to specific budgets and thus necessarily undertake a social classification of eating patterns and a dif-

---

*Inexpensive popular reading matter (bound in blue paper) that was widely sold by ambulant peddlers and even distributed to lending libraries.—Trans.

ferentiated semiology. By eschewing all considerations of this kind and permitting the social connotation of any given foodstuff to remain indistinct, the *Encyclopédie* does not approach the actual food practices from the same perspective. In this manner the statements about cooking in the *Encyclopédie* are in a class by themselves, since they partake neither of the utilitarianism of the cookbooks nor of the discourse of gastronomy, which classifies the various foods according to esthetic criteria and establishes a rigid code of social conventions. The culinary system of the *Encyclopédie* thus reflects, above all, the state of knowledge at the time, as well as the authors' pluralistic and wide-ranging learning.

In the entries concerning natural history, physiology, medicine, and animal economy, the *Encyclopédie* addresses a different order of problems. Learned history, literature, and mythology had sought to apprehend human eating habits through their development over time and the diffusion of customs, while in the entries mentioned above eating is related to the established tenets of learning concerning the body, which provides the framework for a different approach to nutrition. The activity of eating, about which we think quite naturally with the words taken from our own body of knowledge in biology, dietetics, and psychoanalysis, is defined in the *Encyclopédie* by means of words that seem close to our understanding, but which upon close examination reveal how remote from us they are.

In the 1750s Réaumur simulated the process of digestion, and Bordeu defined it as "an effort of the entire body, a general function"; but science was still far from isolating the major functions of life and from having a comprehensive and organized conception of life. The mechanical-physical model alone prevailed, and the body was defined in terms of humoral medicine. Only in this context was a connection made between eating and sexuality. According to the article "Nutrition" [Ingestion], "the means used (by nature) for the preservation of the individual are as hidden as those used for the preservation of the species," for there is a physical connection between these two functions: Chyle and sperm are one and the same substance, defined only by their physical character as "gelatinous juices." In this manner, digestive disorders in masturbators[8] can be explained by an "excessive evacuation of the seminal fluid," a "fluid truly analogous to the gastric juice by its viscous, malleable nature and by the manner in which it is generated" (s.v. "Nutrition"). The relationship between food and sexuality in the *Encyclopédie* has nothing in common with the relationship we can envisage today on the basis of the knowledge at our disposal. In the context of humoral medicine, the Encyclopedists tied these two phenomena together by means of a physical analysis, reinforced perhaps by the religious discourse, which combined under the generic term of concupiscence the excesses of the bed and of the table. It was only by the end of the eighteenth century, with Lavoisiers's analyses of combustion, that the body was defined in depth.[9] By that time digestion and reproduction were to be described as two of the major functions characterizing the organization of living things. As early as 1778 Lamarck defined organic life as "that which breathes, takes nourishment, and reproduces."

Let us now turn to the articles "Diète [Dietetics] and "Régime" [Regimen] and the set of articles to which they refer and find out whether they represent a departure from traditional medicine. In the article "Diète," dietetics is defined as a set of rules indicating what is beneficial and what is harmful to the animal economy and thereby compensating for the failure of the instincts in man. This science is expounded in terms of the most ancient learning: all food is included among the six "Non-Naturals" whose use is prescribed in traditional medicine. Unlike our own dietetics, this system is not based on organic chemistry but on a classification of the various foodstuffs in the context of humoral theory. Bland and gelatinous foods, which are physically closest to chyle, are recommended, while all those with a tart, "aromatic" flavor, the elaborate products of cooking, are considered dangerous to the animal economy since their taste has an "active" character upsetting to the system of humors. The article "Régime" presents a summary of the temperaments and the regimens suitable for each of them. Each temperament is associated with one age of life and one season: Childhood/ sanguine/spring; Puberty/bilious/summer; Manhood/phlegmatic/autumn; Old Age/melancholic/winter. In this manner, the human body in all its aspects is placed under an algebraic grid that seems quite unfamiliar to us and calls for some surprising regimens. Under the humoral theory the phlegmatic temperament, characterized as it is by a "viscous, mucous serosity and languid activity," needs a diet of "spicy and aromatic dishes, good wine, and fermented liquids." Indeed, people of this temperament are advised to engage in "strong passions liable to arouse emotion, agitation, and vivid impressions." In the articles on dietetics the *Encyclopédie* adheres to the eighteenth century's most widely held concepts of the body. Most people thought about their own bodies and their various bodily functions in these terms. Casanova, for example, who in his *Mémoires* expresses the most subtle nuances of his erotic and gastronomical experiences, does not hesitate in the preface to place his body under the grid of the temperaments: "I have successively had all the temperaments: I was pituitous in my childhood, sanguine in my youth, later bilious, and now I am melancholic, which I shall probably remain. Adapting my food to my constitution, I have always enjoyed good health" (Pléiade ed., p. 5). Rousseau, on the other hand, violently criticizes the dietetic rules and the system of regimens. In book 11 of his *Confessions* he actually accuses Bordeu of causing the death of Maréchal de Luxembourg's grandson.[10] These views of diet make it quite clear that a concept of life did not exist in the eighteenth century.[11] Eating was seen as a maintenance operation designed to ensure continuous good health, but "despite every effort," as we are told in the article "Choses Non-Naturelles" [Non-Naturals], "it has been amply demonstrated that it is very difficult to maintain good health and to prevent illness throughout a long life." Death is seen as an unexpected accident that intervenes to upset the state of health that is conceived as an ataraxia. The dietetics of the *Encyclopédie* espouses the tradition of Celsus, Galen, and Boerhaave; to our thinking it perceives the body as a crude machine, fairly similar to Papin's "digester," which is described in the article "Digestion." Anyone who at this point still doubts that this conception of the body is truly foreign to us should take a look at the anatomical plates of the *Encyclopédie,* which can no longer teach us anything and seem utterly fantastic to us. While the dietetics and the global concept of nutrition in the *Encyclopédie* do not mark a new approach to life and to the body, the insistence with which certain questions are raised in a number of scattered articles does seem to suggest an interest in certain new topics.

In his definition of the complex phenomenon of taste, Jaucourt uses banal formulations, such as: "Taste in general is the impulse of an organ which reacts to its object." Or else, he explains the curious variations of taste by physiological reasons: Texture is "the disposition or obstruction of the nervous mamillas"; the fibers of the tastebuds "become blunted or hardened"; the nerves, "more sensitive in youth, become callous and more difficult to arouse in the adult." Yet none of this permits him to explain the vagaries of taste and the mysterious phenomenon of distaste. In the article "Saveur" [Flavor], Jaucourt notes that "imagination, too...enters into the sensation of taste, as into all other sensations." "Why is it that I used to hate the bitter flavor of coffee which today is my delight? It follows that there is no idea intrinsically attached to any given impression; at least none that the soul is not able to change." Gustatory sensations can undergo a change in the process of habituation; moreover, the impression and the idea "that is attached to it" can shift and waver under the influence of the imagination.

All of this provides an opening for the study of deviant behavior, aberrant phenomena, and the "obscure labyrinth of the sensations," which are part of "the monstrous in nature" that is included in the tree of knowledge as defined in the *Prospectus.* Eating is no longer a simple, mechanical action but in man gives rise to the most extraordinary excesses. The *Encyclopédie* describes a whole series of alimentary aberrations when speaking of "pica," which takes us into the world of strange cravings. "Pica" is defined as a "violent appetite for absurd and harmful things that have nothing to do with food":

The etymologists claim that it was given this name, which in its natural sense means magpie, because just as this bird is very wide-ranging in its utterances and variegated in its plumage, so the depraved appetite of persons afflicted with this disease extends to many different things and spawns an infinite number of variations; but could we not have found a more obvious and more striking connection between the notorious chatter of this bird and the persons of the fair sex who are the usual victims of this disorder?

The *Encyclopédie* gives a series of the most curious food fantasies: One woman dreams of "raw fish, green fruits, old herring"; one "pregnant woman had a strong desire to bite into a young baker's arm"; another had such a strong desire to "feed on her husband's flesh" that she killed and salted him. Those aberrations of pica that are chronic are interpreted not in physiological, but in psychic terms. Similar to such phenomena as "the frantic pursuit of some disagreeable smell, such as that of rotten old books, candles, smoldering lamps, or even excrement," they are related to the "retention of strong passion, the smothering of violent desires and the failure to satisfy pressing natural needs from a sense of virtue, fear, or shame." All the vices of the appetite, of the "concupiscient" faculty, are laid to a "lesion" of the imagination. Some persons of "depraved" appetite have contracted this disorder "from an overly intense contemplation of something in a picture that could become the object of this depravity." In the world of cravings, the activity of eating takes on a certain depth, for it is related to the body as a whole, and especially to language: "Is it not quite natural that they (the women suffering from pica) refuse to confess that their appetite gives them a violent desire to eat rotten leather, for example, or fecal matter? And if the cause of this disease happens to be a wish to marry which they are forbidden to express, and even less to satisfy, will it not cause them a great deal of pain to break their silence? And yet, how useful would such a confession be to the physician!" One might deduce from such texts that the *Encyclopédie* describes quite well what we today call the "oral" dimension. But this would be to forget that the catalogue of aberrations is part of an ancient learned tradition that is largely based on hearsay, and that Jaucourt also attempts to explain the phenomenon of cravings as the result of "vitiated humors." Nonetheless, it can be said that the articles dealing with taste, distaste, craving, pica, pallor, and canine hunger, by raising particular kinds of questions, outline a somewhat novel appoach to the area of eating habits. The study of faulty eating and deviant behavior removes the body from the mechanical grid of the humoral theory and opens it to the strange dimensions of desire, fantasy, and tabu. Thus, the history of "the monstrous in nature" approaches the complex activity of eating in terms that are more satisfactory to us than the humoral theory and the dietetics of the eighteenth century.

Related on the one hand to the prevailing knowledge about the body, the approach to eating habits is also related to the prevailing knowledge about food. Can it be said that in the *Encyclopédie* the definition of what is a foodstuff and what is edible is envisaged in a new way on the basis of natural history? In the article "Encyclopédie" Diderot responds to "those who have objected that (our) botany is neither complete nor interesting enough, . . . that these objections are completely unfounded; that it was impossible to go beyond the genera without writing in-folio volumes; that none of the common plants have been omitted; that they have been described; that their chemical analysis has been given along with their properties as remedies or as foodstuffs." While Diderot does not really answer these objections, he does make it clear that in the pluralistic approach of the *Encyclopédie* the plant is placed into the context of a multifaceted discourse that goes far beyond the classifications of natural history. The plant or animal is not described in the *Encyclopédie* by means of the strict nomenclature of botany or zoology, which, in any case, had not yet been fully developed at that point in the eighteenth century; nor are the edible things, the whole area of edibility with which we are concerned here, completely caught up in the imperialism of the visible and the describable that is the hallmark of classical learning. This is why they have the splendor of things that are not described and which, since they have no exact name, are spoken about in everyday language. The strawberry, for example, is presented in these terms: "a small red or white fruit; it looks like the tip of a nurse's breast." How does one deal with such a statement, where the metaphorical classification of the strawberry leads us straight to the core of the "oral" dimension, since the description of the fruit as a delicacy calls forth a process of fantasizing about the infantile or erotic sucking of a breast. Here observation has nothing to do with classification, but serves to cover pure desire in all its depth. This is the exact opposite of the classification of natural history in the context of an old structure harking back to Ambroise Paré and Aldrovandi, a structure that was dominated by the use of similarity and analogy.[12] In the *Encyclopédie,* plants and animals are not desemanticized (in the sense that Michel Foucault has given to this expression in *Les Mots et les choses*);[13] rather, they have an underlying meaning and a history that can be seized upon by desire. In certain cases, they are considered above all from the standpoint of their edibility, their flavor, and their taste. Thus the orange: "The flesh, pith, or pulp of the sweet orange contains a superabundant, sweet and pungent juice, which makes this fruit very refreshing and thirst quenching. This flesh is eaten without the skin, either plain or with sugar; in most subjects' stomachs this food manifestly gives rise to the sensation that in most books on dietetics is referred to as rejoicing of the stomach." In the *Encyclopédie* food is not described by means of the nomenclature of natural history, but in an open-ended language that places imagination above taxonomy.

Due to its manner of defining and describing food, the *Encyclopédie* can be said to be pregastronomical in its discourse, for on the level of discourse, gastronomy is, at least in the writings of Grimod de la Reynière, a kind of compensation for the desemantization of things brought about by natural history. To be sure, Grimod, too, in his own way might make a connection between the strawberry and a nurse's breast, but for him such a statement would have a very different meaning. For gastronomy is a strictly literary game that uses the metaphorical classification of things to break out of the rigid taxonomical classification. Here the nomenclature of flavors is created by means of an esthetic transposition, and a given food item is systematically reinvested with its full weight of desire and orality in a methodical and calculated literary endeavor. While the *Encyclopédie* harks back to a learned tradition, gastronomy is a party to the birth of "literature."

The two sectors in which the *Encyclopédie* deals with the history of food practices and nutrition are composed of heterogeneous statements that do not proceed from a single level of knowledge. They define the activity of eating by probing it from all sides in a complex approach combining old and new elements. These two sectors share a certain instability of the "nomenclature," which shatters, as it were, as it is dispersed throughout the system and the culinary subject matter. By contrast, when dealing with the technical aspects of food, the *Encyclopédie* in its role as "dictionary of the arts" makes use of a new kind of language. In this area the culinary system is relatively homogeneous.

In this sector, which is far removed from the sometimes insoluble problems involved in the social, scientific, or cultural classification of food, the *Encyclopédie* describes the multifarious activities of production in a self-assured and positive manner. Here eating is no longer dealt with in the words of a complex and heterogeneous learning, for the language of the arts makes it possible to adopt a clear, technical approach to food. Here the *Encyclopédie* does not limit itself to summing up what is known about a specific subject matter, but produces new statements.

This technical sector does not identify the historical or social position of a given food item. Evaluated solely in terms of the "art," it is stripped of its social connotations, as it were. Owing to the technical focus on the anonymous manual labor that processes the raw material, certain aspects are left in the dark. We do not find out who produces, who sells, and who consumes. In this manner, the description of the crafts throws a veil of innocence over certain food items that are obtained by the most questionable means. Sugar and coffee, for example, were the fruits of the slave trade; they were denounced by Montesquieu and by Bernardin de Saint-Pierre, who noted in the diary of his voyage to Ile-Bourbon: "I do not know whether coffee or sugar are needed for Europe's happiness, but I do know that these two plants have brought unhappiness to two continents. America has been depopulated to make room for planting them; and now Africa is being depopulated in order to have a nation for cultivating them" (25 April 1760). But the writers of the *Encyclopédie* see these colonial products as fashionable substances that have brought about the appearance of cafés and yielded the subtle art of confectionery. They therefore describe the many uses of sugar in confectionery making, the various stages in sugar production, and also devote a long article and a plate to "Sucreries" [Sugar plantations]. But even this purely technical description provides a glimpse of the prisonlike structure of the colony. The plate shows the spatial arrangement of the master's house and the "Negroes' cabins," for it is necessary, "whenever possible, to place the master's house and its outbuildings on a high place from which it is possible to see what is happening in the quarters." Standard anticolonial sentiments and virtuous indignation have no place in the *Encyclopédie,* for it is exclusively interested in the production and use of sugar. The development of productive forces, human labor, and trade are treated favorably and enthusiastically throughout. This is why the description of the practical arts does not evaluate a foodstuff in terms of the blood it may have cost, but seeks out and marvels at its marks of human endeavor and cultural mediation. This the *Encyclopédie* does with a clear conscience, for it considers the colonization of the eighteenth century to be a different matter from the Spanish conquest. The eighteenth century contrasts the pillage and coldhearted pursuit of gold with its own dynamic of progress, which, through the concerted efforts of scholars and merchants, enhances the value of nature's gifts, the true sources of wealth. Food production in all of its technical aspects is considered an innocent, beneficial, and joyful activity by which trade becomes a truly civilized pursuit.[14]

Unlike the gastronomical approach, the technical approach to food is not a description limited to the art of cooking, for it follows the food through all the stages of its transformation, from the raw material to the table. The *Encyclopédie* is not interested in cooking as an artifice, for it sees culinary magic as a perversion of the art. All the special effects that are so greatly appreciated by Grimod de la Reynière, who presents the cook as a miracle worker and esthete capable of changing fish into meat, the whole world of forcemeats, decorations, and sculptures in lard and sugar that is cursorily evoked in the article "Confiseur" [Confectioner]—all this is of no more than secondary importance in the *Encyclopédie*. The art of cooking must not be a sybaritic, corrupting luxury, but an honest and innocent art that gives sustenance and wholesome pleasure. Not for the *Encyclopédie* the gastronomic obsession that keeps the culinary discourse within the confines of esthetics or sexual innuendo. The capon and the steer, which inspire Grimod to lewd verses on the virginity of castrates, are depicted live in the stable or the barnyard. With a certain levity, but also with all the seriousness of one who has useful information to impart, Diderot explains how to make a rooster into a capon by using butter so as not to cause it unnecessary pain, how to have chicks raised by a capon,[15] and how to bring a new rooster into the barnyard. The culinary system includes the domestic economy, and the master chef is flanked by a good country housewife. Food is the end result of a chain of activities, none of which is ignored by the *Dictionnaire Encyclopédique*. Healthy curiosity takes the place of the game of gastronomy; and desire is focused more on the joys of production and the multiplication of wealth by human industry than on the ultimate oral satisfaction. Any given food item is thus defined in terms of a general technique of food production, including agronomy and animal husbandry, rather than in terms of the culinary art that derives prestige from its seeming effortlessness. At the revolving table of Trianon, which made cumbersome serving unnecessary—an idea that was later revived by mad King Louis II [of Bavaria]—the appearance of food became a spectacular feat of staging, orchestrated by a Circe-like chef. In an opposite sense, the *Encyclopédie* deploys an array of techniques and experiments, contrasting a baroque black magic with the straightforward but multifaceted wealth of production.

The experimental bent makes it possible to sidestep the polemic about luxury and to treat refined and costly foodstuffs on the same footing as all others. This was not peculiar to the *Encyclopédie;* Louis-Sébastien Mercier, who castigated excess of any kind and condemned the cuisine of the rich, nonetheless approved, in his *Tableau de Paris,* of the orange trees grown in the hothouses of noble households, seeing this as a matter of experimenting, of acclimatizing an exotic product for the benefit of all. Agricultural science was expected to end food shortages once and for all. This is why the importation of foreign species was considered not a superfluous game, but an activity of public interest. With food thus at the core of scientific endeavor, hunger acquired a new dimension. Food, which in the eighteenth century was distributed in a marketing system and by a variety of trade guilds that no longer exist today, was encompassed with a system of precautions and operations that conferred a certain prestige upon it. The pharmacists made decorative sugarwork, roasted coffee beans, sold coffee extract, and made cocoa: "They form one and the same guild with the grocers." A novelty such as the chocolate bar was seen less as a delicacy than as a pharmaceutical concentrate: "Chocolate composed in this manner is a very convenient item; for whenever one has to leave the house hurriedly or is traveling and therefore lacks the time to make it into a beverage, one can eat a one-ounce bar and drink afterward, leaving it to the stomach to dissolve this impromptu breakfast." For us, chocolate in either of its two forms no longer has this pharmaceutical appeal, nor that of an amusing novelty. The distillation of wine, the roasting of coffee and cocoa, all involved operations of a scientific character. The ceremony of coffee was a ritual of experimentation whose appeal lay in the utensils used. To this day the glass percolator partakes of this ancient prestige of chemistry. In the eighteenth century, techniques for the preservation of food (drying and cooling) also availed themselves of the newest discoveries of physics and chemistry. In the article "Glace" [Ice], Jaucourt refers directly to the works of Réaumur, who "teaches us how to make ice cream inexpensively." It was a happy moment when science could invest sherbet with this very special importance.

The human body itself was one of the main areas of experimentation. There was a great interest in experiencing new sensations; it was felt that just as the glottis should be made to articulate all languages, so the tastebuds should be systematically exposed to different tastes and made to experience new flavors that would shock the old body. On 20 June 1768, [Captain] Cook ate dog-meat and stated: "All those who had tasted it declared that they had never eaten any tastier meat, and that they would henceforth no longer look down on dog-meat." In the same manner Bernardin de Saint-Pierre at Ile-Bourbon tasted all the unknown plants he found in the course of his botanical research, at the risk of poisoning himself. As Brillat noted, everything had changed in two centuries; the culinary horizon had become completely transformed since the Renaissance. It was therefore felt that the human body is anchored directly in history through its use of food, and that Fontenelle's Apicius was right when he proclaimed that the progress of reason cannot be dissociated from the progress of the senses, for food is part of human history. The conscious attention to flavors and tastes in the *Encyclopédie* is not a matter of catering to the fantasies of the gourmet, but of intellectual curiosity and openness to the world. Orality is made a part of experience, and pleasure is reinforced by an element of experimentation. Because of its interest in technology and new experiences, the *Encyclopédie* thus transcends the dichotomy between frugality and luxury and, in this sector, adopts a resolutely new position with respect to food. Once it has defined cooking as a useful art and accepted the culinary endeavor as one aspect of progress and civilization, it must find a new language in which to speak of it.

The *Encyclopédie* offers a whole *corpus* of scattered recipes, which it either presents as separate articles or under the heading "Diète" in certain articles. But what is a recipe? Are the texts that we today define as recipes of the same nature as those of the *Encyclopédie?* Are the recipes of the *Encyclopédie* similar to those of the cookbooks, or of the same order as the treatises on gastronomy? In order to define that a recipe is in the *Encyclopédie,* we must try to establish exactly to which schema of classification these recipes refer and what kind of nomenclature they employ. The fact that the scattered recipes are rather difficult to gather together in one set indicates the lack of firm criteria. The list of recipes can include many things, since it is not subject to any exclusive rule, such as budgetary considerations or national preference. The mango and the different ways of preparing it appear in the *Encyclopédie* on the same footing with rabbit stew.

It can be said that the series of recipes of the *Encyclopédie* does not lay out any particular program of consumption, but rather attests to a general curiosity about what can be eaten. The nomenclature is not formal, like that of "Louis XV" cooking, because it is not interested in the gastronomical ritual that consists of giving a name to everything. Gastronomy is a cult, the fostering of a mystery. In its exclusive preoccupation with taste, it seeks to define what makes for a glorious culinary achievement. The central gesture of the "panel of tasters" presided over by Grimod is a baptismal ceremony. The critics want to enjoy unexpected culinary effects as they would enjoy an esthetic event; they formulate a synthetic appraisal of the tonality of a combination of flavors, of their symphonic effect, without entering the sacred den of the chef. The gastronomical recipe thus partakes of a mythology. Grimod, in his *Manuel des Amphytrions*, wants to bring back the great names of "Louis XV" cooking: "We would render these illustrious Fathers of the gourmand Church a great service by restoring these names to their original purity and clearly establishing the origins of these various dishes." Here the recipe is reduced to a name that, far from having a directly explanatory character, swathes the food item in a cloud of splendor. Plays on words and anecdotes are loosely connected to these recipes; they take us away from the kitchen and into a social and historical environment.[16]

The *Encyclopédie*, on the other hand, presents anonymous recipes. Here the emphasis is not on the name of the dish or on the menu, but on the detailed exposition of how it is made. Preceded by a discussion of the raw material (beef) or a broad culinary category (roast, *ragoût*), the recipe speaks the language of the kitchen and constantly refers to a body of practical knowledge. It does not describe the end product, but the various operations the foodstuff must undergo. It violates the forbidden space of the kitchen and betrays the secrets of the trade. Frequently representing the transcription of a regional recipe, it marks the advent of a written, urban culture, the centralization of a scattered oral tradition. Uninterested in the gourmet's system of flavors, the recipe of the *Encyclopédie* proceeds to reduce the various techniques to their essentials. Here is what is said about *confitures:* "All *confitures* can be reduced to eight kinds: stewed fruit, jam, jelly, paste, dry preserves, whole candied fruit, candied fruit pieces, and crystallized fruit." Each one of these is precisely defined by color and consistency ("delicately sticky," "crystalline transparency") throughout the various stages of cooking: "If they (syrups) do not contain enough sugar, they will curdle; if they contain too much, they will crystallize." The article "Cuisson" [Boiling] deploys all the subtleties of the confectioner's art: "The boiling of sugar is the mainstay of the art of confectionary. There are different kinds of boiling, such as the boiling of sugar to the ball, thread, puffed, spun and crack stages, as well as caramelizing;

and some of these can still be subdivided and marked by lesser degrees, such as the medium and the full thread stage, the soft and the hard ball stage, the small and the large puffed stage." The recipe of the *Encyclopédie* takes care of the problem of flavors and tastes by using the language of the art with greater precision, that is, by straightforward words about individual dishes.

Even though Diderot had left the treatment of the basic problems of food to Jaucourt, he made occasional contributions in this area. Marked by an asterisk,[17] these amount to more than the superficial connivance of a man who liked to live well and frequently dined at d'Holbach's table at Grand'val. Diderot was equally and impartially interested in esthetics, still lives, and recipes. His articles about cooking provide a definition of a new type of recipe, new at least in its form. The articles are often secondhand, copied from some specialized work. This is true, for example, in the article "Cacao," which by an unexpurgated "I" betrays that it is borrowed from a traveler to faraway lands. But Diderot does more than an editor's work; in certain articles he creates a special culinary style. In the article "Chocolat" he clearly states the problem of the recipe and notes its conventional character: "For since with respect to taste the diversity of opinions is infinite, everyone wants his own to be heard, and one person will add what another omits; and even if everyone agreed as to the ingredients, it would be impossible to establish universally approved proportions among them; and it will be sufficient to choose them in such a way that they are acceptable to the greatest number and thus result in the most popular flavor." In preparing one's own chocolate, one is not at all obliged to follow any rule of average but can vary the proportions according to one's taste and temperament. In an industrial society where the ingredients are rarely prepared by the consumer, the recipe calls for invariable proportions; whereas in the eighteenth century, when ingredients were often processed at home, they were not standardized. The recipe for chocolate "after the manner of the French islands of America" takes us into the domestic intimacy of the pantry: "Place this mixture (cinnamon and sugar) into a chocolate pot and add one whole fresh egg, that is to say the white and the yolk; mix well with a beater until the mixture reaches the consistency of liquid honey; then have someone pour the boiling liquid (milk or water, according to taste) over it while continuing to beat vigorously in order to blend it well." By becoming involved in the preparation, one can give oneself the pleasure of a practical accomplishment and gain direct access to the culinary art, which makes it possible to enjoy a gamut of flavors by means of precise dosages. As Brillat-Savarin put it: "Those who have not manipulated them have no idea of the difficulties entailed in bringing any substance to perfection; nor do they know how much attention, tact, and experience are needed to produce a chocolate that is sweet but not insipid, firm but not hard, pungent but not unwholesome, and smooth but not starchy." (*Physiologie du goût*, Meditation 6). The *Encyclopédie* gives recipes for those who "manipulate" and who can thus make sure that their chocolate is "well prepared, of exquisite scent, and great delicacy of flavor." Since the preparation of a food is never immutably fixed by a rigid definition, one can improvise according to one's own mood and desire without ever falling into monotony. This is a far cry from today's recipes, with their emphasis on precision, their compulsory proportions, and their cold technicality. The *Encyclopédie*'s recipes for cookies and biscuits present, in addition to their informative dimension, a special style of writing that pursues the striking formula and a certain semantic saturation. Here the technical language of the art has a depth of signification that is quite surprising. The recipe outlines a whole program of subtle operations. Orangeade, for example, is good if "by rubbing a small piece of sugar against the skin of the same orange," one blends "the perfume of the skin with the flavor of the sugar." Such delicate precision confers true nobility on the food, yet also preserves its simplicity. At such special moments, the recipe of the *Encyclopédie* becomes as sensuous as it can be.

If the recipes of the *Encyclopédie* constitute, in principle, an open and rather undefined series, some actual preferences do emerge, although they are not premeditated but, rather, due to the mood of the collaborators and the material circumstances of the encyclopedic undertaking. The large number of recipes for *ragoûts* initially strikes us as a logical inconsistency, since in the medical-dietetic sector of the culinary system Jaucourt had defined the *ragoût* as the harmful aspect of cooking. Yet Diderot slips recipes for *ragoûts* into the interstices of this culinary discourse and into added passages and even gives precise definitions of their preparation. He thus mentions the *fricassée,* characterized by "rapid cooking," the *fricandeau* [larded veal braised], the *civet* [venison stew], the *persillade* [beef salad garnished with parsley], and the fish stew, "a *ragoût* that is very popular at riverside inns." All these dishes are characteristic of a provincial cooking that may well be the basis of "à la mode" bourgeois cooking. From personal or regional preference, Diderot dwells at length on the various kinds of fowl: the woodcock, the snipe, and the warbler, "which are prepared with verjuice of grain and white pepper." While the roast is simply presented as the minimum of preparation, the *petit ragoût* calls for a complex and sensuous formula that is obviously enjoyed by Diderot. "Snipes can be treated like woodcocks if they are to be eaten roasted; but if they are to be made into a *ragoût* they are split in half without being emptied. They are then browned in fatback and seasoned with pepper and chives. The same pan is used for drawing out the juice of the mushrooms with a little lemon. The *ragoût* is finished when the snipes are cooked through. Keep in mind that they must be half done before they are split." In its disregard for the strictures of dietetics, the series of *ragoûts* amounts to a bit of lust of the palate that is very French. But while *ragoûts* do appear occasionally in these delightful little recipes, they do not have a positive symbolic value. They are not the totemic foods of the *Encyclopédie.*

These must be sought in two areas, namely, in the exotic dish and in the sugary sphere of sweetmeats and pastries, with the former representing, as it were, modernity and the era of commerce, and the latter serving as the emblem of a civilization that perceived itself as peaceful. The exotic product has the charm of the unknown, for it is part of an unfamiliar nature and used in distant culinary traditions. The culinary classification of the mango, for example, is one of the specific contributions of the *Encyclopédie:* "Its fruit is rounded, oblong, and flat.... Shaped like a kidney, larger than a goose-egg, smooth and shiny,...its flesh is yellowish and succulent, rather similar to that of the peach, or rather the plum, tart at first, then sour, mild and agreeable to the taste.... It is cut up and eaten either raw or marinated in wine. It is also kept as a preserve. The Indians sometimes open it with a knife and fill it with fresh ginger, garlic, mustard, and salt, to eat it with rice or like pickled olives." Vanilla, cocoa, and sugar are totemic foods on two counts, for they not only retain the prestige of the exotic, but are also used in pastry making. Sweet dishes and sweetmeats compose the *Encyclopédie*'s favorite culinary register because they have a symbolic value of "sweetness" and innocence. The eighteenth century saw eating habits as a deep sign of a person's nature or character; recall Rousseau's verses about the cruel, meat-eating Englishmen. In the same vein, Lapérouse was surprised that cruel savages should eat raspberries. In the *Encyclopédie* the great emphasis on sweet foods is a kind of collective affirmation of a happy, lighthearted orality that takes a particular delight in sherbets, ice creams, and sweetmeats in general. Diderot speaks joyfully about the whole series of sweet pastries, cookies, biscuits, macaroons, and so forth. Voltaire constantly uses pastry for the values it connotes, and Marivaux, in *Le paysan parvenu,* uses it to characterize the innocent aspect of the gourmandise of the Habert sisters, while their liking for *ragoût* is the dark and forbidden side of this trait. In Diderot's *Père de famille,* chocolate is the occasion of a touching and intimate domestic ceremony. The *Encyclopédie* as well draws a literary effect from the connotation of "sweets" to represent a certain conception of sociability and festive dining whose underlying character-istic is not yet the deep obsessive appetite (*boulimie*) of the bourgeois dinner, but a forthright, permissible, and joyful sensuality.

Among the plates devoted to the area of food (dishes, dairy production, sugar making, cultivation of the vineyard), those depicting confectionery and pastry making form a coherent and significant set. In the figures at the bottom of the plate, the kitchen implements are clearly lined up: mold for candied fruits, oven for making *praliné,* cream shaker. The vignette at the top depicts the various techniques: One worker is making sugar-coated almonds by "pearling," another by "spinning," another by "tumbling." The vignette also shows the successive stages in the preparation of a product: one worker torrifies the coffee, another winnows the almonds, a third one crushes them in a mortar. The plates are thus an exact illustration of the recipes and techniques, for they visualize the precise and coded system of activities defined in the language of the craft. Here the culinary activity becomes pure spectacle, but one that takes place behind the scenes of the gastronomical achievement, at the workplace. The set of plates about confectionery and pastry making with its figures, vignettes, and com-mentary conveys the impression of a happy activity described and pictured with sensuous precision.

Conveying the very opposite impression and as if to form a counterpoint, the two plates devoted to the butcher, and particularly the plate on "Tuerie"

[Slaughter] open onto a sphere of malediction. Bearing the title: "Slaughtering and the butcher's tools that are used for it," this plate, which, like all the others, is designed to explain, becomes rather frightening as soon as one looks at the figures showing these instruments of torture: "Poleax for felling the ox, trimming knife for slitting the oxen's throat, small carving knife for opening sheep." Here the technical information is insufficient to redeem an occupation that is horrifying and cannot be integrated into the honorable arts. The commentary on the vignette precisely explains the various operations involved in slaughtering. The vignette itself totally transcends this explicit meaning in a phenomenon that Roland Barthes has called "resistence to meaning." "It can be said that every single plate of the Encyclopédie vibrates far beyond its demonstrative purpose."* The figures [of the vignette], when analyzed in isolation, show a very striking elaboration of the detail: the ox that is being felled, standing next to a row of skinned and split beef carcasses, has the ugly snout of a monstrous beast, the butchers show all the distinctive traits of their guild: sharp chins, sunken eyes, a sly expression, razor-thin lips, predatory ease of movement contrasting with huge, muscular arms. Their coarse and vicious grin is the opposite of the laughter of the young errand-boys in the plates on confectionery. But what makes this one of the strangest plates of the *Encyclopédie* is the staged setting of the scene: Barred windows, stone-tiled floors, and, leaning over a railing, the attentive figure of a sad (?) child watching the scene. Here the traumatic character of the "slaughter" is clearly expressed. This second meaning is not the fortuitous result of our reading or of the mood of the master engraver. Is is bolstered by a series of statements about butchers in the *Encyclopédie* itself. Diderot, in a learned article about this guild since Antiquity, elaborates the usual themes: "They are all violent people who cannot be disciplined; their hands and their eyes are accustomed to blood." He takes pleasure in evoking another, pagan, epoch, when "slaughter" was not a curse, but a noble ritual. "Homer's heroes often dismembered and roasted their meat themselves; there was nothing repulsive about this operation that is so unpleasant to behold." By the end of the century, Louis-Sébastien Mercier still gives a horrified description of the streets where slaughtering took place in his *Tableau de Paris*.[18] While the technical sector of the culinary system of the *Encyclopédie* is permeated by the idea of a happy and peaceful activity, one unexpected plate about "an occupation that is so unpleasant to behold," as Diderot puts it, serves to reintroduce the crude violence of the activity of eating.

The culinary statements of the *Encyclopédie* do not define cooking as one narrowly circumscribed subject matter. Because of the material circumstances involved in the editing, the encyclopedic undertaking did not develop strictly in accordance with a uniform plan; instead, the vicissitudes of bringing it to fruition produced a whole array of heterogeneous discourses. Moreover, since the

---

*Roland Barthes, Robert Mauzi, Jean-Pierre Séguin, *L'Univers de l'Encyclopédie: Images d'une civilisation* (Paris, 1964).

principle of the encyclopedic mode is the systematic multiplication of references, the treatment of cooking in the *Dictionnaire Encyclopédique* constitutes an open and very extensive subject. Responding to a wide variety of concerns, the culinary system is a wheel with many spokes, devised in such a way that all the elements refer to each other, so that the activity of eating is not evaluated from the narrow point of view of the housewife or the gourmet, but defined within the framework of a multitiered body of knowledge and a wide-ranging curiosity. The culinary system clearly shows historical and economic transformations, as well as changes in the discourse of cooking. Summing up a body of information about the physiology of nutrition in a language that reflects a number of different states of knowledge, it produces new statements characteristic of its particular cultural moment in the area of technology. For us, this disparity of language is more than an empiric fact or simply a sign of anarchy, for it makes us see that certain choices were made. While special attention was given to the technical sector, a decision was clearly made to ignore the social dimension of the activity of eating and the normative aspect of social conventions. All of this amounts to a particular mode of openness to orality. Hunger is not painful in the *Encyclopédie;* eating does not involve any violence, nor is it fraught with fear or frustration of any kind. An innocent and slight experience, marked neither by obsessive appetite nor by "sado-oral" cravings, it is a learned game involving both knowledge and sensuous enjoyment of food. The characteristic statements about food it produced, their distribution throughout the work, and its varied approaches to the activity of eating are so many indications that the *Encyclopédie* preceeded the era of gastronomy.

NOTES

1. In the article "Encyclopédie," [*Encyclopédie, ou dictionnaire raisonné des sciences, des arts, et des lettres, par une société de gens de lettres,* 17 vols. (Paris, 1762-72)] Diderot writes: "the encyclopedic mode in general will be like the map of the world, where one will find only the major regions; the mode of treating particular topics will be like maps of particular kingdoms, provinces, and territories; and the dictionary will be like the detailed geographical history of every place, the general and critical topography of what we know in the intelligible world and the visible world."

2. Jacques Proust, in *Diderot et l'Encyclopédie* (Paris, 1967), pp. 133, 134, challenges the myth of Diderot's massive participation in the writing and tallies the contribution of Jaucourt, who wrote close to one third of the articles and was the real author of the last four volumes of the *Encyclopédie.* Proust cites Diderot's hommage to Jaucourt. In a letter to Sophie he says: "The Chevalier de Jaucourt? Do not fear that he will get bored with grinding out articles; God has made him for this," and in the foreword to volume 8: "Never has there been a more complete and a more absolute sacrifice of rest, self-interest, and health: he has not shrunk from the most painstaking and the most thankless research, which he has relentlessly pursued, always happy to relieve others of this distasteful task."

3. Michel Foucault writes, in *Les Mots et les choses* (Paris, 1966), p. 132 (English translation, *The Order of Things* [New York: Random House, 1970]): "Observation, from the seventeenth century onward, is a perceptible knowledge furnished with a series of systematically negative conditions. Hearsay is excluded, that goes without saying; but so are taste and smell, because their lack of certainty and their variability render impossible any analysis into distinct elements that could be universally acceptable."

Jean Anthelme Brillat-Savarin, in Meditation 2 of his *Physiologie du goût* (Paris, 1825), states the problem of classifying flavors very clearly and hopes that chemistry, which studies compounds, will be able to solve it:

Flavors are also modified by their simple, double, or multiple aggregation; so that it is impossible to classify them, from the most pleasant to the most disagreeable, from the strawberry to the colocynth. Thus, every one who has yet tried to do this has almost failed.

This result ought not to amaze us, for, it being granted that endless series of simple flavors exist, which may be modified by their reciprocal union, in any number and in any quantity, a new language would be necessary to explain all these results, mountains of folios to describe them, and as yet unknown numeric characters to label them.

Now, as until today no circumstance has yet presented itself in which any flavor could have been appreciated with perfect exactness, we have been obliged to be satisfied with a restricted number of general epithets, such as sweet, sugary, acid, sharp, and similar ones, which are expressed in the final analysis by the words "agreeable" and "disagreeable," and which suffice to make us be understood, and to indicate more or less the gustatory properties of any sapid substance with which we are dealing.

Those who come after us will know more about it, and it is no longer permitted to doubt that chemistry will reveal to them the causes or the primitive elements of flavors.

(English translation, with slight modifications, by C. C. Nimmo and N. Bain [London, 1884; reprint ed. New York, 1926], pp. 14-15.) A. B. L. Grimod de la Reynière, for his part, solved the problem in a literary fashion and thus became the founder of gastronomy. And indeed, the only possible classification of flavors makes use of metaphorical transpositions and connotations.

4. Le Père Louis Thomassin, in *Traité des jeûnes*, 2nd ed. (Paris, 1700), writes: "I wanted to make the world admire the ingenious charity and the insuperable firmness of the Church in maintaining the old rigor of fasting against the relaxation that has crept in, in increasing the number of fast-days when their severity declined, and in compensating by new pious exercises for a certain slackening it could not avoid."

Brillat-Savarin, saying that he had "seen this relaxation arise, and that gradually," fondly recalls these days of the past, for there was a sensuous side to fasting: "I must admit that this habit of fasting has singularly fallen into disuse; and, as it may serve for the edification or for the conversion of unbelievers, I will relate here how it was done toward the middle of the eighteenth century.... The strict observance of the Lenten fast gave rise to a pleasure unknown at present—namely, that of breaking our fast by breakfasting on Easter Day." (*Physiology of Taste*, pp. 218, 219).

5. Ernest Labrousse writes in his *Histoire économique et sociale de la France* (Paris, 1970), vol. 2, p. 695: "Thus, the immemorial tragedy of hunger, of massive, "cyclical" dying, gave way to another era. Terrible years no longer occurred. How did this come about? Perhaps by the grace of Heaven, by a more favorable meteorology that lessened the fluctuations of harvests, by the climatic changes that Emmanuel Le Roy Ladurie has brought into human history. Perhaps also, in addition to this free gift, by human endeavor, which had improved the techniques of agriculture. And even more probably, by commercial relations, which had also been improved."

6. Jean Paul Aron writes in *Le Mangeur au XIXe siècle* (Paris, 1973), p. 229: "In private houses, the dining room, a vaste, austere room, is a creation of the post-revolutionary bourgeoisie. It is well-nigh impossible to find in antique stores authentic dining-furniture from before the late Louis XVI period."

7. Here is a small contribution to the very serious history of the potato in the eighteenth century. In chapter 325 of the *Tableau de Paris*, 12 vols. (Amsterdam, 1782-88), entitled: "Potato Bread," Louis-Sébastien Mercier writes: "Concerned about food for the poor, whose number is truly frightening, I do not want to pass over the method of a friend of humanity who, unlike so many artisans of luxury who work for the tables of the rich, has thought about those of the indigent." The "panification" [making into bread] of the potato would produce a bread "less costly to buy, and less under the control of the great landlords, these tyrants of society who always protect the avid speculators because they share profits with them." For Mercier, the potato has an ideological weight because it is essentially the food of the poor, and a symbolic weight because it is the equivalent of the bread of the Gospel, except that it is given to the suffering poor by a "great man," a friend of humanity. Taking off from the potato, Mercier constructs a Utopia of food, dreaming of an absolute foodstuff, a manna to be provided by chemistry. Here a preoccupation with agronomy blends into the dream of an alchemistic Land of Plenty: "I may be deceived in my ardent desire, but I believe that chemistry may one day be able to extract from all bodies a nourishing principle, and that then it will be as easy for man to satisfy all his needs as to draw water from lakes and wells." Grimod, for his part (although he accepts the potato for every table and recognizes the blessings bestowed by "the illustrious and respectable Parmentier," who has "sheltered the poor, once and for all, against the threat of food shortages" and

given new pleasures to the "rich"), does not dwell on humanitarian considerations, which lie totally outside his concerns.

8. From the same perspective Tissot explains that "fumigation" upsets the digestion as much as masturbation, since it produces salivation. Chyle, sperm, and saliva are thus analyzed as analogous substances: "Having exposed the dangers of a bad digestion in some detail, I do not have to dwell on the dangers of an excessive evacuation that leads to it. It is for this reason that M. Lewis absolutely forbids his patients to smoke, since smoking, among other disadvantages, tends to produce abundant salivation by irritating the glands that generate this secretion" (Samuel Auguste Tissot, L'Onanisme [Paris, 1775], p. 144).

9. As François Jacob has pointed out, the physicochemical model of the steam engine led to a complete transformation in the representation of living beings in the late eighteenth century: "On the one hand, the work of Lavoisier reversed the relative importance attributed to organs and to their functions, imposed the concept of basic functions that satisfy the needs of the whole organism and revealed the necessity of coordinating them" (La Logique du vivant [Paris, 1970], p. 96. English translation by Betty E. Spillmann, The Logic of Life [New York, 1973], p. 83).

10. We read in book 2 of the Confessions (Geneva, 1782) (English translation by the Bibliophilist Society, London, 1923), vol. 2, p. 296: "Madame de Montmorency felt a confidence in Bordeu of which her son finally became the victim. How delighted the poor child was when he was able to get permission to come to Mont Louis with Madame de Boufflers, to ask Thérèse for something to eat and to put a little nourishment into his famished stomach! . . . But it was no use for me to say or to do anything; the physician triumphed and the child starved."

11. François Jacob writes in The Logic of Life, p. 89: "As long as the classical period was primarily concerned with demonstrating the unity of the universe, living beings had to conform to the laws of mechanics governing inanimate objects. The forces animating organized bodies were characterized in terms used to describe the movement continually occurring in their fluids or solid parts. The concept of life did not exist, as shown by the definition in the Grande Encyclopédie, an almost self-evident truth: life is 'the opposite of death'."

12. "Only towards the end of the seventeenth century were all the doubtful analogies rejected, all the invisible bonds and obscure similitudes, all which, said Linaeus, 'is not clear and obvious to the lowest capacity and has been introduced only to the great detriment of the art.' Only then could natural history develop, with the visible structure of living beings as its object and their classification as its aim" (Jacob, The Logic of Life, p. 44).

13. The history of a living being was that being itself, within the whole semantic network that connected it to the world. . . . The whole of animal semantic has disappeared, like a dead and useless limb. The words that had been interwoven into the very being of the beast have been unravelled and removed: and the living being, in its anatomy, its form, its habits, its birth and death, appears as though stripped naked. Natural history finds its locus in the gap that is now opened up between things and words— a silent gap, pure of all verbal sedimentation, and yet articulated according to the elements of representation, those same elements that can now without let or hindrance be named. (The Order of Things, pp. 129-30)

14. The Spaniards, in their exclusive preoccupation with spurious wealth, totally failed to appreciate the truly precious products of the New World. Bent only on slothful enjoyment, they had little interest in new knowledge and useful techniques. In the article "Vanille" we read: "in addition the Spaniards, satisfied with the wealth they had taken away from them (the natives), and also accustomed to a lazy way of life and to a double ignorance, scorn the curiosities of natural history and those who study them. In short, with the exception of only two Spaniards, Hernandez and Father Ignatio, it is to inquisitive persons from other nations, to travelers, merchants, and consuls established at Cadix that we owe the few details about this precious drug that have come to our attention and will be used in this article."

15. The capon is "inebriated" with wine-soaked bread, and his underbelly is plucked bare and rubbed with nettles: "When the chicks sit under his belly they soothe the burning of the stings . . . and so he loves them and calls them." It amuses Diderot to report this undoubtedly ancient bit of savoir faire. This method for augmenting the productivity of the barnyard bears a decidedly preindustrial stamp.

16. The gastronomical title always has an outward connection with the dish: chicken Villeroy, soufflet Montgolfier. In the Almanach des gourmands (1803), p. 191, Grimod describes the meeting of a taster's panel that gives to a "neophyte, amiable, and nameless" biscuit the name of a vaudeville actress: "Delicate, pretty, slight, breathing excellent taste and esprit through every pore, these biscuits met with general approval; and when the time came to baptize them, the panel scanned the audience for a similarity between their quality and those of one of the amiable candidates present at the session

in order to determine the name that should be given to them. In this manner the panel of tasters unanimously decided to proclaim them 'Gâteaux à la Minette.'"

17. Jacques Proust, in *Diderot et l'Encyclopédie* (p. 136), comes to the following conclusion: "the articles marked with an asterisk definitely constitute the minimum body of texts clearly by Diderot with which one can work. Yet the articles marked with an asterisk must not be used without caution. For while the asterisk indicates without doubt that Diderot wrote the article, its meaning is ambiguous as to the exact share he had in its elaboration. We have seen that, at least beginning with volume 3, the asterisk marked both the articles Diderot wrote and those he edited."

18. The butchers are men whose faces bear a ferocious and bloodthirsty stamp; they have bare arms, thick necks, bloodshot eyes, dirty legs, and bloodstained aprons; they carry massive, knotty sticks in their heavy hands, always ready for a fight, which they love. These fights are punished more severely than in other trades in order to mitigate their ferocity; and experience shows that there is reason to do so.

The blood they shed seems to inflame their faces and their temperaments. Their distinguishing mark is a coarse and wild lewdness, and there are streets close to the butcheries where a cadaverous odor prevails, and where vile prostitutes, sitting on the milestones in the full noonday light, make a public spectacle of their debauchery. There is nothing attractive about it: these females, all painted up and plastered over with *mouches*, monstrous and disgusting objects, invariably big and heavy, glower at you more threateningly than bulls. Yet these are the beauties pleasing to these men of blood who seek voluptuous pleasure in the arms of these Pasiphaës. (Mercier, *Tableau de Paris*, vol. 1, ch. 42)

11
Toward a Psychosociology of Contemporary Food Consumption

Roland Barthes

The inhabitants of the United States consume almost twice as much sugar as the French.[1] Such a fact is usually a concern of economics and politics. But this is by no means all. One needs only to take the step from sugar as merchandise, an abstract item in accounts, to sugar as food, a concrete item that is "eaten" rather than "consumed," to get an inkling of the (probably unexplored) depth of the phenomenon. For the Americans must do something with all that sugar. And as a matter of fact, anyone who has spent time in the United States knows that sugar permeates a considerable part of American cooking; that it saturates ordinarily sweet foods, such as pastries; makes for a great variety of sweets served, such as ice creams, jellies, or syrups; and is used in many dishes that French people do not sweeten, such as meats, fish, salads, and relishes. This is something that would be of interest to scholars in fields other than economics, to the psychosociologist, for example, who will have something to say about the presumably invariable relation between standard of living and sugar consumption. (But is this relation really invariable today? And if so, why?)[2] It could be of interest to the historian also, who might find it worthwhile to study the ways in which the use of sugar evolved as part of American culture (the influence of Dutch and German immigrants who were used to "sweet-salty" cooking?). Nor is this all. Sugar is not just a foodstuff, even when it is used in conjunction with other foods; it is, if you will, an "attitude," bound to certain usages, certain "protocols," that have to do with more than food. Serving a sweet relish or drinking a Coca-Cola with a meal are things that are confined to eating habits proper; but to go regularly to a dairy bar, where the absence of alcohol coincides with a great abundance of sweet beverages, means more than to consume sugar; through the sugar, it also means to experience the day, periods of rest, traveling, and leisure in a specific fashion that is certain to have its impact

Annales, E.S.C. 16 (September-October 1961): 977-86. Translated by Elborg Forster.

on the American. For who would claim that in France wine is only wine? Sugar or wine, these two superabundant substances are also institutions. And these institutions necessarily imply a set of images, dreams, tastes, choices, and values. I remember an American hit song: *Sugar Time*. Sugar is a time, a category of the world.[3]

I have started out with the example of the American use of sugar because it permits us to get outside of what we, as Frenchmen, consider "obvious." For we do not see our own food or, worse, we assume that it is insignificant. Even—or perhaps especially—to the scholar, the subject of food connotes triviality or guilt.[4] This may explain in part why the psychosociology of French eating habits is still approached only indirectly and in passing when more weighty subjects, such as life-styles, budgets, and advertising, are under discussion. But at least the sociologists, the historians of the present (since we are talking only about contemporary eating habits here) and the economists are already aware that there is such a thing.

Thus, P. H. Chombart de Lauwe has made an excellent study of the behavior of French working-class families with respect to food. He was able to define areas of frustration and to outline some of the mechanisms by which needs are transformed into values, necessities into alibis.[5] In her book *Le Mode de vie des familles bourgeoises de 1873 à 1953*, M. Perrot came to the conclusion that economic factors played a less important role in the changes that have taken place in middle-class food habits in the last hundred years than changing tastes; and this really means ideas, especially about nutrition.[6] Finally, the development of advertising has enabled the economists to become quite conscious of the ideal nature of consumer goods; by now everyone knows that the product as bought —that is, experienced—by the consumer is by no means the real product; between the former and the latter there is a considerable production of false perceptions and values. By being faithful to a certain brand and by justifying this loyalty with a set of "natural" reasons, the consumer gives diversity to products that are technically so identical that frequently even the manufacturer cannot find any differences. This is notably the case with most cooking oils.[7]

It is obvious that such deformations or reconstructions are not only the manifestation of individual, anomic prejudices, but also elements of a veritable collective imagination showing the outlines of a certain mental framework. All of this, we might say, points to the (necessary) widening of the very notion of food. For what is food? It is not only a collection of products that can be used for statistical or nutritional studies. It is also, and at the same time, a system of communication, a body of images, a protocol of usages, situations, and behavior. Information about food must be gathered wherever it can be found: by direct observation in the economy, in techniques, usages, and advertising; and by indirect observation of the mental life in a given society.[8] And once these data are assembled, they should no doubt be subjected to an internal analysis that should try to establish what is significant about the way in which they have been assembled before any economic or even ideological determinism is brought into play. I should like to give a brief outline of what such an analysis might be.

When he buys an item of food, consumes it, or serves it, modern man does not manipulate a simple object in a purely transitive fashion; this item of food sums up and transmits a situation; it constitutes an information; it signifies. That is to say that it is not just an indicator of a set of more or less conscious motivations, but that it is a real sign, perhaps the functional unit of a system of communication. By this I mean not only the elements of *display* in food, such as foods involved in rites of hospitality,[9] for all food serves as a sign among the members of a given society. As soon as a need is satisfied by standardized production and consumption, in short, as soon as it takes on the characteristics of an institution, its function can no longer be dissociated from the sign of that function. This is true for clothing;[10] it is also true for food. No doubt, food is, anthropologically speaking (though very much in the abstract), the first need; but ever since man has ceased living off wild berries, this need has been highly structured. Substances, techniques of preparation, habits, all become part of a system of differences in signification; and as soon as this happens, we have communication by way of food. For the fact that there is communication is proven, not by the more or less vague consciousness that its users may have of it, but by the ease with which all the facts concerning food form a structure analogous to other systems of communication.[11] People may very well continue to believe that food is an immediate reality (necessity or pleasure), but this does not prevent it from carrying a system of communication: it would not be the first thing that people continue to experience as a simple function at the very moment when they constitute it into a sign.

If food is a system, what might be its constituent units? In order to find out, it would obviously be necessary to start out with a complete inventory of all we know of the food in a given society (products, techniques, habits), and then to subject these facts to what the linguists call transformational analysis, that is, to observe whether the passage from one fact to another produces a difference in signification. Here is an example: the changeover from ordinary bread to *pain de mie* involves a difference in what is signified: the former signifies day-to-day life, the latter a party. Similarly, in contemporary terms, the changeover from white to brown bread corresponds to a change in what is signified in social terms, because, paradoxically, brown bread has become a sign of refinement. We are, therefore, justified in considering the varieties of bread—at least these varieties —as units of signification, for the same test can also show that there are insignificant varieties as well, whose use has nothing to do with a collective institution, but simply with individual taste. In this manner, one could, proceeding step by step, make a compendium of the differences in signification regulating the system of our food. In other words, it would be a matter of separating the significant from the insignificant and then of reconstructing the differential system of signification by constructing, if I may be permitted to use such a metaphor, a veritable grammar of foods.

It must be added that the units of our system would probably coincide only rarely with the products in current use in the economy. Within French society, for example, bread as such does not constitute a signifying unit: in order to find these we must go further and look for certain of its varieties. In other words, these signifying units are more subtle than the commercial units and, above all, they have to do with subdivisions with which production is not concerned, so that the sense of the subdivision can differentiate a single product. Thus, it is not at the level of its production that the sense of a food item is elaborated, but at the level of its preparation and use. There is perhaps no unprepared food item that signifies anything in itself, except for a few deluxe items such as salmon, caviar, truffles, and so on, whose preparation is less important than their absolute cost.

If the units of our system of food are not the *products* of our economy, can we at least have some preliminary idea of what they might be? In the absence of a systematic inventory, we may risk a few hypotheses. A study by P. F. Lazarsfeld[12] (it is old, concerned with particulars, and I cite it only as an example) has shown that certain sensorial "tastes" can vary according to the income level of the social groups interviewed: lower-income persons like sweet chocolates, smooth materials, strong perfumes; the upper classes, on the other hand, prefer bitter substances, irregular materials, and light perfumes. To remain within the area of food, we can see that signification (which, itself, refers to a twofold social phenomenon: upper classes/lower classes) does not involve kinds of products, but flavors: *sweet* and *bitter* make up the opposition in signification, so that we must place certain units of the system of food on that level. We can imagine other classes of units, for example, opposite substances such as dry, creamy, watery ones, which immediately show their great psychoanalytical potential (and it is obvious that if the subject of food had not been so trivialized and invested with guilt, it could easily be subjected to the kind of "poetic" analysis that G. Bachelard applied to language). As for what is considered tasty, C. Lévi-Strauss has already shown that this might very well constitute a class of oppositions that refers to national characters (French versus English cuisine, French versus Chinese or German cuisine, and so on).[13]

Finally, one can imagine opposites that are even more encompassing, but also more subtle. Why not speak, if the facts are sufficiently numerous and sufficiently clear, of a certain "spirit" of food, if I may be permitted to use this romantic term? By this I mean that a coherent set of food traits and habits can constitute a complex but homogeneous dominant feature useful for defining a general system of tastes and habits. This "spirit" brings together different units (such as flavor or substance), forming a composite unit with a single signification, somewhat analogous to the suprasegmental prosodic units of language. I should like to suggest here two very different examples. The ancient Greeks unified in a single (euphoric) notion the ideas of succulence, brightness, and moistness, and they called it γάνος. Honey had γάνος, and wine was the γάνος of the vineyard.[14] Now this would certainly be a signifying unit if we were to establish the system of food of the Greeks, even though it does not refer to any particular item. And here is another example, modern this time. In the United States, the Americans seem to oppose the category of sweet (and we have already seen to how many different varieties of foods this applies) with an equally general category that is not, however, that of salty—understandably so, since their food is salty and sweet to begin with—but that of *crisp* or *crispy*. *Crisp* designates everything that crunches, crackles, grates, sparkles, from potato chips to certain brands of beer; *crisp*—and this shows that the unit of food can overthrow logical categories—may be applied to a product just because it is ice cold, to another because it is sour, to a third because it is brittle. Quite obviously, such a notion goes beyond the purely physical nature of the product: *crispness* in a food designates an almost magical quality, a certain briskness and sharpness, as opposed to the soft, soothing character of sweet foods.

Now then, how will we use the units established in this manner? We will use them to reconstruct systems, syntaxes ("menus"), and styles ("diets")[15] no longer in an empirical but in a semantic way—in a way, that is, that will enable us to compare them to each other. We now must show, not that which is, but that which signifies. Why? Because we are interested in human communication and because communication always implies a system of signification, that is, a body of discrete signs standing out from a mass of indifferent materials. For this reason, sociology must, as soon as it deals with cultural "objects" such as clothing, food, and—not quite as clearly—housing, structure these objects before trying to find out what society does with them. For what society does with them is precisely to structure them in order to make use of them.

To what, then, can these significations of food refer? As I have already pointed out, they refer not only to display,[16] but to a much larger set of themes and situations. One could say that an entire "world" (social environment) is present in and signified by food. Today we have a tool with which to isolate these themes and situations, namely, advertising. There is no question that advertising provides only a projected image of reality; but the sociology of mass communication has become increasingly inclined to think that large-scale advertising, even though technically the work of a particular group, reflects the collective psychology much more than it shapes it. Furthermore, studies of motivation are now so advanced that it is possible to analyze cases in which the response of the public is negative. (I already mentioned the feelings of guilt fostered by an advertising for sugar that emphasized pure enjoyment. It was bad advertising, but the response of the public was nonetheless psychologically most interesting.)

A rapid glance at food advertising permits us rather easily, I think, to identify three groups of themes. The first of these assigns to food a function that is, in some sense, commemorative: food permits a person (and I am here speaking of French themes) to partake each day of the national past. In this case, the historical quality is obviously linked to food techniques (preparation and cooking). These have long roots, reaching back to the depth of the French past. They are, we are told, the repository of a whole experience, of the accumulated wisdom of our ancestors. French food is never supposed to be innovative, except when it rediscovers long-forgotten secrets. The historical theme, which was so often sounded in our advertising, mobilizes two different values: on the one hand, it implies an aristocratic tradition (dynasties of manufacturers, *moutarde du Roy,* the Brandy of Napoleon); on the other hand, food frequently carries notions of representing the flavorful survival of an old, rural society that is itself highly idealized.[17] In this manner, food brings the memory of the soil into our very contemporary life; hence the paradoxical association of gastronomy and indus-trialization in the form of canned "gourmet dishes." No doubt the myth of

French cooking abroad (or as expressed to foreigners) strengthens this "nostalgic" value of food considerably; but since the French themselves actively participate in this myth (especially when traveling), it is fair to say that through his food the Frenchman experiences a certain national continuity. By way of a thousand detours, food permits him to insert himself daily into his own past and to believe in a certain culinary "being" of France.[18]

A second group of values concerns what we might call the anthropological situation of the French consumer. Motivation studies have shown that feelings of inferiority were attached to certain foods and that people therefore abstained from them.[19] For example, there are supposed to be masculine and feminine kinds of food. Furthermore, visual advertising makes it possible to associate certain kinds of foods with images connoting a sublimated sexuality. In a certain sense, advertising eroticizes food and thereby transforms our consciousness of it, bringing it into a new sphere of situations by means of a pseudocausal relationship.

Finally, a third area of consciousness is constituted by a whole set of ambiguous values of a somatic as well as psychic nature, clustering around the concept of *health*. In a mythical way, health is indeed a simple relay midway between the body and the mind; it is the alibi food gives to itself in order to signify materially a pattern of immaterial realities. Health is thus experienced through food only in the form of "conditioning," which implies that the body is able to cope with a certain number of day-to-day situations. Conditioning originates with the body but goes beyond it. It produces *energy* (sugar, the "powerhouse of foods," at least in France, maintains an "uninterrupted flow of energy"; margarine "builds solid muscles"; coffee "dissolves fatigue"); *alertness* ("Be alert with Lustucru") and *relaxation* (coffee, mineral water, fruit juices, Coca-Cola, and so on). In this manner, food does indeed retain its physiological function by giving strength to the organism, but this strength is immediately sublimated and placed into a specific situation (I shall come back to this in a moment). This situation may be one of conquest (alertness, aggressiveness) or a response to the stress of modern life (relaxation). No doubt, the existence of such themes is related to the spectacular development of the science of nutrition, to which, as we have seen, one historian unequivocally attributes the evolution of food budgets over the last fifty years. It seems, then, that the acceptance of this new value by the masses has brought about a new phenomenon, which must be the first item of study in any psychosociology of food: it is what might be called nutritional consciousness. In the developed countries, food is henceforth *thought out*, not by specialists, but by the entire public, even if this thinking is done within a framework of highly mythical notions. Nor is this all. This nutritional rationalizing is aimed in a specific direction. Modern nutritional science (at least according to what can be observed in France) is not bound to any moral values, such as asceticism, wisdom, or purity,[20] but, on the contrary, to values of *power*. The energy furnished by a consciously worked out diet is mythically directed, it seems, toward an adaptation of man to the modern world. In the final analysis, therefore, a representation of contemporary existence is implied in the consciousness we have of the function of our food.[21]

For, as I said before, food serves as a sign not only for themes, but also for situations; and this, all told, means for a way of life that is emphasized, much more than expressed, by it. To eat is a behavior that develops beyond its own ends, replacing, summing up, and signalizing other behaviors, and it is precisely for these reasons that it is a sign. What are these other behaviors? Today, we might say all of them: activity, work, sports, effort, leisure, celebration—every one of these situations is expressed through food. We might almost say that this "polysemia" of food characterizes modernity; in the past, only festive occasions were signalized by food in any positive and organized manner. But today, work also has its own kind of food (on the level of a sign, that is): energy-giving and light food is experienced as the very sign of, rather than only a help toward, participation in modern life. The snack bar not only responds to a new need, it also gives a certain dramatic expression to this need and shows those who frequent it to be modern men, managers who exercise power and control over the extreme rapidity of modern life. Let us say that there is an element of "Napoleonism" in this ritually condensed, light, and rapid kind of eating. On the level of institutions, there is also the business lunch, a very different kind of thing, which has become commercialized in the form of special menus: here, on the contrary, the emphasis is placed on comfort and long discussions; there even remains a trace of the mythical conciliatory power of conviviality. Hence, the business lunch emphasizes the gastronomic, and under certain circumstances traditional, value of the dishes served and uses this value to stimulate the euphoria needed to facilitate the transaction of business. Snack bar and business lunch are two very closely related work situations, yet the food connected with them signalizes their differences in a perfectly readable manner. We can imagine many others that should be catalogued.

This much can be said already: today, at least in France, we are witnessing an extraordinary expansion of the areas associated with food: food is becoming incorporated into an ever-lengthening list of situations. This adaptation is usually made in the name of hygiene and better living, but in reality, to stress this fact once more, food is also charged with signifying the situation in which it is used. It has a twofold value, being nutrition as well as protocol, and its value as protocol becomes increasingly more important as soon as the basic needs are satisfied, as they are in France. In other words, we might say that in contemporary French society *food has a constant tendency to transform itself into situation.*

There is no better illustration for this trend than the advertising mythology about coffee. For centuries, coffee was considered a stimulant to the nervous system (recall that Michelet claimed that it led to the Revolution), but contemporary advertising, while not expressly denying this traditional function, paradoxically associates it more and more with images of "breaks," rest, and even relaxation. What is the reason for this shift? It is that coffee is felt to be not so much a substance[22] as a circumstance. It is the recognized occasion for interrupting work and using this respite in a precise protocol of taking sustenance. It stands to reason that if this transferral of the food substance to its use becomes really all-encompassing, the power of signification of food will be vastly increased. Food, in short, will lose in substance and gain in function; this function will be general and point to activity (such as the business lunch) or to times of rest (such as coffee); but since there is a very marked opposition between work and relaxation, the traditionally festive function of food is apt to disappear gradually, and society will arrange the signifying system of its food around two major focal points: on the one hand, activity (and no longer work), and on the other hand, leisure (no longer celebration). All of this goes to show, if indeed it needs to be shown, to what extent food is an organic system, organically integrated into its specific type of civilization.

NOTES

1. Annual sugar consumption in the United States is 43 kg. per person; in France, 25 kg. per person.
2. F. Charny, *Le Sucre,* Collection "Que sais-je?" (Paris, 1950), p. 8.
3. I do not wish to deal here with the problem of sugar "metaphors" or paradoxes, such as the "sweet" rock singers or the sweet milk beverages of certain "toughs."
4. Motivation studies have shown that food advertisements openly based on enjoyment are apt to fail, since they make the reader feel guilty (J. Marcus-Steiff, *Les Etudes de motivation* [Paris, 1961], pp. 44-45).
5. P. H. Chombart de Lauve, *La Vie quotidienne des familles ouvières* (Paris, 1956).
6. Marguerite Perrot, *Le Mode de vie des familles bourgeoises, 1873-1953* (Paris, 1961). "Since the end of the nineteenth century, there has been a very marked evolution in the dietary habits of the middle-class families we have investigated in this study. This evolution seems related, not to a change in the standard of living, but rather to a transformation of individual tastes under the influence of a greater awareness of the rules of nutrition" (p. 292).
7. Marcus-Steiff, *Les Etudes de motivation,* p. 28.
8. On the latest techniques of investigation, see Marcus-Steiff, *Les Etudes de motivation.*
9. Yet on this point alone, there are many known facts that should be assembled and systematized: cocktail parties, formal dinners, degrees and kinds of display by way of food according to the different social groups.
10. R. Barthes, "Le Bleu est à la mode cette année: Note sur la recherche des unités signifiantes dans le vêtement de mode," *Revue française de sociologie* 1 (1960): 147-62.
11. I am using the word *structure* in the sense that it has in linguistics: "an autonomous entity of internal dependencies" (L. Hjelnislev, *Essais linguistiques* [Copenhagen, 1959], p. 1).
12. P. F. Lazarsfeld, "The Psychological Aspect of Market Research," *Harvard Business Review* 13 (1934): 54-71.
13. C. Lévi-Strauss, *Anthropologie structurale* (Paris, 1958), p. 99.
14. H. Jeanmaire, *Dionysos* (Paris, 1951), p. 510.
15. In a semantic analysis, vegetarianism, for example (at least at the level of specialized restaurants), would appear as an attempt to copy the appearance of meat dishes by means of a series of artifices that are somewhat similar to "costume jewelry" in clothing, at least the jewelry that is meant to be seen as such.
16. The idea of social *display* must not be associated purely and simply with vanity; the analysis of motivation, when conducted by indirect questioning, reveals that worry about appearances is part of an extremely subtle reaction and that social strictures are very strong, even with respect to food.
17. The expression *cuisine bourgeoise,* used at first in a literal, then in a metaphoric way, seems to be gradually disappearing; while the "peasant stew" is periodically featured in the photographic pages of the major ladies' magazines.
18. The exotic nature of food can, of course, be a value, but in the French public at large it seems limited to coffee (tropical) and pasta (Italian).
19. This would be the place to ask just what is meant by "strong" food. Obviously, there is no psychic quality inherent in the thing itself. A food becomes "masculine" as soon as women, children, and old people, for nutritional (and thus fairly historical) reasons, do not consume it.
20. We need only to compare the development of vegetarianism in England and France.
21. Right now, in France, there is a conflict between traditional (gastronomic) and modern (nutritional) values.
22. It seems that this stimulating, reenergizing power is now assigned to sugar, at least in France.

Library of Congress Cataloging in Publication Data
Main entry under title:

Food and drink in history.

    Includes bibliographical references.
    CONTENTS: Aymard, M. Toward the history of nutrition. Morineau, M. The potato in the
eighteenth century.—Revel J. A capital city's privileges.—Hemardinquer, J. J. The family pig of
the ancien régime.—Frijhoff, W. and Julia, D. The diet in boarding schools at the end of the
ancien régime.—Leclant, J. Coffee and cafes in Paris, 1644-1693. [etc.]
    1. Food—History—Addresses, essays, lectures. 2. Diet—History—Addresses, essays,
lectures. I. Forster, Robert, 1926-   II. Ranum, Orest A. III. Series: Annales, économies,
sociétés, civilisations.

TX353.F59   641'.09   78-21920
ISBN 0-8018-2156-8
ISBN 0-8018-2157-6 pbk.